PASSING

PASSING
The Vision of Death in America

edited by
Charles O. Jackson

Contributions in Family Studies, Number 2

GREENWOOD PRESS
WESTPORT, CONNECTICUT • LONDON, ENGLAND

Library of Congress Cataloging in Publication Data

Main entry under title:

Passing.

(Contributions in family studies ; no. 2)
CONTENTS: Prepare for death and follow me, Colonial America: Covey, C. Destination death. Earle, A. M. Death ritual in Colonial New York. Livingston, W. Of the extravagance of our funerals. Dethlefsen, E. and Deetz, J. Death's heads, cherubs, and willow trees. [etc.]
Bibliography: p.
Includes index.
1. Funeral rites and ceremonies—United States—Addresses, essays, lectures. 2. Death—Addresses, essays, lectures. I. Jackson, Charles O. II. Series.
GT3203.P37 393'.0973 77-23794
ISBN 0-8371-9757-0

Library of Congress Catalog Card Number: 77-23794
ISBN: 0-8371-9757-0
ISSN: 0147-1023

First published in 1977

Greenwood Press, Inc.
51 Riverside Avenue, Westport, Connecticut 06880

Printed in the United States of America

10 9 8 7 6 5 4 3 2 1

Although generally base metal, he always wanted to be—and occasionally was—a bit of gold. He was grateful for periodic wizards, and especially for his wife, who believed in alchemy.

CONTENTS

PREFACE

My basic aim in this volume has been to create a brief and compact body of material which provides historical perspective on death in American culture. In addition to its general interest value, this collection is designed to fill the need for an historical text in the growing number of undergraduate courses on death and dying. The lack of appropriate material has thus far forced the omission of that perspective from these settings. The volume should prove equally useful in American studies courses, and in history courses which focus on the social and cultural aspects of the national past. Mortality has always been, though regretfully, a dynamic part of life. Full appreciation of that life requires that the cultural manifestations of death receive at least as much attention as that given in study to the various other powerful forces at work in American history. Indeed, the absence of such comment from texts typically employed in such courses further validates the now common observation that death has been, at least until recent years, a taboo topic in the United States.

This volume differs somewhat from most edited collections in that it argues an overall thesis. All selections included here relate in some way to that thesis, though most go beyond my particular concern. Opening comments provided before each of the three major sections are designed to highlight data in the selections which speak specifically to the volume's general theme. My introductory and concluding remarks in the book are additional attempts to guide the reader toward a particular frame of vision. The volume is characterized, therefore, by an interrelatedness and conceptual continuity which places it somewhere between that of the typical collection of readings and the standard historical monograph.

My decision to organize materials around a given thesis has meant, unfortunately, that certain dimensions of American response to death have had to be omitted. Thus I have not sought to develop the matter of racial, ethnic, or regional variation because to accord such topics appropriate attention would have diluted my chosen central focus and/or have violated my sense of correct proportion in the volume. I have also included very little material which utilizes a cross-cultural approach. In part this omission reflects the relative absence of comment suitable for inclusion. However, it also represents an effort to preserve my original design, whereby I chose not to substitute such approaches for selections which provided greater detail on, or insight into, the American story. Needless to say, I do not claim that all aspects of the history developed here are uniquely American. Some are; others are dimensions of broader movements, a fact which I would contend does not diminish the importance of clarifying them for a given location. For my purposes the distinction between the two is not a significant one.

I freely admit that this collection of readings does have limitations. My single objective has been to delineate the particulars of certain broad currents of the life-death relationship in the United States, emphasizing consistently commonality rather than diversity of response to mortality. On the other hand, I believe this knowledge has been the essential thing missing from the contemporary discussion among Americans on the topics of death and dying. Hopefully, the strength of this volume is that it meets in an interpretive and concise fashion the terms of that basic need.

To the extent that the collection does have worth, I owe thanks and acknowledgements to a number of people. Two are my colleagues, Dr. Samuel Wallace (Department of Sociology) and Dr. Lee Humphreys (Department of Religious

Studies). For some time we have team taught in the University an undergraduate course on death and dying. This most rewarding interaction with them, as well as with students in the class, has been of invaluable assistance to me in identifying historical questions which warranted pursuit, and in clarifying my own thoughts about the answers. I owe thanks as well to my friends and departmental colleagues, Dr. LeRoy Graf and Dr. Milton Klein, for the continued encouragement they gave me to complete this collection. I must acknowledge a very special dept of gratitude to Phyllis Cole and Sandra Westmoreland. They not only assisted me significantly in the physical preparation of the manuscript, but listened with enormous patience to my continued concerns about completing it. In the end, it was because of their substantial ability that I was allowed the time to do so on schedule. In this regard, I wish also to thank my student assistant Susan Fowler. She aided me substantially, and, by her light heart, kept an otherwise cranky author/editor generally civil during the final stages of preparing this material. Needless to say, I remain most appreciative to James Sabin and to Greenwood Press for their interest in my project.

Charles O. Jackson

Knoxville, Tennessee

PASSING

INTRODUCTION

Death and dying are basic and unalterable conditions of life, though they were realities not admitted into polite society for much of the present century. In recent years, however, a great deal has come to be said as well as written about both in the United States. The popularity of such literature would suggest a highly significant change in the national mood. Perhaps Americans have determined that these previously taboo topics are once more respectable areas of consideration and concern. The judgment could be premature, but at any rate, the new scholarly outpouring is a striking phenomenon. The present volume is directed toward a matter largely neglected in this scholarship, the historical dimension of death and response to death. It rests on the belief that full appreciation of contemporary social problems cannot be obtained without an understanding of their history. In brief, all such problems come to us with their past built in.

I should like to open this volume with several observations on death for which I claim no originality. The primary one is that death has always been much more than a simple biological event. It is an occurrence with multiple social dimensions. Thus while one's hereditary composition may predispose him toward a certain type of death, social environment may help put off or advance that event in time, or change its nature completely. Such matters as population density, standard of living, and socioeconomic status can have an effect. Public health and medical technology also have significant consequences, defining at least statistically the number of years of life the individual may expect, providing the basis for more or less effective intervention in life-threatening illness, and even making probable the final causes of death. So in the United States where medical science has been able to control dramatically the contagious killers of the nineteenth century, more citizens will reach advanced ages, making them susceptible to the degenerative diseases such as heart ailments and malignancy, characteristic of those years.

Death is social, moreover, because it is defined as well as pronounced by the living, the former recently given substantial recognition in heated popular and legislative debate. But the question is not a new one. Certainly it dates back at least to the late eighteenth century, and the issue of "apparent" versus "true" death raised by so-called Humane Societies here and abroad. The significance of that issue becomes more dramatic and understandable when related to the present. Quite clearly many cases of "death" in the eighteenth century or even late nineteenth would now not be so defined and would respond to standard recovery techniques. Pronouncement of death is complicated. An excellent illustration of this is to be found in David Sudnow's study of the organization of death in the hospital, *Passing On* (1967). As he makes quite clear, there can be significant variation of the label "dead," even among persons in similar physical condition.

The social dimension of death is reflected in the additional fact that individuals die through a whole cluster of societal definitions and value-laden categories. The worth of their particular type of death is assessed. If assigned the judgment "heroic" the deceased is honored and the bereaved are held in high esteem by their fellows. If on the other hand the event obtains a negative evaluation, generally the case with suicides, even friends may turn away from the bereaved. Social assignment is made also on the "appropriateness" of death. Death of the elderly after a long illness is "appropriate." Deaths out of due time, the child or promising young adult, are not.

Death has social dimension in yet another way. As a number of sociologists have observed, death takes away not merely the deceased, but important portions of "self" among the survivors. We are who we think we are, and our social selves are comprised in large part of relationships with significant others. Death terminates relationships. The deceased can no longer treat survivors as mother, sister, wife, etc. To think oneself a brother for twenty years and have that relationship suddenly concluded is a grievous assault on self-identity. A part of the living has also died.

Finally, death is social in that the living determine, with more or less awareness, the meaning of that event, e.g., a beginning or an end. They determine as well what will be the place of death in, and relationship of death to, life. These two matters are the primary concern of the following readings. The volume offers a collection of selections drawn from a variety of perspectives and organized around three general topics: societal view of death as an event, social response to death, the cemetery as a cultural institution. Selections fall further into three general chronological periods with short introductions to each selection by the editor: the colonial era, the nineteenth century, and the twentieth century. The volume concludes with an epilogue by the editor which acts to summarize major changes in the American vision of death examined in Parts One through Three, and relates those changes directly to the role of the dead in the life world. It contains also some brief comments on the new contemporary interest in death and dying.

Unlike many edited volumes, the present one has been developed around an overall thesis on death in the American past. Basically the thesis holds that the history of the vision of death and of social response to death in America revolve around two major occurrences. The first was what might be called a domestication and beautification of death which took place between the late eighteenth and late nineteenth centuries. The effect of this movement was to increase significantly the place of death and the dead in the world of the living. The second development becomes recognizable by the opening of the twentieth century and increased in consequence with each decade at least until challenged by the death and bereavement-related literature of recent years. The period was characterized by a major withdrawal on the part of the living from communion with and commitment to the dying and the dead. Death became alienated from life and the world of the dead and dying was essentially lost. Elaboration and analysis of these broad movements are the primary objectives of this volume.

PART ONE

"Prepare for Death and Follow Me"

Colonial America

Characteristics of mortality-related behavior and outlook were very different in seventeenth- and eighteenth-century British America from what they have become in the secular urban environment of the twentieth century. For one thing, death was never denied or "hidden away" as has been the case in contemporary America; nor could it be. There was too much of it around. Even late in the eighteenth century burial records for Boston indicate an average mortality of thirty-three per 1,000 white population.[1] A corresponding figure for the present-day United States would be approximately nine per 1,000 total population. Life expectancy at birth was probably only thirty years in the seventeenth century and increased to no more than thirty-five by the close of the next century.

Secondly, there was in this earlier period a much more widely held belief in the existence of an omnipotent and concerned God, as well as in personal immortality. To the degree that belief in a future life was accepted, death did not constitute so serious a challenge as it now does to the individual's sense of self. It was a frightening event to be sure, especially within Puritan New England where the devout were confronted by an ambivalent conception of death as both reward and punishment and where they were denied theologically any secure assurance of their own salvation.[2] Still, the afterlife was a reality and the righteous could hope, even in New England. They knew also where their vision should be focused. As Cyclone Covey has pointed out, despite constant defection and despite the fact that some groups never subscribed, it is possible to identify for at least 150 years in colonial thought a guiding vision of life as a symbolic pilgrimage through the wilderness of this world to an ultimate home in the next.[3] The future state was the important one and dying, a commonplace if grim reality, was a beginning not an end. Covey's discussion of this concept is the first essay in this section.

Moreover, because the great majority of inhabitants of British North America lived in small communities where mutual dependency and primary relationships between individuals were the norm, death of even a single individual was experienced as a community loss. In turn, the community rallied in a variety of very direct ways to assist the bereaved family in this crisis. Between the two groups, the grim business of final disposition of the deceased was accomplished. This normally included "laying out" and attending the body in the home (very often the location of the funeral as well) until burial, constructing the wooden coffin, bearing the body to the burial site, and digging as well as covering the grave. In sharp contrast to contemporary America, where funerary activities are closeted and participation is more or less limited, such activity in the colonial period had the quality of a social function and public event. They involved, and were expected to involve, large numbers of people, children among them.[4]

Mourning practice in particular took on an extensive social character. Customs, such as gifts made to the living as an announcement of death and funeral feasts following a burial, became sufficiently costly and extravagant so as to provoke periodic governmental concerns. The General Court of Massachusetts passed laws three times during the first half of the eighteenth century which sought to restrict excessive expenditures on funeral activity.[5] The colony of New

York was among the places where funerary rites were the most elaborate and lavish. The selection by Alice Morse Earle describes response to death in that colony. Extravagance in funerals was not merely a concern of colonial governments, however; it also drew public criticism from time to time. William Livingston's 1753 statement on New York is included to illustrate the nature of popular discontent. It should be noted that such criticism fell largely on deaf ears, even within Livingston's own family. When his father died in 1749, two ceremonies and gifts cost approximately £500. When his mother's death occured seven years later, the rites were as elaborate as for his father.[6]

Basically the cemetery is for the living and serves the functions they assign it. In the seventeenth century those functions were essentially two. One was merely a location for disposal of the body, a mortal casing not particularly important or worth elaborate permanent commemoration to the extent that the "pilgrim" posture held sway. Second, it sat amid the living as a socially useful if cold reminder of the brevity of life and certainty of judgment summed up in the common New England epitaph: "Prepare for death and follow me." Yet as a large-scale study of Massachusetts' gravestones by Edwin Dethlefsen and James Deetz indicates, even within Puritan society that harsh view of mortality suggested by such phrases gradually changed. Stones progressed through two additional states, implying by the mid-nineteenth century a much softer and more sentimentalized vision of death. As will be noted, such changes were reflections of popular yearnings which would alter appreciably the social purposes of the cemetery. Results of the Dethlefsen and Deetz research is provided as the final selection in this section.

NOTES

1. Richard Shryock, *Medicine and Society in America: 1660-1860* (New York, 1960), 108.

2. David Stannard, "Death and Dying in Puritan New England," *American Historical Review*, 78 (December 1973), 1313, 1317.

3. Cyclone Covey, *The American Pilgrimage: The Roots of American History, Religion and Culture* (New York, 1961), 7.

4. Robert W. Habenstein and William M. Lamers, *The History of American Funeral Directing* (Milwaukee, 1955).

5. *Ibid*.

6. William Livingston, *The Independent Reflector*, ed. by Milton M. Klein (Cambridge, 1963), 262.

Cyclone Covey

DESTINATION: DEATH

"As I walk'd through the wilderness of this world," Bunyan begins *The Pilgrim's Progress,* "I lighted on a certain place, where was a Denn [Bedford Jail]," and there dreamed a dream of the pilgrim, Christian, trudging with a burden on his back to Mount Zion. Christian reads in his book that he must die and come to judgment, but is unwilling to do the first and unable to do the second: He looks as though he would run if he knew which way to go. *"What shall I do to be saved?"* his anguished cry echoes down the centuries—itself re-echoing the question of the Macedonian jailer in *Acts* 16. Jonathan Edwards reports that this was a common cry in the Connecticut Valley early in the Great Awakening.[1] Edward's father Timothy, on the one occasion of his life when he preached the big election sermon before the Connecticut General Assembly (1732) chose the overriding topic *All the living must surely die, and go to judgment.* Meanwhile, all the living are but pilgrims in a wilderness on their way to a permanent, restful abode in the Celestial City.

The Biblical authority for conceiving the Christian life as a pilgrimage comes from the reinterpretation of Old Testament history in the eleventh chapter of *Hebrews:*

> By faith Abraham . . . sojourned in the land of promise, as in a strange country . . . for he looked for a city which hath foundations, whose builder and maker is God.

Abraham and innumerable descendants

> all died in faith, not having received the promises, but having seen them afar off, and embraced them, and confessed that they were strangers and pilgrims on the earth. For they that say such things declare plainly that they seek . . . a better country that is, a heavenly . . . .

Thus the King James version of 1611. The Wyclif, Tyndale, Cranmer, Geneva, and Rheims versions before it also used the word "pilgrims," whether spelled "pilgryms," "pylgrems," or "pilgrimes."[2] It was this chapter in *Hebrews*—doubtless the Geneva version of 1557—that William Bradford cited in a marginal note when he chronicled the departure of the America-bound Pilgrims from Leyden:

> So they lefte that goodly, & Pleasant citie, which had been ther resting place, nere .12. years; but they knew they were pilgrimes, & looked not much on these things; but lift vp their eyes to the heauens, their dearest cuntrie; and quieted their spirits.[3]

Bradford refers to himself personally as a pilgrim in a poem he composed in his last years:

> *In fears and wants, through weal and woe,*
> *A pilgrim, past I to and fro . . . .*[4]

The child born to Mrs. William White on the *Mayflower* in Provincetown Harbor was named Peregrine, a synonym for "pilgrim." The reason the Pilgrims called themselves pilgrims is not that they made a long trip to a wilderness, but that they regarded every moment of their lives as part of a trip to Zion. They had been exiles in Holland, but their whole earthly tenure, wherever, was to them an exile in a wilderness.

It may not need explaining that Zion was the hill in Jerusalem which David stormed and whereon he established his capital, his palace, and the altar of Israel. In the wilderness the Israelites had called their place of worship the Tabernacle; atop Zion it became the Temple and, for Christians, symbolized the gateway to the Celestial City. Here was the point of contact, in Hebrew tradition, between God and His chosen people. With the New Testament it came also to represent the Church (and so Augustine defines "Tabernacle"), the only portal through which God's people could gain salvation. Hence the pilgrimage must culminate at God's house on earth, the highest one may get in this life; but through it as the gate, one ascends to God's house in heaven. The existence of an actual Zion Gate facilitated the symbolism.

The westward journey of Abraham and his progeny complicates this Zion imagery; for the unknown author of *Hebrews* saw the crossing of the River Jordan into the Promised Land as the after-death ascent into the heavenly country—the crossing of the bar, or boundary between this world and the next. The Puritans in particular regarded Israel, also Zion and Jordan, as "types" prefiguring the New Testament. To them Massachusetts could be as much an Israel as Israel had been, and so they called it. Increase Mather more strictly defined "Israel" (which Augustine points out meant "seeing God") as "the Lord's Covenant People," with New England Congregationalists in mind.[5] Puritan Zionism had no commitment to any geographical locus.

John Bunyan found he had to shift the site of his House Beautiful from Zion to another eminence; otherwise, the pilgrim would have to cross Jordan before he could enter the church. While thinking of themselves as in transit and in the church, the American Puritans and sectarians also thought of themselves as Israelites already planted, with their churches, on the summit of Zion. At least, they thought of themselves as replicas of the Israelites; they never really confused their American Zion with the height they ultimately hoped to scale.

The pilgrimage, in summary, signified an inner quest of the Christian within a church context involving a mystical crossing of Jordan and an ascent up Zion to see God on His throne in His City and join Him there for eternity. The whole of a Christian's life was conceived to be an up-hill struggle.

Jonathan Edwards says in his *Christian Pilgrim* that those who lead holy lives journey through a wilderness with much labor and toil towards heaven, "up the hill toward Zion, against the inclinations and tendency of the flesh . . . ."

> This world was made for a place of preparation for another. Man's mortal life was given him, that he might be prepared for his fixed state.[6]

To go back even before *Hebrews* in the western tradition, we find the pilgrimage idea already fully developed by the beginning of the 4th century B.C. (To go back many centuries before Plato in the *eastern* tradition, we find the philosophical poets of India already regarding every man as a pilgrim [*śramana*] wandering, or disciplining himself, through the stages of his life along the Sacred Way to the "farther shore" or celestial strand of the river of life. They also liken this spiritual pilgrimage to the smoke from an altar that ascends to the eye of the dome; so one seeks to ascend through the eye of the dome of heaven; and to die is to "become one" with God.) In Plato's *Phaedo* Socrates talks of the soul's internal pilgrimage, first returning into itself and reflecting, then passing into "the realm of purity, and eternity, and immortality, and unchangeableness"; where it ceases from its erring ways, "and being in communion with the unchanging is unchanging." This state of the soul Plato calls wisdom and equates with virtue.

The philosopher growing in virtue prepares his soul for a more propitious after-death pilgrimage. Anticipating the hemlock, Socrates says that "as I am going to another place, I ought to be thinking and talking of the nature of the pilgrimage which I am about to make." What he meant by "pilgrimage" here was the journey of the soul to the other world after death, a journey involving many partings of the road and many wanderings. Those, he says, who have led holy lives purified by philosophy go to their home above and dwell in mansions "fairer far than these."

Then there is the return pilgrimage of the soul back into

life, described in the Myth of Er which concludes the *Republic*. This pilgrimage in reverse culminates with the crossing of Lethe, the River of Forgetfulness, which brings the soul back into earthly life, as in Bunyan the crossing of Jordan brings the soul into everlasting life. While rejecting Plato's belief in transmigration of souls and in partial recollection of a previous state, Christianity retains a counterpart longing to go home and to recall the perfect vision clouded since the Fall.

Plato immediately concerns himself, however, with the earthly pilgrimage—the aspiration via reason divorced from the senses to grasp "essential reality," "the very nature of Goodness itself." This journey, the "travelling up to the first principle of all," "the passion to see the truth," Plato calls Dialectic.[7]

Plotinus, the main link between Plato and Augustine, defines "dialectic" as "the Upward Way." The mounting wayfarer, says Plotinus, is a godlike man, one who has "clear vision of the splendor above," toward which he rises from the cloud and fog of earth. Looking beyond all here, he delights in that other world, "the place of reality," his "native land,"

> like a man returning after long wanderings to the pleasant ways of his own country.[8]

Augustine, who freely admits that his conversion to Christianity came by way of the Platonists, resumes the question-and-answer technique of Plato's dialectic (as adapted in Latin by Cicero) in his *Soliloquies*. He calls this scholarly-conversational pursuit the "going to God" or the virtue "whereby we journey"; in his *Sermon 92* he defines God as "the home whither we go" and "the way whereby we go." The Church, he says in his *Tractate on John*, knows two lives divinely preached and commended unto her:

> one is in the time of pilgrimage, the other in eternity of abiding; the one is in labor, the other in rest; the one is on the way, the other in the [true] country . . . .[9]

The real theme of the first two books of his great treatise, *On Christian Doctrine*, is the pilgrimage. Suppose, says Augustine, that we were wanderers in a strange country feeling wretched away from our fatherland and, to put an end to our misery, determined to return home, but that the beauty of the countryside and the very pleasure of our motion diverted our thoughts from what would make us truly happy. So we have wandered far from God and, if we wish to return to our Father's home, the soul must be purified so it can discriminate clearly the invisible things of our Father's country—use this world but not enjoy it. "And let us look upon this purification as a kind of journey or voyage to our native land." The more we enjoy Him in this life as through a giass darkly, the more easily we are able to bear out our pilgrimage and the more eagerly we long for its termination. It is while one wanders as a stranger in the world and fixes his affections entirely upon the future unchangeable life that he is in his optimum state; and the way he takes is "not a way through space, but through a change of affections."[10]

The pilgrimage also becomes a theme of certain parts of Augustine's long, trenchant classic, *The City of God*. Book XIX, chapter 17, makes the most use of the pilgrimage figure and most fully recapitulates the concept. From the beginning of the work as a whole, however, Augustine is distinguishing between the earthly city that lives according to men, and the heavenly that is mingled with it but lives according to God. The citizen of the latter "is as yet a pilgrim journeying on to the celestial city" which is eternal. The desire for that promised, peaceful habitation is what draws the Christian on, through faith, "in this miserable pilgrimage." By bearing one another's burdens and growing in grace, "the citizens of the city of God are healed while still they sojourn in this earth and sigh for the peace of their heavenly country." In this world, in these evil days, from the time of Abel and thenceforth even to the end of this world, "the Church has gone forward on pilgrimage amid the persecutions of the world and the consolations of God."[11] Augustine's City of God is therefore the Pilgrim City.

Now the Puritans were before everything else Augustinian,[12] though they are commonly called Calvinist. But Calvin was also before everything else Augustinian. In his monumental systematic theology Calvin repeated that "while we are aspiring towards our true country, we be pilgrims on earth."[13] His *Catechism* underscores that

> our happiness is not located on earth . . . . we are to live in this world as foreigners, thinking continually of departure, and not allowing our hearts to be involved in earthly delights.[14]

Calvin's sermons return to the theme; for instance, one on 2 *Timothy* 2. 16-18:

> We must learn to . . . . walk fearfully and carefully . . . . St. Paul hath shown us, that . . . we must walk in death before we can come to life. How long will this death continue? As long as we are in this world . . . . Until God shall take us out of this world, we must be as pilgrims in a strange country . . . .[15]

Dante opens his *Commedia* "in the middle of the journey" of his life, having strayed from the way. When he comes to his senses, he tries to proceed on uphill toward or on a mountain but has not the strength to overcome the temptations of this world. The mountain he is trying to scale is Zion, which turns out to be the same as Mount Purgatory. He cannot negotiate it directly but must go down through hell first, at length gaining the Mountain's summit from within, crossing "the sacred river" (Lethe), and ascending, escorted, to the realm of peace and light.

Shakespeare has Richard II unfeelingly intone the pilgrim concept on the death of Lancaster: "His time is spent, our pilgrimage must be." Francis Bacon invokes it contritely in April 1621: "my soul hath been a stranger in the course of my pilgrimage." Sir Walter Raleigh, beneath his taciturnity, clasps it:

Give me my scallop-shell of quiet,
My staff of faith to walk upon.
My scrip of joy, immortal diet,
My bottle of salvation,
My gown of glory, hope's true gage;
And thus I'll take my pilgrimage . . . .

Whilst my soul, like quiet palmer,
Travelleth towards the land of heaven;
Over the silver mountains . . . .

But this is an age-old idea, found fully formed in antiquity and in familiar usage in western Europe at least from the 12th century. One of its most striking restatements in England in the period of the first colonizing of New England occurs in a funeral sermon that John Taylor delivered in 1622 or earlier, entitled *The Pilgrims Profession*. Taylor was a disciple of the Cambridge professor, William Perkins, who decisively influenced John Cotton, among countless others. Taylor took for his text on this occasion one that Increase Mather later made much of: "I am a stranger with thee, and a sojourner," from Psalm 39. The carriage (deportment) of the saint through this life, Taylor said, is like that of the traveler going home through a strange country, bearing the threefold burden of sin, worldly care, and fear of death.

Hee will through thicke and thin, through drops and drout and all because he is going home . . . . Now how happily shall this man compasse his journey and goe singing through the most tedious wayes of his Pilgrimage that hath . . . furnished himselfe with the understanding of the way . . . .[16]

John Winthrop, the most influential political figure of first-generation Massachusetts, had long been a pilgrim when he won the 1629 election in London as governor of the Bay Company. Back in March or April 1618, a few weeks before his marriage to Margaret Tyndal, he bade her let worldly minds that savor not the things of God bend all their care and study to secure themselves an earthly happiness.

But you, whom God hathe ordayned to a better ende, he lookes you should be guided by an other rule; he telles you that you are a pilgrime & stranger in this life, that you have no abidinge cytye heerebut must looke for one to come . . .

In the black-looking spring of 1629, on April 28, he wrote her from London that he trusted God's mercy "to carry us along through this course of our pilgrimage, in the peace of a good conscience . . . .[17]

John Winthrop Jr. had sojourned to Constantinople and had participated in the British naval failure to relieve the Huguenots at La Rochelle when he wrote his father rather world wearily 21 August 1629 about embarking for New England:

I have seene so much of the vanity of the world that I esteeme noe more of the diversities of Countries then as so many Innes, wherof the travailer, that hath lodged in the best, or in the worst findeth noe difference when he commeth to his Journies end . . . .[18]

The Roxbury minister Thomas Welde, in his preface to Winthrop Sr.'s account of the Antinomian convulsion, published 1644, observes that "our wise God . . . seldome suffers his owne, in this their wearysome Pilgrimage to be long without trouble . . . .[19]

"The city where I hope to dwell," says another first generation Puritan, Ann Bradstreet, "There's none on earth can parallel . . ." This in her poem of 1678, *The Flesh and the Spirit.*

If I of Heaven may have my fill
Take thou the world, and all that will.

She follows the time-honored custom of referring to her pilgrimage as "weary." One of her poems (dated 31 August 1669) bears the actual title *A Pilgrim* and goes in part:

A Pilgrim I on Earth, perplext,
With sins with cares and sorrows vext.[20]

Roger Williams sounds Bunyanesque in 1672, six years before Bunyan's classic, when he says that we wilfully stumble into the Ditch Eternal by refusing the word of Scripture, which is a light to our feet and lantern to our paths. "Thus the Heavenly Sun-Dial is one and constant in its guidance and direction to us poor Travellers."[21]

Williams's local enemy William Harris refers to himself in a petition to the king 11 June 1675 as "A weary traueller for the Space of almoste forty years In the wildernes of New England . . . .[22]

Increase Mather, the leading Puritan during the last quarter of the 17th century, talks in his old age of "the dayes of my pilgrimage now drawing to their close";[23] he speaks of his wife as "the Dear Companion of my Pilgrimage on Earth,"[24] and of the years that his and his son's lives overlapped as "Our Peregrination together thro' the Wilderness."[25] To one of his funeral sermons he appends a coda-section: "Meditations on death, and on the heavenly-countrey which believers go into at the hour of death," on the text: "For we are Strangers before thee, and Sojourners, as were all our Fathers: Our Dayes on the Earth are as a Shadow, and there is none abiding."[26]

Solomon Stoddard, who dominated Connecticut-Valley Puritanism as Increase Mather did that of the seaboard in their time, designed his 1714 *Guide to Christ* mostly, he says on the title page, for young ministers and partly for private Christians "who are enquiring the way to Zion."

When Cotton Mather, the dominant Puritan of the generation between Increase's and Edwards's, called himself a "Fellow Traveller" and addressed his readers: "O my *Fellow Travellers*," no one would mistake that he meant pilgrims "to that Glorius World." He characteristically calls it "the *Heavenly World*" rather than the more customary Heavenly Country or Celestial City, but it is the identical destination.

> Look upwards, and you shall soon say . . . . *We faint not, while we look to the Things that are not seen.* Look and see there what you have to encourage you under the Difficulties of your *Pilgrimage.*[27]

In his autobiography Cotton Mather epitomizes his life as a "poor *walk with god*."[28] In *Coheleth* he speaks of himself as "Hastening to the *Conclusion* of my *Pilgrimage*, thro' *this present Evil World* . . . . while you [*my Son*] are yet . . . . no further from the *Beginning* of your *Pilgrimage* . . . ."[29] In his metaphorical *Agricola* he inserts a poem between chapters entitled "The Plain Songs of the Pious Husbandman; In the *Work* of his *Husbandry*, and the *House* of his *Pilgrimage*."[30]

The polished Boston minister, Benjamin Colman, who knew both Cotton Mather and Edwards, advised young ministers in his funeral sermon for Stoddard in 1729 not to "count upon attaining the Days of the Years of their Pilgrimage . . . ."[31] John Dickinson, an anti-Great-Awakening minister at Elizabethtown, New Jersey, recapitulated the pilgrim concept as the orientation of the Christian life at even greater length than Edwards's *Christian Pilgrim*.[32] In the same year as Dickinson's work (1745), a collection of poems by Cotton Mather's young disciple, John Adams, a minister living at Cambridge, came to print posthumously in Boston. It included lines extolling divine grace, a force, says Adams.

Which broke my Soul from all its servile Chains,
And fix'd my Feet on Zion's wid'ning Plains.[33]

The otherwordly destination of the pilgrimage explains why Puritans focally emphasized death, even as the 2nd-century church father Irenaeus had said: "The business of the Christian is nothing else than to be ever preparing for death."[34] "Do you not know," Paul wrote the Romans, "that all of us who have been baptized into Christ Jesus were baptized into his death?" Long before Christ, Socrates had said (according to Plato's *Phaedo*) that other men do not perceive that the true disciple of philosophy "is ever pursuing death and dying." This disciple, says Socrates, has reason to be of good cheer when about to die, for "after death he may hope to receive the greatest good in the other world." "Men see Him just so far as they die to this world," says Augustine (*On Christian Doctrine,* II.7). Augustine chides his friend

Nebridius in a letter of 389 for wanting him to make the long journey for a visit:

> To go through life planning journeys that cannot be undertaken without disturbance and trouble does not become one who is planning for that last journey we call death; with it alone, as you are aware, should our real plans be concerned.[35]

Montaigne reaffirms this whole set of traditional views in his famous essay, *That to study philosophy is to learn to die*.

Cotton Mather said in 1726: "the Contemplation of DEATH shall be the FIRST Point of the *Wisdom* that my Advice must lead you to." As the leading Puritan of the entire first quarter of the 18th century, he was giving his final advice to ministerial candidates who would soon assume the burden of maintaining Puritanism.

> Place yourself in the *Circumstances* of a *Dying Person*; your Breth failing, your *Throat* rattling, your *Eyes* with a dim Cloud, and your *Heads* with a damp Sweat upon them: And *then* entertain such Sentiments of *this World*, and of the *Work* to be done in this World, that such a *View* must needs inspire you withal.[36]

"So teach us to number our Days, that we may apply our Hearts to Wisdom." Mather quotes Psalm 90 for a sermon, *Death Made Happy*, published in London in 1701. God, he, says, seems to entertain many of us with a handwriting somewhat like that which terrified Belshazzar of old. It should stir us "to renounce this *World*, the *Flesh*, and the *Devil* . . . ."[37] Mather comes directly to grips with the pilgrim theme in a companion discourse, *Death Made Easie*, on the text from Psalm 119.19, "I am a Stranger in the Earth":

> It is usually the delirious, but the observable Fancy of *Dying Men, That they are not at Home*. And yet it would be . . . the highest *Reasonableness*, in every Man *living,* to count himself, *not at Home,* until he dies . . . . Yea, let a Man *live* like a *Stranger* in this, and that Man shall *die* as a *Citizen* of another, and a better World . . . . The Life of *a Stranger in the World*, is that which all the servants of God have

evermore espoused; it is the *Epitaph* which the Spirit of God has at last inscribed upon their Tombs, in *Heb.* 11. 13. *These dyed in Faith and confess that they were Strangers and Pilgrims on the Earth* . . . .[38]

"Let your *Meditations* upon your Death be solemn, serious, and very frequent," Mather says in the last discourse of this trilogy, *Serious Thoughts in Dying Times.*

THE THOUGHTS of DEATH, are *at all Times* too *seasonable,* and too *profitable,* to be *justly* laid aside; were our Deaths more considered, our Lives would be more circumspect, serious, gracious; and if the *Contemplation of Death,* were with any Reason of old assigned as the Great *Exercise* of true *Philosophy,* it may much more be accounted the Grand incentive of right *Christianity* . . . .[39]

Mather explains the mystery (though a mystery only to moderns) of why the autocratic Salem Puritan, John Endecott, should have sealed all his letters with a skull: "That Man is like to die comfortably," says Mather, "who is every Day minding himself, that he is to die shortly. Let us look upon every thing as a short of *Death's-Head* set before us, with a *Memento mortis* written upon it."[40] This view had been a late medieval commonplace.

And what was the nature of this death that should preoccupy one's mind in life? In the Celestial City, Augustine thought, the soul would enjoy eternal and perpetual Sabbath. The Christian doctrine of the re-creation and resurrection of a new body identical to the distintegrating one proved something of an embarrassment to the Platonic notion of the immortality of the soul alone and unfettered. Like Augustine, Cotton Mather tended to ignore the corporeal side of the afterlife. Yet he thought that some matter from the head served as a vehicle to convey the spirit away from the body.[41] Like Luther, among others, Mather fell back on the metaphor of sleep in conceiving of death.

Death to the Faithful, is a SLEEP . . . . The Great Thing to be now pressed upon us all, is this. *Make due provision for it,* That when you *Dy,* you may *Sleep Comfortably.*[43]

Fifteen years later, in his last sermon, Mather returned to the question of the sleep of death which the saint has made sure will be without bad dreams.

'Tis indeed a *Rest* . . . . And yet the chief sweet of the *rest*, is that it is *without rest*. It is a *rest* from *irksome* and *vexing* things; Not a *rest* from the *joyful praises* of God . . . . The *spirits* of them who *sleep* in *Jesus* are not lull'd into *sleep* of utter *inactivity* and *insensibility there*. How the disengaged *spirits* of good men exert their operations, who can tell . . . .[43]

Mather had done most of his speculating back before the turn of the century on what God has in store at the climactic moment of dissolution:

Let us Believe, that He has Legions and Myriads, and Millions of Blessed *Spirits,* to be our Convoy, and safeguard from those *Evil Spirits,* which are waiting to arrest our *Spirits* . . .

Thousands of angels from God's Holy Place will "fly like swift Flashes of Lightning to succour us . . . ." But whoever is without the Grant of Grace will be doomed unto Outer Darkness.[44]

"Oh long for the harvest, long for your departure, and for *the appearing of Christ,*" Cotton's grandfather, Richard Mather, said in his farewell address to his congregation at Dorchester (six miles south of Boston) in 1657.[45] Richard's contemporary, John Robinson, the pastor of the Pilgrims in Leyden, said in his 1625 essay *Of Death* that we should not live "in a senseless blockishness, overcoming death, as they most do, by forgetting it; as if a man overcame his enemy, by getting as far from him as he could"; we should instead take occasion by the death of friends "to love this world less . . . and heaven the more . . ."[46]

The death of the imperious Solomon Stoddard in February 1729 at the age of 86, moved young William Williams, who preached his funeral sermon at Northampton, to enjoine everybody "to *make ready for Death* . . . . This is the great Business of Life . . . ."[47] Colman in his funeral sermon for

Stoddard at Boston eleven days after Williams's, concluded that "The *Crown* of Life is to finish well, in *happy Death.* And the way to *this* is to pass our Days here under the governing Tho'ts of Death and *Eternity.*"[48]

Jonathan Edwards, who more than once in his notes alludes specifically to the City of God, talks as though he had taken all these men's advice. But he was taking it largely from the same traditional sources as they. "Frequently in my Pursuits of whatever Kind," Edwards writes in his diary, "let this come into my Mind; 'How much shall I value this on my Death Bed?' "[49] His ninth resolution says: "Resolved, to think much on all Occasions of my own dying, and of the Common Circumstances which attend Death."[50] And why? "To obtain for myself as much happiness, in the other world, as I possibly can."[51]

In his culminative sermon, *The Christian Pilgrim*, he elaborates:

> Our whole lives ought to be spent in travelling this road. We ought to begin *early*. This should be the *first* concern, when persons become capable of acting. When they first set out in the *world*, they should set out on *this* journey. And we ought to travel with *assiduity.* It ought to be the work of every day. We should often think of our journey's end; and make it our daily work to travel on in the way that leads to it. He who is on a journey, is often thinking of the destined place; and it is his daily care and business to get along; and to improve his time to get towards his journey's end. Thus should heaven be continually in our thoughts; and the immediate entrance or passage to it, *viz.* death, should be present with us . . . . All other concerns of life, ought to be entirely subordinate to this.[52]

But to turn to that impetuous Puritan preacher whom the "orthodox" Puritans banished from Massachusetts, the rigid Separatist and radical democrat, Roger Williams. Did *he* regard himself a pilgrim who should be thinking constantly about death? Ah, listen. Let us, he tells his wife, "live the rest of your *short uncertaine span*, more as *strangers*, longing and breathing after another *Home* and *Country* . . . ." It is of "great and sweet use," says he, daily to thinke each day our *last,* the day of our last *farewell* . . . . we are but strangers in an *In*, but passengers in a Ship, and though we dreame of long *Summer* dayes, yet our very life and being is but a swift short *passage* from the bank of *time* to the other side or *Banck* of a doleful *eternity* . . . ."[53]

"Eternitie (O Eternitie) is our business," he reminds Governor Simon Bradstreet.[54]

Yes, even a democratic Puritan was still a pilgrim. Williams made a literal pilgrimage through wilderness in deep snow and suffered severe privations before finally founding Providence. When his puzzled old friend Governor Winthrop wrote him, why did he bring this suffering on himself? "To what end do you drive?" Williams replied in the language of the pilgrim, forty years before Bunyan's book: "I aske the way to lost Zion . . . ."[55]

NOTES

1. *A Faithful Narrative of the Surprizing Work of God in the Conversion of Many Hundred Souls in Northampton, and the Neighbouring Towns and Villages of New-Hampshire in New England. In a Letter to the Revd. Dr. Benjamin Colman of Boston . . . Nov. 6 1736* (London 1737), p. 32.

2. Albert Matthews, "The Term Pilgrim Fathers and Early Celebrations of Forefathers' Day," Col. Soc. Mass. *Pubs.,* XVII, 355. The Greek word translated "pilgrims" was (transliterated) *parepidemoi.*

3. *Of Plimmoth Plantation,* fac. edition (London 1896), p. 91.

4. Nathaniel Morton, *New England's Memorial,* 5th edition, ed. John Davis (Boston 1826), p. 264.

5. *Returning unto God the Great Concernment of a Covenant People* (Boston 1680), p. 1.

6. Jonathan Edwards, *The Christian Pilgrim, or The Christian Life a Journey towards Heaven,* in *Works,* ed. Sereno Dwight (N.Y. 1830), VII, 137, 140-41.

7. Quotations from *Phaedo* are in the Benjamin Jowett translation, numerous editions; from the *Republic,* the translation of Francis MacDonald Cornford (N.Y. & London: Oxford U. 1945). Many editions of *Pilgrim's Progress,* old and new, have been used; princi-

pally: John Bunyan. *The Pilgrim's Progress from this World, to that which is to come: delivered under the Similitude of a Dream* [Part I] (London 1678), fac. edition (London: Noel Douglas Replicas 1928) and both Parts, ed. J. B. Warey (Oxford: Clarendon Press 1928). Part II was first published in 1685. The two Parts went into innumerable editions both separately and combined.

8. First Ennead, 3. 3; Fifth Ennead, 9. 1, *The Six Enneads,* tr. Stephen MacKenna and B. S. Page, *Great Books of the Western World,* ed. Robert Maynard Hutchins (Chicago, London, Toronto: Encyclopedia Britannica 1952), XVII, 10-11, 246.

9. Cuthbert Butler, *Western Mysticism: the Teaching of SS. Augustine, Gregory and Bernard on Contemplation and the Contemplative Life,* 2nd edition (London: Dutton 1926; reprint 1951), pp. 157, 158, 163.

10. *On Christian Doctrine,* tr. J. F. Shaw [T & T Clark, Edinburgh], *Great Books,* XVIII, 625, 627, 628, 629, 632, 639.

11. *The City of God,* tr. Marcus Dods [T & T Clark, Edinburgh], *ibid.,* 401, 421, 464, 503, 507, 520, 522-23.

12. See particularly Perry Miller, *The New England Mind: the Seventeenth Century* (Cambridge: Harvard U. 1939), chap. 1: "The Augustinian Strain of Piety," pp. 4-10.

13. *Institutes of the Christian Religion,* Bk. IV, chap. 20, par 2.

14. "The Catechism of the Church of Geneva that is a Plan for Instructing Children in the Doctrine of Christ," *Theological Treatises,* tr. J.K.S. Reid (London: SCM 1954), p. 104.

15. *A Selection of the Most Celebrated Sermons of John Calvin* (Philadelphia 1860), pp. 69-70.

16. Quoted in William Haller, *The Rise of Puritanism* (N.Y.: Columbia U. 1938), p. 149.

17. R. C. Winthrop, *Life and Letters of John Winthrop,* 2nd edition, 2 vols. (Boston, 1869), I, 129-30, 290.

18. *The Winthrop Papers,* 5 vols. (Boston: MHS 1929-47), II, 151.

19. *A Short Story of the Rise, Reign, and Ruine of the Antinomians* (London 1644), preface.

20. Charles Eliot Norton, ed., *The Poems of Mrs. Anne Bradstreet* (n.p. 1897), p. 262; A. B., *Meditations Divine and Morall* (msc. in Houghton Library), p. 98.

21. *George Fox Digg'd out of his Burrovves* (Boston 1676), Narr. Club *Pubs.,* V. (Providence 1872), p. 276.

22. *Harris Papers,* ed. Clarence S. Brigham, RIHS *Colls.,* X (1902), p. 150.

23. *The Mystery of Christ Opened and Applyed* (Boston 1686) p. 2.

24. *A Sermon concerning Obedience & Resignation to the Will of God* (Boston 1714), p. 38.

25. "An Attestation," in Cotton Mather, *Coelestinus* (Boston 1723), p. i. (D3).

26. *Meditations on Death and on the Believers Deliverance from the Fear of it* (Boston 1717), p. 111.

27. *Coelestinus,* p. 45.

28. *Paterna* (msc. in Alderman Library), p. 2. He also calls it "my *private* Walk," p. 111.

29. *Coheleth* (Boston 1720), pp. 1-2.

30. *Agricola* (Boston 1727), p. 21.

31. *The Faithful Ministers of Christ Mindful of their own Death* (Boston 1729), p. 24.

32. *Familiar Letters to a Gentleman, upon a Variety of Seasonable and Important Subjects in Religion* (Boston 1745), Letter 19: "Containing particular Advices and Directions, for a close and comfortable *Walk with God,"* pp. 402-24.

33. *Poems on Several Occasions* (Boston 1745), p. 19.

34. "Fragments from the Lost Writings of Irenaeus," *The Ante-Nicene Fathers,* ed. Alexander Roberts, James Donaldson, and A. Cleveland Coxe (Buffalo 1887), I, 570.

35. Epistle X, in *Select Letters,* tr. J. H. Baxter (London: Heinemann; N.Y.: Putnam's 1930), p. 11.

36. *Manuductio ad Ministerium. Directions for a Candidate of the Ministry* (Boston 1726), pp. 1-2.

37. *Death Made Easie & Happy* (London 1701), pp. 28-29, 50.

38. *Ibid.,* 1-3, 23.

39. *Ibid.,* 55, 94, 105.

40. *Ibid.,* 94.

41. *The Comfortable Chambers Opened and Visited* (Boston 1796), p. 12. See Augustine, *The Soliloquies,* tr. Thomas F. Gilligan (N.Y.: Cosmopolitan Science & Art 1943), Bk. II, chap. 13, "Of the Proof of the Soul's Immortality," pp. 121-23.

42. *Awakening Thoughts on the Sleep of Death* (Boston 1712), pp. 5, 29. *Cf.* Martin Luther, preface to *Spiritual Hymns Newly Revised at Wittenberg* (1529), *Works* (Philadelphia: Holman 1932), II, 228.

43. *The Comfortable Chambers,* pp. 11-12.

44. *A Good Man Making A Good End* (Boston 1698), pp. 17, 27. *Cf.* Increase Mather, *The Glorious Throne* (Boston 1702).

45. *A Farewel Exhortation to the Church and People of Dorchester in New-England* (Cambridge 1657), p. 26.

46. *Works,* ed. Robert Ashton (Boston 1851), I, 257, 259.

47. *The Death of a Prophet Lamented and Improved* (Boston 1729), pp. 12-13.

48. *The Faithful Ministers of Christ,* pp. 23-25.

49. [Samuel Hopkins,] *The Life and Character of the Late Reverend Mr. Jonathan Edwards* (Boston 1765), p. 19; 3 Feb. 1725.

50. *Ibid.,* p. 6.

51. [S. E. Dwight,] *The Life of President Edwards* (N.Y. 1830), p. 69.

52. *The Christian Pilgrim,* p. 138.

53. *Experiments of Spiritual Life & Health, and their Preservatives* (London 1652; reprint Providence 1863), pp. 1, 57-59.

54. Letter (6 May 1682), 2 Mass. Hist. Soc. *Colls.,* VIII, 198.

55. *Letters and Papers of Roger Williams,* comp. Howard M. Chapin (Boston: MHS 1924), unnumbered photostat.

Alice Morse Earle

DEATH RITUAL IN COLONIAL NEW YORK

As soon as a death had been announced to the dwellers in any little town in colonial New York, by the slow ringing or tolling of the church-bell, there went forth solemnly from his home the *aanspreecker*, or funeral inviter (who might well be grave-digger, bell ringer, schoolmaster, or chorister, and who was usually all four), attired in gloomy black, with hat fluttering long streamers of crape; and with much punctilio he visited all the relatives and friends of the deceased person, notified them of the death, advised them of the day and hour of the funeral, and requested their honorable presence. This inviting was a matter of most rigid etiquette; no one in these Dutch-American communities of slightest dignity or regard for social proprieties would attend a funeral unbidden. The *aanspreecker* was paid at regular rates for his service as living perambulating obituary notice, according to the distance travelled and the time spent, if he lived in a country town where distances between houses were great.

In 1691 the "inviters to the buryiall of deceased persons" in New York were public officers, appointed and licensed by the Mayor. Their names were Conrad Vanderbeck and Richard Chapman, and they were bidden to give their atten-

---

Reprinted from *Colonial Days in Old New York* by Alice Morse Earle. Published by Charles Scribner's Sons, 1896, pp. 293-312.

dance gratis to the poor. A law was passed in New York in 1731, setting the fees of "inviters to funerals" at eighteen shillings for the funeral of any one over twenty years of age; for a person between twelve and twenty years, twelve shillings; for one under twelve years, eight shillings. For a large circle of friends these sums seem small. The Flatbush inviter in 1682 had twelve guilders for inviting to the funeral of a grown person, and only four guilders in addition if he invited in New York—which was poor pay enough, when we think of the long ride and the row across. In 1760, we find the New York inviter, Evert Fels, advertising his change of residence, and that he can be found if needed next to King's Stores. It is easy to imagine that the *aanspreecker* must have been a somewhat self-important personage, who doubtless soberly enjoyed his profession of mortuary news-purveyor, and who must have been greeted wherever he went with that grewsome interest which in his colonial days attached to everything pertaining to death.

This public officer and custom was probably derived from the Romans, who used to send a public crier about, inviting the people to the solemnization of a funeral. In the northern counties of England each village had its regular "bidder," who announced his "funeral-bidding" by knocking on each door with a great key. Sometimes he "cried" the funeral through the town with a hand-bell. In New York the fashion was purely of Dutch derivation. In Holland the *aanspreecker* was an official appointed by government, and authorized to invite for the funerals of persons of all faiths and denominations who chanced to die in his parish.

In New York, ever bent on fashions new, the *aanspreecker*, on mournful mission intent, no longer walks our city avenues nor even our country lanes or village streets; but in Holland he still is a familiar form. Not, as of old, the honored schoolmaster, but simply a hired servant of the undertaker, he rushes with haste through the streets of Dutch towns. Still clad in dingy black of ancient fashion, kneebreeches, buckled shoes, long cloak, cocked hat with long streamers of crape, he seems the sombre ghost of old-time manners. Sometimes he bears written invitations deep bordered with black; sometimes he calls the death and time of funeral, as did the Roman *praeco*; and sometimes, with streamers of white, and white cockade on his hat, he goes on a kindred duty—he bears to a circle of friends or relatives the news of a birth.

Before the burial took place, in olden times, a number of persons, usually intimate friends of the dead, watched the body throughout the night. Liberally supplied with various bodily comforts, such as abundant strong drink, plentiful tobacco and pipes, and newly baked cakes, these watchers were not wholly gloomy, nor did the midnight hours lag unsolaced. The great *kamer* in which the body lay, the stateroom of the house, was an apartment so rarely used on other occasions than a funeral that in many households it was known as the *doed-kamer*, or dead-room. Sometimes it had a separate front door by which it was entered, thus giving two front doors to the house. Diedrich Knickerbocker says the front door of New York houses was never opened save for funerals, New Years, and such holidays. The kitchen door certainly offered a more cheerful welcome. In North Holland the custom still exists of reserving a room with separate outside entrance, for use for weddings and funerals. Hence the common saying in Holland that doors are not made for going in and out of the house.

Men and women both served as watchers, and sometimes both were at the funeral services within the *doed-kamer*; but when the body was borne to the grave on the wooden bier resting on the shoulders of the chosen bearers, it was followed by men only. The women remained for a time in the house where the funeral had taken place, and ate *doed-koecks* and sipped Madeira wine.

The coffin, made of well-seasoned boards, was often covered with black cloth. Over it was spread the *doed-kleed*, a pall of fringed black cloth. This *doed-kleed* was the property of the church, as was the pall in New England churches, and was usually stored with the bier in the church-vestibule, or *doop-huys.* In case of a death in childbirth, a heavy white sheet took the place of the black pall. This practice also obtained in Yorkshire, England.

Among the Dutch a funeral was a most costly function. The expenditure upon funeral gloves, scarfs, and rings, which was universal in New England, was augmented in New York by the gift of a bottle of wine and a linen scarf.

When Philip Livingstone died, in 1749, his funeral was held both in New York and at the Manor. He had lived in Broad Street, and the lower rooms of his house and those of his neighbors were thrown open to receive the assemblage. A pipe of wine was spiced for the guests, and the eight bearers were each given a pair of gloves, a mourning-ring, a scarf, a handkerchief, and a monkey-spoon. At the Manor a similar ceremony took place, and a pair of gloves and handkerchief were given to each tenant. The whole expense was five hundred pounds. When Madam Livingstone died, we find her son writing to New York from the Manor for a piece of black Strouds to cover the four hearse-horses; for a "Barrell of Cutt Tobacco and Long Pipes of which I am out;" for six silver tankards and cinnamon for the burnt wine; he said he had bottles, decanters, and glasses enough. The expense of these funerals may have been the inspiration for William Livingstone's paper on extravagance in funerals.

A monkey-spoon was a handsome piece of silver bearing the figure or head of an ape on the handle. *Mannetiens* spoons, also used in New Netherland, were similar in design. At the funeral of Henry De Forest, an early resident of New Harlem in 1637, his bearers were given spoons.

A familiar and extreme example of excess at funerals as told by Judge Egbert Benson was at the obsequies of Lucas Wyngaard, an old bachelor who died in Albany in 1756. The attendance was very large, and after the burial a large number of the friends of the dead man returned to the house, and literally made a night of it. These sober Albany citizens drank up a pipe of wine, and smoked many pounds of tobacco. They broke hundreds of pipes and all the decanters and glasses in the house, and wound up by burning all their funeral scarfs in a heap in the fireplace.

In Albany the expense, as well as the rioting, of funerals seems to have reached a climax. It is said that the obsequies of the first wife of Hon. Stephen Van Rensselaer cost twenty thousand dollars. Two thousand linen scarfs were given, and all the tenants were entertained for several days.

On Long Island every young man of good family began in his youth to lay aside money in gold coin to pay for his funeral; and a superior stock of wine was also saved for the same occasion. In Albany the cask of choice Madeira which was bought for a wedding and used in part, was saved in remainder for the funeral of the bridegroom.

The honor of a lavish funeral was not given to the wealthy and great and distinguished only. The close of every life, no matter how humble, how unsuccessful, was through the dignity conferred by death afforded a triumphal exit by the medium of "a fine burying."

In a preceding chapter the funeral of a penniless Albanian is noted; in 1696 Ryseck Swart also became one of the church-poor of Albany. She was not wholly penniless; she had a little silver and a few petty jewels, and a little strip of pasture land, worth in all about three hundred guilders. These she transferred to the church, for the Consistory to take charge of and dole out to her. A good soul, Marritje Lievertse, was from that time paid by the church thirty-six guilders a month for caring for Ryseck. I do not doubt that she had tender care, for she was the last of the real church-poor (soon they had paupers and an almshouse), and she lived four years, and cost the parish two thousand two hundred and twenty-nine guilders. She died on February 15, 1700, and, though a pauper, she departed this life neither unwept, unhonored, nor unsung. Had she been the cherished wife of a burgomaster or *schepen*, she could scarce have had a more fully rounded or more proper funeral. The bill, which was paid by the church, was as follows:—

	g.	s.
3 dry boards for a coffin	7	10
¾ lb. nails	1	10
Making coffin	24	
Cartage	10	
Half a vat and an anker of good beer	27	
1 gallon Rum	21	
6 gallons Madeira for women and men	84	
Sugar and *cruyery*	5	
150 Sugar cakes	15	
Tobacco and pipes	5	
Grave digger	30	
Use of pall	10	
Wife Jans Lockermans	36	
	232 guilders.	

Rosenboom, for many years the *voor-leeser* and *dood-graver* and *aanspreecker* in Albany, sent in a bill of twelve guilders for delivering invitations to the funeral—which bill was rejected by the deacons as exorbitant. But the invitations were delivered just the same, for even colonial paupers had friends, and her coffin was not made of green wood held together with wooden pegs, which some poor bodies had to endure; and the one hundred and fifty *doed-koecks* and Madeira for the women very evenly balanced the plentiful beer and wine and tobacco for the men. Truly, to quote one of Dyckman's letters from Albany, "the poor's purse here was richly garnisht."

An account of Albany, written by a traveller thereto in 1789, showed the continued existence of these funeral customs. It runs thus:—

"Their funeral customs are equally singular. None attend them without a previous invitation. At the appointed hour they meet at the neighboring houses or stoops until the corpse is brought out. Ten or twelve persons are appointed to take the bier altogether, and are not relieved. The clerk then desires the gentlemen (for ladies never walk to the grave, nor even attend the funeral unless a near relation) to fall into the procession. They go to the grave and return to the house of mourning in the same order. Here the tables are handsomely set and furnished with cold and spiced wine, tobacco and pipes, and candles, paper, etc., to light them. The house of mourning is soon converted into a house of feasting."

In New York we find old citizens leaving directions in their wills that their funeral shall be conducted in "the old Dutch fashion," not liking the comparatively simpler modern modes.

The customs were nearly the same in English families. At the funeral of Hon. Rufus King at Jamaica, Long Island, in 1827, which was held upon an exceptionally hot day in April, silver salvers holding decanters of wine and spirits, glasses and cigars, were constantly passed, both indoors and out, where many stood waiting the bearing of the coffin to the grave.

The transition of the funeral customs of ante-Revolutionary days into those of our own may partially be learned from this account written in 1858 by Rev. Peter Van Pelt, telling Domine Schoonmaker's method of conducting a funeral in the year 1819:

"The deceased had, many years before, provided and laid away the materials for his own coffin. This one was of the best seasoned and smoothest boards and beautifully grained. As I entered the room I observed the coffin elevated on a table in one corner. The Domine, abstracted and grave, was seated at the upper end; and around in solemn silence, the venerable and hoary-headed friends of the deceased. A simple recognition or a half-audible inquiry as one after another arrived was all that passed. Directly the sexton, followed by a servant, made his appearance with glasses and decanters. Wine was handed to each. Some declined, others drank a solitary glass. This ended, again the sexton presented himself with pipes and tobacco. The Domine smoked his pipe and a few followed his example. The custom has become obsolete, and it was well that it has. When the whiffs of smoke had ceased to curl around the head of the Domine, he arose with evident feeling, and in a quiet subdued tone, made a short but apparently impressive address. I judged solely by his appearance and manner; for although boasting a Holland descent, it was to me an unknown tongue. A short prayer concluded the service; and then the sexton taking the lead, followed the Domine, doctor, and pallbearers with white scarfs and black gloves. The corpse and long procession of friends and neighbors proceeded to the churchyard."

Not only were materials for the coffin secured and made ready during the lifetime, but often a shroud was made and kept for use. Instances have been known where a shroud was laid by unused for so many years that it became too yellow and discolored to use at all, and was replaced by another. Sometimes a new unlaundered shirt was laid aside for years to use as a *doed-hemde*. Two curious superstitions were rife in some localities, especially on Long Island; one was the careful covering of all the mirrors in the house, from the time of the death till after the funeral; the other the pathetically picturesque "telling the bees." Whittier's gentle rhyme on the subject has made familiar to modern readers the custom of "telling the bees of one, gone on the journey we all must go."

Both an English and Dutch funeral fashion was the serving to the attendants of the funeral of funeral-cakes. In New York and New Netherland these were a distinctive kind of *koeckje* known as *doed-koecks*, literally dead-cakes. An old receipt for their manufacture is thus given by Mrs. Ferris: "Fourteen pounds of flour, six pounds of sugar, five pounds of butter, one quart of water, two teaspoonfuls of salt, one ounce of Caraway seed. Cut in thick dishes four inches in diameter." They were, therefore, in substance much like our New Year's cakes. Sometimes they were marked with the initials of the deceased person; and often they were carried home and kept for years as a memento of the dead—perhaps of the pleasures of the funeral. One baker in Albany made a specialty of these cakes, but often they were baked at home. Sometimes two of these *doed-koecks* were sent with a bottle of wine and a pair of gloves as a summons to the funeral.

In Whitby, England, a similar cake is still made by bakers and served at funerals; but it is sprinkled with white sugar. In Lincolnshire and Cumberland like customs still exist. "Burial-cakes" were advertised by a baker in 1748 in the Philadelphia newspapers.

It is frequently asserted that funeral rings were commonly given among the Dutch. It seems fair to infer that more of them would have been in existence to-day if the custom had been universal. Scores of them can be found in New England. There is an enamelled ring marked "K.V.R., obit Sept. 16, 1719," which was given at the funeral of Kileaen Van Renssalaer. One of the Earl of Bellomont is also known, and two in the Lefferts family, dating towards the close of the past century. I have heard of a few others in Hudson Valley towns. Perhaps with gifts of gloves, spoons, bottles of wine, *doed-koecks*, scarfs, or handkerchiefs, rings would have been superfluous.

It will be noted in all these references to funerals herein given that the services were held in private houses; it was not until almost our own day that the funerals of those of Dutch descent were held in the churches.

Interments were made under the churches; and, by special payment, a church-attendant could be buried under the seat in which he was wont to sit during his lifetime. The cost of interment in the Flatbush church was two pounds for the body of a child under six years; three pounds for a person from six to sixteen years of age; four pounds for an adult; and in addition "those who are inclined to be permitted to be interred in the church are required to pay the expense of every person." I don't know exactly what this ambiguous sentence can mean, but it was at any rate an extra charge "for the profit of the schoolmaster," who dug the grave and carried the dirt out of the church, and was paid twenty-seven guilders for this sexton's work for an adult, and less for a younger person and hence a smaller grave. Usually the domines were buried in front of the pulpit where they had stood so often in life.

After newspaper-days arrived in the colony, there blossomed in print scores of long death-notices, thoroughly in the taste of the day, but not to our taste. In the "New York Gazette" of December 24, 1750, we find a characteristic one:—

"Last Friday Morning departed this Life after a lingering Illness the Honorable Mrs. Roddam, wife to Robert Roddam, Esq. Commander of his Majesty's Ship Greyhound, now on this Station, and eldest Daughter of his Excellency our Governor. We hear she is to be Interred this Evening.

"Good Mr. Parker—Dont let the Character of our Deceased Friend, Mrs. Roddam, slip through your Fingers, as that of her Person through those of the Doctors. That she was a most affable and perfectly Good-Natured young Lady, with Good Sense and Politeness is well known to all her Acquaintances, and became one of the most affectionate Wives.

"Immatura peri, sed tu felicior, Annos
Vivi mens, Conjux optime, vive tuos

were the Sentiments of her Later Moments when I had the Honour to attend her. As this is intended as a small Tribute to the Manes of my dear departed Friend, your inserting of it will oblige one of your constant Female Readers and Humble Servant."

Another, of a well-known colonial dame, reads thus:—

"Last Monday died in the 80th year of her Age, and on Thursday was recently interred in the Family Vault at Morrisania: Isabella Morris, Widow and Relict of his Excellency Lewis Morris, Esq., Late Governor of the Province of New Jersey: A Lady endowed with every Qualification Requisite to render the Sex agreeable and entertaining, through all the Various scenes of Life. She was a pattern of Conjugal Affection, a tender Parent, a sincere Friend, and an excellent Oeconomist.

She was
Liberal, without Prodigality
Frugal, without Parsimony
Chearful, without Levity
Exalted, without Pride.
In person, Amiable
In conversation, Affable
In friendship, Faithful
Of Envy, void.

She passed through Life endow'd with every Grace
Her virtues! Black Detraction can't deface;
Or Cruel Envy e'er eclipse her Fame;
Nor Mouldering Time obliterate her Name."

The tiresome, pompous, verbose production, Johnsonian in phrase and fulsome in sentiment, which effloresced on the death of any man in public life or of great wealth, need not be repeated here. They were monotonously devoid of imagination and originality, being full of idle repetitions from each other, and whoever has labored through one can judge of them all.

It does not give us a very exalted notion of the sincerity or value of these funeral testimonials, or the mental capacity of our ancestors, to read in the newspapers advertisements of printed circulars of praise for the dead, eulogistic in every aspect of the life of the departed, and suitable for various ages and either sex, to be filled in with the name of the deceased, his late residence, and date of death.

Puttenham in the "Arte of English Poesie," says: "An Epitaph is an inscription such as a man may commodiously write or engrave vpon a tombe in few verses, pithie, quicke, and sententious, for the passer-by to peruse and judge vpon without any long tariaunce."

There need be no "long tariaunce" for either inquisitive or irreverent search over the tombstones of the Dutch, for the dignified and simple inscriptions are in marked contrast to the stilted affectations, the verbose enumerations, the pompous eulogies, which make many English "graveyard lines" a source of ridicule and a gratification of curiousity. Indeed, the Dutch inscriptions can scarcely be called epitaphs; the name, date of birth and death, are simply prefaced with the ever-recurring *Hier rust het lighaam,* Here rests the body; *Hier leydt het stoffelyk deel,* Here lie the earthly remains; or simpler still, *Hier leyt begraven,* Here lies buried. Sometimes is found the touching *Gedachtenis,* In remembrance. More impressive still, from its calm repitition on stone after stone, of an undying faith in a future life, are the ever-present words, *In den Heere Ontslapen,* Sleeping in the Lord.

Not only in memory of those dead-and-gone colonists stand these simple Dutch tombstones, but in suggestive remembrance also of a language forever passed away from daily life in this land. The lichened lettering of those unfamiliar words seems in sombre truth the very voice of those honored dead who, in those green Dutch graveyards, in the shadow of the Old Dutch churches, *in den Heere ontslapen*.

William Livingston

OF THE EXTRAVAGANCE OF OUR FUNERALS

As the Dangers flowing from Luxury are evident from the Reason of Things, so are we assured, by the Voice of History, that all wise Legislators have considered public Prodigality as the Bane of Society, and a Kind of political Cancer which corrodes and demolishes the best regulated Constitution. For this Reason they framed Laws to inhibit this formidable Evil, upon the Introduction of which, they thought it impossible to preserve the State from Ruin and Misery. Upon these Principles LYCURGUS, one of the most celebrated Lawgivers of Antiquity, enacted the severest Penalties against this destructive Vice. From the punctual Execution of the *Roman* Laws, in this respect equally rigorous, is, in a great Measure to be derived, the Splendor and Prowess of antient *Rome*. But when in Process of Time, the ambitious Leaders of Faction introduced the luxurious Modes of living, which they had learn'd from the *Grecians* and *Asiatics,* they accelerated the Fall of that mighty Empire, which had reduced the greatest Part of the then known World, to its Obedience.

By the Luxury of the leading Men of *Athens* was that once illustrious State enslaved by PHILIP, who pav'd the Road to

---

that universal Monarchy which was afterwards completed by his Son ALEXANDER.

The same Causes will invariably produce the same Effects; and that Luxury is the Harbinger of a dying State, is a Truth too obvious to require the Formality of Proof. Hence MACHIAVELLI advises a Prince who would destroy a Country, to introduce Vice and Luxury, as the most effectual Expedients for accomplishing his Designs.

Our extraordinary Success during the late War, has given Rise to a Method of living unknown to our frugal Ancestors. At present our Trade is at a low Ebb, but still our Profusion continues unretrench'd. Amongst other Instances of Extravagance, the following Letter exhibits to our View, a Piece of Luxury that has long been the Complaint of every wise and virtuous Man amongst us. It is wrote by a sincere Lover of his Country, whose Observations I am proud of conveying to the Public.

To the INDEPENDENT REFLECTOR

New-York, March 17, 1753.

Indeed, Sir, it is with Sorrow and Indignation, that I behold your implacable Adversaries, almost weekly violating both Truth and Decency, to malign your Character, and misrepresent your Design. But let it be your Consolation and Crown of rejoicing, that in general you are are only calumniated by those, whose Praise would be the greatest Infamy you could suffer.

It affects me at the same Time with singular Delight, that supported by the Testimony of a good Conscience, you can appeal to the Tribunal of Heaven for your Sincerity; and, being influenced by no View of personal Promotion, are able to pity and despise the Obloquies of an ungrateful, a traducing Generation. This I mention, not by Way of Compliment, but solely to animate you in your Progress, and to enter my Protest against the Discontinuance of your noble Paper, on

Account of the stupid Opposition you have met with. From the Example of your Readiness to serve your Country, already exhibited in several of your Productions, I am emboldened to send you the following indigested Hints, which you will be pleased so to range and methodize as not to derogate from the Character of your Writings.

Tho' we are in many Instances luxurious and extravagant, there is, perhaps, no Article in which we carry our Prodigality to a higher Excess, than that of our Funerals. One would think that the Sorrow we feel at the Death of a Relation, was a sufficient Calamity, without the Aggravation of making ourselves anxious about the Preparation of a pompous Interment. Whoever is not insensible to the tender Emotions of Sorrow and Distress, on so melancholy an Occasion, can but ill relish the additional Load of Solicitude, that the deceased is carried to his Grave with the fashionable Apparatus, and buried Alamode. But this is not the worst Part of the Story. Besides the Loss of, perhaps, him who was the only Support of the Family, and whose Death is to the Survivors the Beginning of Calamity and Indigence, the scanty Remainder, which might afford them a comfortable Subsistence, is expended in the idle Magnificence of committing him to the Tomb. For the Sake of complying with this ruinous Custom, I have known many a Family dissipate at least a fourth Part of their whole Fortune, and disabled to subsist on the Residue without the greatest Shifts and Assiduity. Nor can they, while such is the Fashion, refrain from following it: For were they to consult the deceased's Circumstances instead of his Rank, they would be obnoxious to the illnatur'd Censures of a malicious World, who would interpret their commendable Parsimony into Avarice, or something more unnatural. The most favourable Construction would be that their deviating from the general Practice, proceeded from their Inability to afford a more magnificent Funeral.

Again, if we consider the Manner in which this ridiculous Expence is Conducted, we shall find it a Loss to the Person upon whom it falls, without being an Advantage to any. The

Scarfs and the Rings are generally bestowed on the Rich, to whose Wealth they make, comparatively speaking, no Addition, tho' to the Giver they prove a very considerable Burthen. To the Dead 'tis of no Avail. With the Situation of the Mourner 'tis wholly inconsistent, and a Kind of Burlesque on true and silent Sorrow, which endeavours to avoid Pomp and Noise, and chuses the sequestred Haunts of Solitude and Retirement. The Money squandered in Liquor, is often worse than thrown away; it intoxicates and imbrutes that noble Being who prides himself in the Title of rational, and looks erect on Heaven.

As People in the inferior Stations of Life, are extremely apt to imitate those who move in a more elevated Sphere: It ought to be the Endeavour of the latter to set them the laudable Example of suppressing this fantastical and inconvenient Piece of Luxury. Their Circumstances could not be called in Question, and did they retrench all superfluous Articles, it would meet with universal Approbation; because all would agree it was for the Sake of discountenancing so absurd a Custom; and their Inferiors tho' they imitated, would not pretend to rival them. Thus might there be a proper Subordination in the Charge of Funerals, and at the same Time every Class of Men inter their Dead with suitable Decency and Decorum.

Without entering into nice Calculations about this monstrous Piece of Extravagance, let us only suppose, Mr. *Reflector,* that on the Funerals of those in the higher and middle Stations of Life, there is expended, at least, Fifty Pounds beyond what is really necessary and decent; which I take to be a Computation vastly within the Bounds of Reason and Probability: Yet, at this Rate What immense Sums must the intombing of our Inhabitants, in a few Years, amount to? How many indigent Families might be cherished and supported with what is thus ridiculously lavish'd on the Dead?

Nor have I the least Apprehension of being, on this Occasion, charged with Singularity of Opinion. I am not against shewing that Decency, that Respect and even Reverence for the Dead, which has been practised by all civilized Nations, and seems to be the natural Dictate of Humanity refined and cultivated. What I argue against is the needless and exorbitant Expence of Funerals; and in this I have the general Suffrage of my Fellow Citizens. It is almost universally inveighed against and condemned, and yet no one appears to have sufficient Resolution to attempt a Reformation. Happy would it be was this the only Thing in which no Reformation is attempted. In *Holland,* a Republic famed for the Wisdom of its Laws, and generally celebrated for its public Frugality, this Expence is limited by Law, the Offences against it punished by a Forfeiture. So in *Boston,* where this romantic Affectation of surpassing each other in the Grandeur of their Funerals, was carried to an enormous Profuseness, the legislature was obliged to interpose, and render it penal to exceed a Sum limited by an Act enacted for its Retrenchment.

Where a Clergyman or a Physician hath deserved well of a Family, by his Attendance on the Deceased, I should not be against sending a genteel Present in a private Manner, in Lieu of the Scarfs, or Rings usually given at Funerals. Was this the Practice, it would only be followed by those who could afford it, as it would not fall within public Observation, by whom it was done or neglected. But such is at present, the *ridiculous* Fondness, of Persons in the most indifferent Circumstances, for imitating the Fashion, that a Clergyman of undoubted Veracity told me, he remembered several Instances of Funerals made at the usual Expence, by Persons who have afterwards pleaded Poverty to obtain the Remission of the burial Fees.

Whether the above Remarks are so far worthy the Consideration of our Superiors, as to turn their Thoughts to plan a Law for the Regulation of this Extravagance, I shall not take upon me to determine. I rather wish our Gentlemen of Figure and Influence would, by their laudable Example, so discountenance this absurd Custom, as to render the Interposition of the Legislature unnecessary, and enjoy for their Reward, that inward and Heart-felt Satisfaction, arising from making their Superiority in Life, instrumental in banishing from amongst us a Practice so greatly injurious to their Country. I cannot, at the same Time help thinking, that a Tax on Luxury and Extravagance in general, in Imitation of the *Romans*, and several other wise Nations, who frequently made sumptuary Laws, by which they turned private Vices into public Benefits; would be highly reasonable and proper.

To prevent the little Critics from all future snarling against my Proposals, I hope, Mr. *Reflector*, you will not fail to refine and embellish, by your masterly Pen, these undecorated Hints, which I offer up from a Soul devoted, according to the best of my Judgment, to the Public Weal, wherein I may probably be no less singular, than in the Name by which I have before subscribed myself,

Your most Humble Servant,

Shadrech Plebianus.

Edwin Dethlefsen and James Deetz

DEATH'S HEADS, CHERUBS, AND WILLOW TREES

The problem of deriving meaningful inferences from an artifactual assemblage concerning the culture which created it is an everpresent one with which the prehistorian must be concerned. A number of specific methods have been devised to aid in coping with this problem, and much of the cultural reconstruction which has been done to date is indicative of the success of such methodology. However, in most instances interpretive methods, such as seriation, typology and various space-time unit concepts, are devised, tested, and subsequently employed in situations which are not rigorously controlled. The purpose of this paper is to direct attention to a corpus of artifactual material in which a wide variety of archaeological methods may be tested, refined, and perhaps improved under highly controlled circumstances. Colonial gravestones are uniquely and admirably suited to such a study. Produced by a literate people whose history is known, these markers show design variations in time and space which can be projected against known historical data, thereby detailing the dynamics of change in material objects as a function of changes in the society which produced them.

An excerpt from "Death's Heads, Cherubs, and Willow Trees: Experimental Archaeology in Colonial Cemeteries" by Edwin Dethlefsen and James Deetz. Reproduced by permission of the Society for American Archaeology from *American Antiquity,* 31, No. 4, 1966.

Gravestones are peculiarly suited to such an investigation for a number of specific reasons:

(1) Although produced in a civilized milieu, Colonial gravestones were not carved by full-time specialists. Stonecarvers might have been ropemakers, leatherworkers, smiths or printers who pursued stonecutting as a secondary specialty. Gravestones are therefore true folk products as is much of the artifactual material with which the prehistorian is routinely involved.

(2) New England stonecutters produced stones for the population immediately surrounding the towns in which they lived. There is no evidence of itinerant stonecutters, and few stones were erected at a great distance from the town in which they were carved. In spite of this local pattern and the absence of a professional stonecarving group, all carvers participated in a decorative tradition which extended unbroken over an area vastly larger than that served by any one individual. While local variations can be seen between any two areas at the same point in time, these are minor when compared with the adherence to a larger design tradition, shown by stones over all of eastern Massachusetts, and probably even farther.

(3) Gravestones, by their very function, carry their own elegant chronological control. All are dated, and in those instances when one can determine the time interval between the death of the individual whose resting place is marked by a stone and its purchase and erection, this period is relatively brief, usually within a year.

(4) It is possible to project design patterns against genealogy, since the stones bear kinship data. Thus one can investigate the effect, if any, of familial affiliation on designs employed. Adequate information also exists regarding the carvers of the stones. Many of them are known by name, their products have been identified, and it is possible to investigate the nature of kin-based micro-traditions of design among the carvers.

(5) Since age at death is also stated in most cases, life tables can by constructed and, through them, certain demographic information can be derived.

(6) Since a large number of the stones bear epitaphs, it is possible to arrive at some statement concerning values regarding death, which can be shown to change in harmony with designs. This literary dimension provides a small measure of psychological control.

(7) The distinctive symbols employed as decorative elements are in part a function of religion, and therefore changes in this aspect of culture can be investigated as they relate to other areas of change.

It can be seen that gravestones are probably unique in permitting the anthropologist to investigate interrelated changes in style, religion, population, personal and societal values, and social organization under absolute chronological control with a full historical record against which to project results for accuracy. As such, they form a valuable laboratory in which to test many of the inferential methods employed by the archaeologist who works with material culture.

The present study, which is still in its early stages, began with a tabulation of design types in a number of cemeteries in eastern Massachusetts. The area presently under investigation is approximately 100 mi. long and 50 mi. wide, centering on Boston, with the long axis running north and south along the Atlantic coast. These limits are purely arbitrary and in the near future will be expanded to include all of New England and ultimately the entire eastern seaboard area which formed the sphere of 17th- and 18th-century English Colonial development. The temporal limits extend from about 1680 to the early years of the 19th century. Preservation of gravestones erected before 1680 is generally not so reliable as that of later stones; by 1830, stonecarving had become a full-time specialty, bringing into effect a different set of forces to act upon stylistic selection and change. Between these two dates, nearly all stones in the area are made from native slate. The widely held notion that most of the raw material from which the stones were cut was imported from the British Isles is incorrect. Harriet Forbes (1927: 5-7) makes an excellent case for the extensive utilization of native stone by citing the absence of slate from the shipping bills of merchant ships of the period and by correctly pointing out that the low prices usually paid for these stones precludes their having been imported in either worked or unworked form. In addition to the commonly used slate, sandstones and schists were employed for gravestones in some cases, these mateials being particularly popular in the area south of Boston, where good-quality slate was lacking in any quantity.

Three basic designs are universally present in the Colonial cemeteries of eastern Massachusetts. A number of other design types have a more local distribution, but local styles do not eclipse the universal motifs. The normal location of the primary design is at the top of the headstone. Although decorated footstones are present in many cases, their designs were not included in this study, since they do not seem to provide the regularity of patterning as universally as headstone designs do, nor are they present in adequate numbers for statistical treatment. Beneath the design is the inscription, usually giving the name, age, and date of death of the individual, and the epitaph, if any. In addition to the main top design, the sides of most stones are embellished with various floral, geometric, and anthropomorphic motifs.

The three universally occurring design types are as follows:

(1) *Death's Heads.* Usually some type of winged skull, this design is early in New England and is found on the oldest stones as the most common motif. At times it is combined with other elements such as bones, hourglasses, coffins, and palls. This design undergoes a gradual simplification through time.

(2) *Cherubs.* A human face with wings, this style is characteristic of stones carved after the middle 18th century. Like the death's-head motif, the cherub motif undergoes considerable modification through time, chiefly marked by a trend toward simplification.

(3) *Urns and Willow Trees.* The urn and willow motif appears at the close of the 18th century and becomes universal in a very short

time. It is the latest design of the three, and its appearance signals the end of the slate-gravestone tradition in New England. Associated with this design is a marked alteration in the shape of the stone. Earlier stones have arched shoulders flanking the curved major-design area, while the urn-and-willow design is preponderantly associated with a square-shouldered stone.

The method employed in this study consisted of making photographic collections of all stones in a number of key cemeteries and supplementing these with selections from a number of other locations. Epitaphs were also collected so that a study of the relationship between epitaph and design, if any, could be made. Each complete cemetery sample was then quantified by determining the relative popularity of all designs through the time represented by the cemetery, broken down by decade, and presented in graphic form showing the percentage of each design type used in each ten-year period. This procedure enables one to determine by rapid inspection the time of initial appearance, maximum popularity, and final disappearance of each design involved. After these graphs were prepared, the data were viewed synchronically in an effort to determine the direction of movement of certain designs or attributes thereof, and then both aspects of design distributions were projected against known historical data. Cemeteries at Sudbury, Concord, Lexington, Cambridge, and Plymouth were treated in this manner, although over 40 cemeteries were visited and inspected to ascertain that the pattern in the five intensively treated cemeteries was a valid and universal one. The results of this initial effort are extremely promising in a number of ways.

When the three types are plotted against time, it appears that gravestone designs produce classic examples of the well-known "battleship shaped" curve which is the mainstay of seriation methods. Each cemetery so far examined in depth shows the gradual replacement of skulls by cherubs and the subsequent eclipse of the cherub motif by the urn-and-willow design. While the general pattern of replacement is repeated in each of the cemeteries treated, as well as in each of those visited, there are significant differences in the time and rate of change. While cherubs replace death's heads over the entire area, they do so later in Cambridge and progressively earlier as one moves out from the Boston area, although their time of initial appearance is earlier in the Boston area and correspondingly later in areas farther removed. This change is more marked in the southern direction toward Plymouth.

Another significant difference is in the number of local styles in the cemeteries in question. Although Cambridge has none, many cemeteries in the surrounding area have at least one design type of only local occurrence. Most of these local styles occur with highest frequency during the 20-year period between 1740 and 1760. Gravestone designs in the 5000-square-mile area in question cluster rather naturally by type into three time periods between 1680 and 1820. These are as follows: Period I, 1680-1740; Period II, 1740-1760; and Period III, 1760-1820.

Of the six local styles described in Table 1, four are found in the area south of Boston, two occur primarily to the west,

TABLE 1. LOCAL STYLES IN COLONIAL CEMETERIES

Style	*Carver*	*Dates and Period*	*Known Distribution*
"Roman"	Worcester	1730-1760 (II)	West of Boston (Concord, Lexington, Wayland, Sudbury, Billerica, Bedford, Harvard).
Large, red sandstone portraits	Unknown	1770-1800 (111)	South of Boston, Old Plymouth Colony (Hanover, Hingham, Quincy, Braintree, Weymouth, Norwell, Plymouth).
Black slate, portraits or bulldoglike death's heads	Park	1756-1785 (III)	West of Boston (Lexington, Concord, Billerica, Bedford, Wayland, Sudbury).
Green schist Medusas	Unknown	1745-1770 (II)	South of Boston to Cape Cod (Middleboro, Marshfield, Plymouth, Buzzards Bay, Duxbury).
Birdlike death's head	Vinal?	1740-1770 (11)	A local style of limited distribution, centered on Scituate, home of Vinal. (Scituate, Norwell, Braintree, Marshfield).
Death's Head with heart-shaped mouth	Unknown	1730-1745 (I, II)	Middleboro, Marshfield, Plymouth, Scituate.

and none as yet has been isolated in the area north of Boston in the direction of Salem or Cape Ann. With one exception, these designs are derived in some way from one of the universal motifs. The portraits, which are nearly universal, occurring in most cemeteries outside the Boston area and the region immediately to the north and east, seem to be analogous in many ways to the cherub motif. In fact, many of the cherubs probably have some aspect of portraiture. In the Cambridge and Charlestown cemeteries, cherubs marking male burials differ from those marking females in a single aspect, the style of hair, with male cherubs exhibiting a downward curl and female hair styles done in an upsweep. This distinction is probably an idiosyncrasy of one family of carvers, the Lamsons of Charlestown, since the distinction cannot be shown to carry over to cherub motifs executed by other carvers. The essential functional identity between cherubs and portraits is further indicated by their similar distribution in time, both reaching their highest frequencies in the third quarter of the 18th century or somewhat later. The Medusas and birdlike death's heads of the Plymouth-Scituate area are derived from the death's-head design. In both cases, there seems to have been a change in the features of the lower face, with the typical death's head nose enlarging to form a smiling mouth, with a subsequent reduction or complete loss of the teeth. The curious heart-mouthed death's heads, on the other hand, appear to derive from some other source, as yet unclear.

Among these local styles, the so-called Roman motif is unique in its remarkable conservatism. Although in use for a period of approximately 30 years, little change can be seen between its earliest and latest form. Slight variations in the number of turns in the flanking spirals and the occasional addition of a second, smaller, six-pointed element within the larger ones at the sides are the only changes which take place. This design was probably the product of a single carver, Jonathan Worcester (Forbes 1927: 77-8), but other carvers whose work is known in detail show considerable variation and change in their work over a comparable period of time, as can be seen in the reduction of complexity in the cherub motif employed by Nathaniel and Caleb Lamson between 1740 and 1760. Worcester's work is also unique in that he retains upper-case lettering for inscriptions, a practice which was abandoned for more conventional lower case by all other carvers in the first two decades of the 18th century. It is tempting to view the intense conservatism of Worcester's curious design as resulting from its unique qualities. The design in toto could have been taken as a minimal significant unit, rather than its constituent attributes, while cherubs and death's heads could more easily have been perceived as made up of rather discrete, semi-independently variable elements such as wings, skulls, faces, and different hair styles.

This pattern of design change and replacement, rigidly placed in time and space by the peculiar nature of the material which demonstrates it, reflects a wealth of information concerning the times during which it was produced. The interpretive aspects of this study, only recently begun in detail, already show considerable promise of providing a model of interrelated change in many aspects of culture, based primarily on its material remains. For example, the replacement of one universal motif by another through time over the entire area is certainly a function of changes in religious values combined with significant shifts in views regarding death. Considered synchronically, it can be seen that these changes did not proceed uniformly but were proceeding at different rates and probably for different reasons. It is a safe assumption that Cambridge and Boston were apparently the 18th-century cultural focus in eastern Massachusetts. Harvard was a divinity school at the time, and religious attitudes and beliefs must have been intensified and initially changed in this central area. Since the death's-head motif was the modal design which accompanied early Puritanism in the colony, the shift from death's heads to cherubs may be viewed as indicative of a departure from a prior form of Puritan religion. Such an assumption is strongly supported by the epitaphs normally found on stones of the late 17th and early 18th centuries, which are in close harmony with the major tenets of New England Puritanism. Mortality is stressed, little of no mention being made of an afterlife or resurrection of the dead, as shown by the following example:

> Remember me as you pass by
> As you are now so once was I
> As I am now you soon must be
> Prepare for death and follow me.

Other epitaphs mention moldering dust, worms, and decay. When cherubs become modal after midcentury, epitaphs take on a lighter, more hopeful note, although the earlier type does not disappear, occurring even on urn-and-willow stones. Frequent mention of ascent to God, or afterlife in general, is common on cherub stones:

> Farewell my wife and children dear,
> I leave you for a while
> For God has called and I must go
> And leave you all behind.

It is important to note that while the death's head can be viewed as a graphic representation of one's mortal remains, cherubs are indicative of the immortal component of the deceased. However, both designs are personal representations, while the later urn-and-willow motif is a depersonalized memorial.

In addition to this religious dimension of design change, there may be a significant social dimension. A survey of the literature dealing with English gravestones of the 17th and 18th centuries shows that a change from death's heads to cherubs occurred in the British Isles approximately 70 years before it occurred in New England (Chin 1963; Christison 1902; Graham 1957-58; Yentsch 1963). Cherubs were therefore modal in England in the opening decades of the 18th century, and they appear in small numbers in Cambridge and Charlestown as early as the second decade of that century. The association of these early cherub stones in Cambridge is largely with members of the cosmopolitan minority of the populace. High church officials, a governor's daughter, Harvard College presidents and their wives, and even a Londoner have graves marked by stones bearing elaborate cherub designs. While the cherub motif remains a minor component in Cambridge gravestone designs, the association with members of a higher, more worldly urban class suggests that they are the source of innovation in this case. The remainder of the population still employs stones with the typical death's heads, and cherubs never become a truly popular design in the central Cambridge-Boston area. The upward slope of the horizon marking the initial appearance of cherubs in the cemeteries progressively farther from the center probably indicates that this influence diffused outward. However, from the point in time when cherubs become popular, the slope is in the other direction, downward as one moves out from Boston. This can be most economically interpreted as indicating the progressive reduction in intensity of the Puritan ethic in places farther removed from the center of its formulation and transmission. It appears that change is primarily initiated by a small segment of the population and then spreads to the majority, with the rate of spread being inversely proportional to the strength with which religious belief is regulated by a central authority. This interpretation is tentative, subject to the accumulation of additional data.

The distribution pattern of local styles supports these general interpretations. The preponderance of local stylistic diversity in the area which until 1692 was Plymouth Colony, with a somewhat different religion, is expectable according to the general conclusions drawn from the pattern of change seen through time in all cometeries studied. The only local styles which exist outside of the Old Colony are the two which occur in the Concord-Lexington-Harvard sphere, and these are somewhat different from those to the south. The Roman style was the work of one man, and it continued only during his productive years; William Park's massive black-slate stones, while distinctively local, are usually decorated with one of the universal motifs. In marked contrast, the area south of Boston abounds with designs which are truly peculiar, and the pattern of highly individualistic designs, derived from the universal motifs but quite different from them in detail, is distinctive of this area.

The period from 1740 to 1760 stands out as a time of initial departure from death's heads and of considerable experimentation in new designs. West of Boston it is the peculiar Roman style; to the south, birdlike skulls, Medusas, and the first cherubs in quantity. This sudden variability is not seen in Boston, in Cambridge, or in the area immediately to the north. In all other cemeteries, however, it is the time during which the maximum number of designs occurs. After 1760, cherubs preponderate; prior to 1740, death's heads are virtually universal. This two-decade span was noted at an early stage of this study, and only much later did we discover that it coincided with the time of the "Great Awakening." This movement within New England Puritanism, sparked by Jonathan Edwards, began in 1740 in the Connecticut Valley in Central Massachusetts, and spread rapidly east, reaching but not entering Boston. It was characterized by a newly placed stress on the joys of life after death and resurrection of the dead, rather than the earlier stern emphasis of judgment and mortality. While the cemeteries surrounding Boston on the west and south do not share in the precise motifs introduced during this period, the cherub is one design universally shared, and its subsequent rise to popularity, eclipsing other local styles, in all probability relates in some way to the influence of the Great Awakening.

The end of the Great Awakening is also the time of the final demise of Puritanism. The year 1760 marks the beginning of yet another change in religious views, leading to the rise of Unitarianism and Methodism in the early years of the 19th century. This change is reflected in the cemeteries by the final shift in design types from cherub to urn-and-willow. The urn-and-willow motif becomes the hallmark of Victorian gravemarkers. In direct contrast to the earlier highly personalized designs, urns and willows reflect a trend toward the depersonalization of death and memorial. By the beginning of the 19th century this design becomes absolutely universal, and even today draped urns are a favorite element in gravestone style. The depth to which chroniclers of American funeral custom trace the historic roots of modern practices probably cannot pass this point of time. Much of modern "grief therapy" (Mitford 1963) may be traceable to this initial step in depersonalization, but certainly funeral customs in the period preceding 1800 belong to another age and another set of values.

REFERENCES

1. Chin, Roberta, 1963. English Tombstones: An Attempt to Trace Their Relationship to Social Attitudes and to the Tombstone Trends of Colonial New England. Unpublished manuscript, Peabody Museum, Cambridge.
2. Christison, D., 1902. The Carvings and Inscriptions of the Kirkyard Monuments of the Scottish Lowlands, Particularly in Perth, Fife, Angus, Mearns and Lothian. *Proceedings of the Society of Antiquaries of Scotland,* Series 3, Vol. 12, pp. 280-457.
3. Forbes, Harriet, 1927. *Gravestones of Early New England, 1653-1800.* Houghton Mifflin, Boston.
4. Graham, A., 1957-1958. Headstones in Post Reformation Scotland. *Proceedings of the Society of Antiquaries of Scotland,* Vol. 91, pp. 1-9.
5. Mitford, Jessica, 1963. *The American Way of Death.* Simon and Schuster, New York.
6. Yentsch, Anne E., 1963. Design Elements in Scottish Gravestones. Unpublished manuscript, Peabody Museum, Cambridge.

PART TWO

"Reaching for the Choir Invisible"

The Nineteenth Century

The popular mind of antebellum America was saturated with concern about death. In the first essay of this section Lewis Saum makes the point well and explains why. The intimacy with death was forced, not only by "actuarial prevalence" but by "existential proximity." Life expectancy throughout the century remained limited, measured against today's standards, approximately forty years in 1850 and forty-seven at the close of the century. If aspects of the earlier noted "pilgrim" posture continued, notably the rhetoric of death as an escape from the world's sadness, there was nonetheless a significant change in vision which gradually occurred. Increasingly death was perceived within a context of attachment to life as well as some disquieting uncertainty about the future of the dead.[1]

From that perspective death as an event became less acceptable than had previously been the case. The living demanded that its harsh reality be reduced, muted, and beautified. Those alive became less willing to conclude their relationship with the deceased and would seek comfort through a substantial reduction in social distance between the living world and the dead world. The dead would be drawn into the lives of the living as never before in the American past. One dimension of these new feelings was that the corpse, largely unimportant from the "pilgrim" posture, now became precious. That preciousness would be expressed symbolically through a growing concern for aesthetic luxury in burial containers, and through an elegant elaboration of death-related ritual and paraphernalia. Direction in all aspects of mortuary practice was toward beauty and sublimity.[2] Comments in the selection by Robert Habenstein and William Lamers illustrate the new perspective as it was expressed in late nineteenth-century mourning etiquette, mourning symbols, and death-related verse.

Beautification of death and the trend toward allowing the dead a greater role in life may be further observed in the so-called rural cemetery movement. The initial motivation for the application of landscape gardening techniques to the graveyard, which got underway in the 1830s, sprang from considerations of public health, but much more than sanitation and location for body disposal was expected of the new burial grounds. As the brief selection by Neil Harris points out, the dead would be rescued from their previous and often appallingly unkept conditions, and their abode would become places of leisure and gentle assurance for the living. While original emphasis in the "rural cemetery" was on the beauty of nature, the comments by Habenstein and Lamers suggest that significant changes in gravestone sculpture were occurring also by the late nineteenth century.

The antebellum mood of Americans was also affected profoundly by certain contemporary challenges to the traditional vision of human significance and destiny. These currents at first encouraged a need for greater relationship with the dead, though growing religious doubts engendered by them joined ultimately with other forces to encourage the alienation of death from life which would characterize the next century. A major force behind the spiritual upheaval of the Gilded Age was developments in the natural sciences, more specifically the evolution controversy. Charles Darwin's *Origin of Species* was published in 1859 but, perhaps because of the crushing political problems of the day, it generated little immediate public discussion. Only in the 1870s did the debate around evolution become heated and major. For many religious Americans such theory had shocking implications. It challenged the Biblical account of creation. It meant that the human species lost a godly image and became merely one more category in the animal kingdom. By inference it called into question the very notions of the "soul" and post-death existence. In the next essay historian Paul Carter describes the impact of this threat to the concept of afterlife and the efforts to deal with it.

Large numbers of Americans could neither live nor die with either the mere "trembling hope" about their future state, which Saum identifies as central to the antebellum popular mind, or the even greater uncertainty seemingly imposed by Darwin's "heartless" science. One effort at reassurance, as Carter notes, was to affirm that immortality was a logical extension of the evolutionary process itself. A second, also identified by Carter, but which began before the Civil War, was spiritualism. Defined as varying types of reciprocal contact between the living and the dead, here was positive proof that departed loved ones did survive the grave and did remain near at hand, anxious indeed for continued relationship on life terms. It is estimated that at one point spiritualism commanded the allegiance of one million Americans.[3]

Another form of earthly comfort against doubts was volumes and visions such as those of the popular novelist Elizabeth Stuart Phelps. Casting off the traditional imagery of heaven, her detailed depictions of the afterlife reduced the once awesome mystery of the spiritual world into a state much like that of a splendid, though quite familiar, middle-class American community. As one scholar put it, in Phelps' *The Gates Ajar* (1868), *Beyond the Gates* (1883), and *The Gates Between* (1887), "heaven becomes a utopian analogue of the world she knew, complete with hospitals for sick souls who receive the ministrations of spirit doctors until they can assume full citizenship in the city of God."[4] Thus was the line between the world of the living and that of the dead significantly blurred. Two brief selections from *The Gates Ajar* are provided as the final material in this section. Here Winnifred Forceythe discusses the nature of the eternal life with Mary Cabot, grief-stricken over the death of her brother Roy.

NOTES

1. Covey identifies this change but believes it occurred in the eighteenth century. *The American Pilgrimage,* 105. Saum emphasizes, in his essay, the extent to which the "pilgrim" posture remained active through the antebellum period.

2. Habenstein and Lamers, *History of American Funeral Directing,* 393, 417-20.

3. E. D. Branch, *The Sentimental Years,* 1836-1860 (New York, 1934), 378.

4. Elizabeth Stuart Phelps, *The Gates Ajar,* ed. Helen Sootin Smith (Cambridge, 1964), xxi.

Lewis O. Saum

DEATH IN THE POPULAR MIND OF PRE-CIVIL WAR AMERICA

"And when men die, we do not mention them." With those words Emerson concluded his gloomy forecast for a society suffering a "decaying church and a wasting unbelief."[1] In time, cultural commentators saw something resembling Emerson's contention. Over a century later the Spanish scholar Julián Marías wrote of the United States that death assumes here "the air of an undesirable alien and has therefore made no progress towards citizenship."[2] Neither of the two philosophers, Emerson or Marías, spoke quite accurately. Marías allowed a faulty inference. Death had once had full citizenship, but had suffered exile, probably with the rise of naturalistic and materialistic moods emergent in the late 19th century. Emerson in 1838 played Jeremiah with overmuch intensity. As forecast, his observation had accuracy; but as description, it fell very wide of the mark. In fact his was a society saturated with concern with death, and fastidious to a fault in observances pertaining to it. Carl Bode in *The Anatomy of American Popular Culture, 1840-1860* concluded with "A Trio for Columbia," three themes about which American culture of that era might be focused. Two of the three, Love and Suc-

---

"Death in the Popular Mind of Pre-Civil War America" by Lewis O. Saum, *American Quarterly,* 26 (December 1974), pp. 477-495.

cess, involved aspiration and possibility. The third, Death, had certainty and universality.

Interestingly, however, Bode showed some impatience in his handling of the appreciation of death evidenced in poetry, plays and novels. Aspects of that theme seemed to impress him as fulsome and, perhaps, emotionally exploitative. Bode's readers have difficulty forgetting that, after Little Mary Morgan of *Ten Nights in a Bar-Room* fell at the strike of a hurled whiskey glass, author Timothy Shay Arthur devoted "most of the next sixty pages to her lingering, pathetic demise." Nor can one readily disassociate the fact that Mrs. Sigourney was "a classical example of an extremely pcpular bad poet" from the fact that "her favorite single subject" was death.[3] Kenneth S. Lynn more abruptly showed a later age's misgiving about the presentation of death in pre-Civil War culture. In an essay praising the artistry of *Uncle Tom's Cabin,* Lynn spoke of Harriet Beecher Stowe's characters as "shockingly believable." But, he allowed, Stowe did employ some "factitious" dramatic situations, most notably the death of Augustine St. Clare. To Lynn, it was an exercise in "saccharine phoniness," one that "strikes us today as hackneyed from beginning to end."[4] It would not do justice to Bode and Lynn to suggest that their artistic and cultural criticisms illustrate what Geoffrey Gorer called "an unremarked shift in prudery" in the 20th century—from sex to death. But there seems to be little hazard in suggesting, as Gorer did, that theatrical, poetical and literary mileage gotten from deathly dramatics derived from the fact that such situations were among the relatively few "that an author could be fairly sure would have been shared by the vast majority of his readers."[5]

The following essay seeks to get at certain perceptions and moods of the comparatively unelevated by what seems to me the sensible, if not always inspiring method of reading the diaries, the letters and the commonplace jottings of people in unprepossessing circumstances. Possibly this will circumvent the inferential leaps inherent in efforts to derive a portrayal of humble sentiments from expressions directed at them or written about them by those in positions of intellectual, literary, journalistic, political or some other form of attainment. Simply, the essay attempts to convey what ordinary people themselves said about death, and, in part, it attempts to relate those attitudes and beliefs to the depictions rendered by better minds both at the time and later.

At the end of his diary Connecticut cook and sailor William Sprague inscribed a toast:

> Here is to the world that goes
> round on wheels
> Death is a thing that all
> man feels
> If death was a thing that
> the rich could buy
> The rich would live and
> the poor would die[6]

Death was indeed that thing "that all man feels"; and it behooved all men to give that fact sober consideration. A great many assiduously fulfilled their obligation, giving almost ceaseless advice to self and others to keep death firmly in mind. Here we encounter a persuasion and an appetite that would seem by later standards a blend of the gargantuan and the pathological. Thus a New Yorker's diary page titled "Needful Counsel" had, centered to the left, the injunctive opening, "let your." To the right of that came a vertical series of subjects—"Conduct," "Diet" and "Sleep," among others—followed, in turn, by the single verb "be." At the right came an appropriately arranged vertical series of compound predicates, thus giving, for example, "let your Diet be temperate, wholesome sober." Appropriately, this diagrammatic didacticism concluded with: "let your Reflection be of death and future state."[7] In Alabama, schoolboy Isaac Barr filled entire pages of his penmanship book with reminders, most of which have a more solemn tone than the following: "School expires Isaac on the 8th day of May 1852." Whatever his exact age, young Isaac had an ample number of years to contemplate sobering ultimates, and thus, far outnumbering the notices of the end of school, came reminders of the end of life. "Death takes the young as well as the old"; "Remember this life is not long"; or simply "Remember you must die."[8]

The risk of idle supererogation or even impertinence looms large in any effort to explain the superabundant musings and dotings on death. Accepting the hazard, one must note first that death was an ever present fact of life. As a normally unreflective Maine farmer cited the conventional wisdom, "in life we are in the midst of death."[9] Few cultural commentaries on that era fail to remark the intimacy most people had with death. Theirs was an immediate, not a derivative or vicarious, awareness. Thus, in the context of melancholy poetry Carl Bode reminded his readers of the "somber story" told by mortality statistics.[10] In this case, Bode mentioned figures from New York City. But the condition was general, not particular; and, as Perry Miller remarked about Concord, "the supreme fact was death."[11] Others, however, have shown puzzlement bordering on impatience when treating the popular inclination to dwell on death at the expense of what a later age would deem more important. One editor of humble writings, though he took satisfaction from the "few references to political and social events" that appeared in his material, had to admit that, of such, there were "not as many as one might hope for." That illness and death should receive so much attention he guardedly ascribed to "the uncertainty of individual life."[12] In that conclusion he was right at least in part.

When upstate New York common schoolteacher Sophronia Beebe opened a letter to an old friend, she did so in this way: "The grim messenger has been at work all over the land calling for his thousands. The lovely child has been taken from its sports; the youth has been taken from its circle of loved ones; the teacher from his arduous duties, the lawyer from the bar, the doctor from his office, the statesman from the senate chamber . . ."[13] This doleful overture left matters in the comparatively abstract, as perhaps befit the lady's calling. Far more commonly, the immediacy took on almost awesome proportions. Farm woman Annis Pierce sent what consolation she could to a daughter who had lost an infant child. Mother Pierce expressed herself awkwardly, but not with the callousness one might infer from the following: "I wast not any disappointed when we heard of the death of little Emma. I was very sure that I would hear of the death of some one of those dear little ones . . ."[14] Routinely people specified what proportion their living offspring bore to the total. If Little Eva and Little Mary Morgan were accorded so much time and attention in dying, it probably had much to do with the fact that mortality among children was staggering.

> My brothers [and] sister kind & dear
> How soon youve passid away
> Your friendly faces now I hear
> Are mowldren in the clay

This Indiana youngster can well be forgiven his or her contribution, "On the death of my 2 brothers & sister," to the melancholy poetry of the period.[15]

The immediacy reflected in mortality rates conjoined in deathly impact with the lack or incipient condition of professional or institutional services for handling the dying and the dead. Ineluctable realities brought people to most direct contact with fundamentals. In February of 1846 Brigham Nims of New Hampshire recorded what may have been his first full participation in handling the dying and the dead, and he did so in a straightforward way that suggests the routineness of the function. On the night of the 10th he "watched with Seth Towns he was very wild the fore part of the night, more calm toward morning." Nims visited Seth again on the 11th, and, when word came that all was over, he returned to prepare the deceased for burial: "I went and helped Lay him out, and shaved him the first person that I tried to shave."[16] Late in 1834 a young Maryland store clerk did such duty at the end of September, again in the middle of November, and again on the last day of the year. In one case it was a friend, in another it was the daughter of a friend, and the third was a cousin. In the case of the dying friend, he sat by the deathbed for several nights consecutively. The end came at 11:40 at night. "I then shaved & washed him," the clerk wrote, "& Marker assisted me in dressing him *(he died hard).*"[17]

In turn, the familiarity with death may have been intensified by urges that were, on the one hand reportorial, and, on the other, therapeutic. In the former regard, letters of the period partake so heavily of the deathly aura in part because communications had not kept pace with population mobility. People at far remove and in infrequent contact concentrated on fundamentals, among which the death list came foremost. Letters often had, given the circumstances of the time, a quality that brought this reflection from a Carolina woman: "I dread mail days . . . the sight of a letter makes me so nervous."[18]

It did not always suffice to tell who had died. The manner of their going received a good deal of attention, and not just in terms of the spiritual considerations to be treated later. Time and again, descriptive comments on death incorporated so much physiological detail as to suggest a purposive eye to medical or therapeutic concerns. Humble people probably communicated and pooled empirical data because there was not a ready resort to trusted and respected experts. Little in the shape of an institutional shield stood between the lay person and the untidy details of disease and dying. Left often to their own needs and devices, common folk recorded and conveyed, not gratuitous morbidity, but the information of pathology. Her daughter "little Lydia," an Ohio woman wrote in an account of the child's death, "did not swell as much as some." This is only an earnest of the graphic description of the course of Lydia's trials: measles in January, then the whooping cough, then smallpox and on to this May day on which she died and on which her mother wrote.[19] On his way west to work as foreman of a carpenter crew on the Illinois Central construction, Charles Rich wrote from Bangor, Maine, to his wife back on the farm at Milo. At the very outset of this long and particularly revealing correspondence, the 45-year-old husband wrote of death. One Gilman, a man who had started with Rich on the way to the West, had fallen ill almost at the outset and died in a tavern at Waterville. Charles stood not on delicacy in addressing his 26-year-old wife, Albina, nor did he spare her the details. The deceased carpenter had been constipated for several days, Rich noted, and the pills and the oil had worked no relief. At the tavern, when Gilman had become incapacitated, some others "took hold and helped" Rich administer enemas. Lobelia and thoroughwort in two or three such applications yielded a half-pint "of what appeared more like sheep manure only in larger rolls and very black." The pathological particulars changed when a doctor arrived with the predictable calomel. Shortly, the dead carpenter was on his way back to Milo.[20]

Gilman would build no more houses, Albina mused as she wrote late in the night after the funeral. At the service itself "while looking at his dead bodie," she had entertained other questions and other associations: "I thought who heard his last words, who laid him out, it was my own *dear husband*." With that dead body before her, she felt "as if I wanted to see you and ask many questions."[21] To ask and receive the details of a person's death was standard. Here it appears that Albina had in mind some spiritual concerns. Her husband had probably given satisfactory account of the temporal, physical and medical aspects of Gilman's demise. It would be fair to assume that Charles Rich had not burdened his wife with idle unsavory details, but that, out of some positive, informative urge, he had sought to share his knowledge of a particular path from disease to death. In more than the ultimate sense, death was inescapable. People knew it by its existential proximity as well as by its actuarial prevalence.

If there was a powerful intimacy with death, a spiritual fascination with death—the outlines of which will be discussed shortly—there was as well a seeming insouciance, a capacity to register without questioning. At one level that capacity represented no more than an extension of the resignation to Providence of the time. At another level it may have been little more than being inured, inevitably, to the sorts of situations described by the Maryland store clerk and so many others. "Not simply as a matter of rhetoric," Fred Somkin wrote, "but in frightening actuality, Americans seemed strangely able to accept the possibility of violent death on a mass scale." That most indiscriminate killer, the steamboat, appeared as no more than the "most recent embodiment of the elemental power."[22] Mark Twain provided an illustration that Somkin might well have used. Writing of antebellum America, and assuring us in footnote that he was not fictionalizing, Mark Twain told in *The Gilded Age* of the race between the *Boreas* and the *Amaranth.* There was pride, "hurrah," juvenile swagger, a "nigger roosting on the safety-valve," and "then there was a booming roar." When the horror and the screams of the dying subsided, 39 were injured, 22 were dead and 96 were missing. The head engineer of the *Amaranth* took off his ring, peeling steam-eaten flesh with it, and handed it and his eternal curse to the man who had been in command at the time. But the court of enquiry returned "the inevitable American verdict which has been so familiar to our ears all the days of our lives—'NOBODY TO BLAME.'"[23]

Mark Twain did more than indulge an intense and mordant irony. On his way from St. Louis to Glasgow, Missouri, in 1842, New Englander Walter B. Foster's boat, the *Satan*, tied up for the night at the mouth of the Missouri. As the *Satan* pulled away in the morning, another boat near by, the *Edna of the Platte,* exploded. Writing a few days later in Glasgow, Foster took some care to describe the ghastly scenes that unfolded as the *Satan* went to assist. For explicit horror, his account far exceeds the *Amaranth* episode in *The Gilded Age.* The "screams and groans, curses and prayers" that "resounded from all sides" established the general aura. Foster then pressed on into the particulars of the pathology of disaster. Some begged "in piteous accents" to be killed forthwith; others lay perfectly still and quiet; those who had inhaled steam screeched hideously; a "respectable looking" man with a demolished hand and various scald wounds graciously accepted a glass of wine; a German woman scalded over most of her body pleaded with Foster to remove the skin of her arm and hand that now hung from her nails like a rolled-off glove. He did. Foster's was an eye to clinical detail, an eye that observed the quick as well as the dying. Some of the sound aided as they could; some shrank in horror; some suffered such shock as to be rendered "incapable of attending to anything"; and some "drank, smoked, and laughed." Some did worse. Around the body of a German killed and denuded by the blast and the steam hung a "belt of sovereigns." "An Irishman standing by pocketed it." Almost at the end of his account, Foster found it "strange" that anyone "could be so depraved!" "But enough," he concluded, not bothering to ask how or why it was that the *Edna of the Platte* had taken so many to such a dreadful end.[24]

It has been common to see ambition as much of the causal context for the seeming heedlessness of American society. Fred Somkin's previously quoted observation about the American ability to accept violent death came, for example, in a chapter titled "Prosperity the Riddle." And one finds intimations of that theme in humble writing. As did so many others, A. P. Moss of Texas related in an 1853 letter "some quite melanchollly" news, an account of the ravages of the flux in his area. But then, "laying aside mortality," he wrote that Smith County was prospering. It was "live with enterprise," and "Railroads is all the go."[25] Here, of course we are edging into Colonel Beriah Sellers' neighborhood. But, however inviting, the idea of progress and its various concomitants do not fit very well with common views of that era. If people showed a seeming indifference or a stoic equanimity, it probably stemmed far more from enforced intimacy with death and, in turn, from what they would have considered a Christian, providential resignation.

The tentative mood reigned supreme. After a New Hampshire mountain tour young Josiah Chaney gave a typical expression of it. He thought it probable that he would some day travel more, but he added the necessary qualifier—if he lived.[26] Walter Foster, before going up the Mississippi to the scene of the *Edna* explosion, had a birthday while at New Orleans. In the diary entry of the preceding day he announced it this way: "Tomorrow I'm twenty-three if I live . . . ."[27] That grimly remindful reservation—if life is spared—resonated around pre-Civil War America. It went to the self, where perhaps it was most needed; but with palsying frequency it went to others, to the old who least required reminding, to the sound and the active who might forget, and to the very young who might not understand.

Christian doctrine joined with hard fact to emphasize the emotional desirability of approaching life with a tentative, almost interrogative mien. When "hannah marthy" of Indiana drowned for venturing onto a shaky footbridge over a freshet-swollen stream, Mary Jane Crane gave poetic statement of the proper reaction to the fate of this "blooming youth":

> But there is something says bestill
> Tis God's most righteous holy will[28]

From such an attitude could come that "great comfort" enjoyed by Melville's Turkish "Fatalists," a type that suddenly merged for him into almost everyone.[29] Melville probably saw Emerson as one of those "amiable philosophers of either the 'Compensation' or 'Optimist' school."[30] But in "Fate" Emerson brought together in mood the Turk, the Arab, the Hindoo and "our Calvinists"—our Calvinists "in the last generation."[31] For seeing the *persisting* similarity, Melville, it seems to me, came nearer the truth. Emerson saw American fatalists in the past but not in the present; had he looked more closely he might well have shared Melville's conviction that they were all about him.

Less than eloquent testimony of the trembling quality of hope can be seen in the census files of the period. Very frequently the family list that ran from husband and wife through the children in order of age would end with "anonymous," "not named" or "unnamed." Infants so designated often had attained several months, sometimes over a year of age. In keeping with this practice J. S. Brown of Phillips, Maine, concluded a letter-listing of the names and ages of his seven children with one who was "a year old has no name yet."[32] Upstate New York farmer Francis Squires made frequent diary references to a son born in July of 1852. But only after weathering a severe illness in March 1853, did "bub" assume full identity in his father's writings. In an entry that probably marked the naming, Squires wrote: "*Clarence Augustine Pierce Squires* weighs 20 lbs."[33]

On the occasion of the birth of a daugher, Josiah Crosby of Westernville, New York, received a letter conveying congratulations and the hope that the child would be a great blessing. "But dont," came the ritual warning, "set too mutch by it."[34] George and Fidelia Baldwin of the same state indulged in the happiness that came with their healthy new baby; "but how long we shal be allowed to keep him is inknown to us." This same letter referred to a previous child they had lost, and that fact as well as the general mood probably accounts for their use of a fairly common designation for the new arrival—the "little stranger."[35] However high the hopes, caution dominated as the admonitory byword. A letter from Carrolton, Alabama, to a grieving brother and sister had the comparative sophistication and the crushing personal experience that allowed fuller explicit expression of the dilemma of loving indifference. In their bereavement the couple must, this writer urged, turn to their remaining children for comfort.

> But do not O do not I beseech you lean too much on this fond hope lest in a moment you least suspect it shall be torn away *forever* . . . O how heart-rending it is for us to be told that we must call off our

affections from these dear second selves and yet if we do not in some degree turn our affections away from them we sharpen the Arrow that is to pierce our vitals.[36]

In the full despondence that ensued—"the heart withers and joy sickens & dies and existance becomes a troubled dream"—this Alabaman went beyond that quiet resignation counseled and sought by most. But a situation incorporating "little strangers" and involving the self-preservative need to "in some degree turn our affections away from them" tells much about childhood, life and death in pre-Civil War America.

Philosophy has been referred to as the learning to die, and insofar as humble Americans philosophized they did indeed learn to die. Countering the assertive optimism of the Emersonian position, Melville bespoke that older resigned mood. *Pierre* becomes an almost angry rejection of the specious felicity of the Transcendental war on circumstances. Pierre Glendinning's insurgency leads only to "conclusive proof that he has no power over his condition." Involuted into the "author-hero, Vivia," Pierre comes to "deep-down, unutterable mournfulness": "'Away, ye chattering apes of a sophomorean Spinoza and Plato, who once didst all but delude me that night was day, and pain only a tickle.'" Here, young Pierre "is fitting himself for the highest life, by thinning his blood and collapsing his heart. He is learning how to live, by rehearsing the part of death."[37] The common man arrived at that position somewhat more readily for having no "'chattering apes'" to circumvent.

The American drift to comfortable worldliness had not run its course by the pre-Civil War period. Cyclone Covey has given us a brief and imaginative account of the move away from a world-view centered on "a symbolic pilgrimage through the wilderness of this world to an ultimate hometown in the next." At the outset of our history the mood appeared in the Augustinian equation: "Destination: Death." By the end of a century in the new world, the Pilgrim found himself in "Vanity Fair," and, a moment later, "The Big Switch" had been completed. With this 18th century, "revolution to modernity," Covey wrote, "death has been the subject to be most avoided of most considered."[38] The conspiracy of silence settled in, and Abraham Lincoln's deathly melancholia assumes the guise of atavistic epilogue. Covey's trenchant work notwithstanding, the move to "modernity" probably came far more slowly than such an overview indicates. What he called "The Psychology of Bereavement" took expression in ever-lessening eloquence and intensity; but the humble writings of mid-19th century bear powerful resemblance in thrust to the elevated statements of three centuries before.

When Francis Squires' wife died in March 1860 the minister chose Romans 13:12 to elucidate the meaning for the survivors: "The night is far spent, the day is at hand: let us therefore cast off the works of darkness, and let us put on the armour of light." "I am very lonesome today," the forty-year-old widower wrote, "& feel that the world is not our home."[39] Most directly, death partook of warning. As a dying man in Sterling, Massachusetts, stated it to the wife who conveyed his words to others, "Tell them that my being about to be cut off in the midst of my years may prove a warning to my dear friends to be ready."[40] The bridegroom cometh, the lamps must be kept trimmed. With a litany's regularity the metaphor of Matthew 25 informed the mood of the period. The fullness of God's purpose was, of course, never clear; but patently the death of a loved one alerted the survivors, and, in turn, it prepared them by weaning them from worldly attachments. When Lawrence Parker's baby died (and his wife was soon to follow), relatives did what they could to explain: "You have now one less object to attach you to the earth, and one more to draw you towards heaven. Undoubtedly this was God's design in taking the *Dear Babe*."[41] To be sure, the "Pilgrim" was indeed in "Vanity Fair," and "the ties of nature are strong."[42] But people resisted the allurements and did what they could to keep the ties loose. Lincoln's poetic statement differs in quality but not in essence from the bereaved sense of his humbler counterparts:

> O memory! thou mid-way world
> 'Twixt Earth and Paradise,
> Where things decayed, and loved ones lost
> In dreamy shadows rise . . . .
> Till every sound appears a knell,
> And every spot a grave.[43]

"And every spot a grave" involved less poetic license than one might suppose. In the writing of the unelevated, that could be illustrated by the superabundant reflections on some "interesting" spot, by courtship walks through graveyards, by school compositions treating weeping willows bending to caress the mounded turf. For the sophisticated, such things had extensions or parallels in the graveyard poetry that abounded in the periodicals, in the blend of the sanitary and the aesthetic in the rural cemetery movement, and perhaps even in what Mario Praz called "The Romantic Agony." But participation in the ritual of death centered more directly on the deathbed than on the grave. Indeed, to an almost unnerving degree, the imagination, emotion and memory of humble America hovered about that sacrosanct place. Small wonder that dramatic and literary creators gravitated to it, or that, when the muse moved the pen of a lesser sort, it might seek to express the poetic perception of "the Death Bed of my friend."[44] Geoffrey Gorer knew well whereof he spoke in emphasizing its genuine rather than contrived or spurious significance.

Postulates and conditions must have varied widely; still, a discernible generic format emerges from the descriptions of and reflections about that hallowed setting. The imperious finality allowed no neat programming, but within death's small sanctions and flexibilities efforts and hopes went to assure certain preparations and meet certain prescriptions. First and most simply there was the solicitude, the emotional comfort and reassurance that the loved ones could give the departing. In turn, for the gathered circle there was the hope of receiving inspiration—the reciprocal reassurance—by witnessing a calm clear-eyed death. Finally, and inseparable from the former, there was the guarded hope for the soul of the deceased that derived from a demonstration of Christian fortitude and resignation. Death could be a powerful lesson and reassurance for the living, and, as well, a spiritual earnest or a final outward sign of an inward grace evidenced by the departing.

A preliminary though important ingredient of the setting for final transformations involved the gathering of family and most intimate friends. In the general mode of expression of the time this desideratum appeared as "among friends," the word here designating more intense connections than the indiscriminate host it would later come to cover. Humble folk gave negative description of the gathering of the friends by noting the terror and the spiritual and emotional loss incurred by an unattended death in the wilderness. "On the death of Ephraim Beeson who died in Iowa territory of the Chills and Fever in the fall of 1843" gave emphasis to the painful disparity between proper and improper setting:

> But if no parents near him stand
> To raise the drooping head
> If no kind sister lend a hand
> To smooth the sufferers bed
>
> Oh then let pitty more and more
> Tears of affection shed
> For him who on the strangers shore
> Now sleeps among the dead[45]

Surely, an unappreciated dimension of the fear of westering centers on this matter. The blurring of its significance in the passing of time probably involves the transmutation of death from profound consecration to what William James called "nothing but"[46]—in this case nothing but statistic and biological process. At the end of his trek, Forty-Niner E. D. Perkins perceived the "grim monster" now grown "doubly" ominous; "the grave has more terrors than I ever before felt."[47]

Whether the "grim monster" came to one who was in solitude or "among friends," it was deemed essential that death's presence be recognized. An East Texas woman gave the concern a characteristic statement in asking about the death of her sister, especially if the departed "wose in her senses . . . and if she read enny thing about ding [dying]."[48] Indeed, a part of the function of those gathered about the afflicted seems to have been to assure that matters were faced squarely. Visiting a sick friend or relative who had been married only three weeks, Minerva Bacon of Ogdensburg, New York, found her "pale as death." Minerva evidently shuffled delicacy into a position of low priority in conversing with this woman who had but a week to live: "I told her thene she was worse of than she had a ware of."[49] When a friend was dying there were considerations far greater than tact. Just who generally performed Minerva's function is difficult to ascertain; but evidently someone did. Time and again it would be marked as a source of satisfaction that the dying person was "sensible" of the situation. Indeed, someone unwilling or unable to recognize his condition, as was a man in Pawlet, Vermont, might be described as "very stupid."[50]

With the circle gathered, and with all alerted to the imminent issue, it was in turn important that all be resigned to the working of Providence. The sober, explicit statement of submission to God's will by the dying became central. It was a thing much hoped for, though of course not always forthcoming. In the fictive ideal, Harriet Beecher Stowe and Timothy Shay Arthur gave paradigmatic illustrations in Little Eva and Little Mary Morgan. And Parson Weems' Washington, one might contend, endeared himself quite as much to the two succeeding generations for his deathbed patience and submission as for his inability to tell a lie. Melville, whose philosophical meanderings often put him on the track of death and the posture appropriate thereto, concluded a disquisition on the subject in this way: "To expire mild-eyed in one's bed transcends the death of Epaminondas."[51]

"To expire mild-eyed" had a beatific quality the presence or absence of which almost always received mention. Mrs. Andrew Adams, herself bearing the privations of Minnesota pioneering, took great satisfaction from knowing that a dead neighbor had departed conscious and resigned: "Am rejoiced to know these facts."[52] With the more intense emotional involvement of a family relation, A. J. Hayter of Saline County, Missouri, wrote to his mother to get the details of the death of "dear old pappy." "Mother i should have liked to have node whither he was resined to gow Joseph could not tell me exackly whither or not you must tell A to rite to me and let me now all about that gives me eas if he was perfectly resined to gow mother in that triing ower if he was prepared to gow what sweet thoughts to himself and all of his children."[53] The style was characteristically faulty; the sentiment was characteristically central.

Evidently there were deviations in the path from time to eternity. Not all died to expectations. But the passing of a fellow mortal always had instructive quality. If all went well it could be a privilege to behold the death. At one level this could involve a celebration of man in humanist terms—the witnessing of a person's calmly and rationally putting the things of the world into order, and unflinchingly accepting the bodily change. Mark Twain, in emphasizing the "privilege" it was to Laura to attend her dying father, left things, by and large, in that realm. Indeed Si Hawkins expired with dimming eye and halting tongue still on the chimerical Tennessee land grant.[54]

Mark Twain did not seek to be ironically macabre in presenting Laura's deathwatch as a "privilege." Frequently the term itself, and nearly always the sentiment appear in humble writings of the time. Not to be able to attend at the deathbed was almost routinely set down as a striking deprivation. Six years after leaving Nicholville, New York, a Wisconsin couple wrote back to express grief at the death of a mother. The sense of loss involved more than the death itself: "if I could have had the privilege of being with her in her sickness & have felt her loss, it would have been a great satisfaction . . . ."[55] Apparently, normal relations had to degenerate to outright sourness before any contrary mood received expression. A rare instance appears in the diary kept by the wife of a small Virginia slaveowner. Driven to her emotional and physical limits by sickness and death among her children, and suffering the endless vexation of directing four or five slave women, Pauline Stratton found it not within her resources to react properly when her mother-in-law took to the deathbed. Relations between the two had long been bad, and now, when Pauline made soup for the apparently dying woman, her effort and thoughtfulness brought only complaint. Much given to self-recrimination, Pauline assumed yet another emotional burden by becoming "so hard-hearted that I felt . . . I did not want to see her die . . . ."[56] Much rancor must have been needed to make her willing to forego that "privilege." Positive and fully enunciated expression of the theme came from a New England woman Lizzie Robbins while she ministered endlessly to her dying husband. Though the expiring man was a "great sufferer," Lizzie felt the toll, and now she slipped into a reference to her "task." The correction and clarification came immediately: "'task,' *indeed it is not*; it is not only my duty but my great privilege."[57]

The acme of privilege came in witnessing a "triumphant" death. In the abstract one encounters the contention that "holy dying" represented the logical finality of "holy living." Moved by a Northeast Pennsylvania revival to contemplate general matters, visitor Horatio Chandler of New Hampshire put it this way: "The last act, on earth, of our gratitude to our deer Redeemer, to set the example of *holy dying,* as well as *holy living*; surely in proportion do we glorify God; & do a real blessing to those around us. May we be prepared to say with the martyrs,—'Welcome death.'"[58] This restatement of Jeremy Taylor's *Holy Living and Dying* seems an unimpeachable expression of Christian mood; but people employed it in comprehensive rather than specific or existential context. "Holy" dying adumbrated more than unpretentious folk were wont to hazard. What was "holy" in the abstract became "triumphant" or "happy" in the concrete.

Of course there were many gradations between a "very stupid" death and one that was "triumphant." And it is well to recognize that, in letters particularly and in diaries to a lesser degree, motivation toward prevarication or omission occasionally obtained. But humble people probably had full preparation for accepting the fact that, in death as in life, high hopes came reluctantly to realization. Writing back to Connecticut in regard to a grandmother's death, an Ohio man noted the "pleasing evidence of her interest in the L. Jesus Christ. This is all we could have expected & nearly all we could have wished. We should indeed have been glad if her departure had been of the more extatic and triumphant cast. . . ."[59]

That "extatic and triumphant cast" came as the final intensification of the knowing acquiescence in God's will. Grief, fatigue, pain and spiritual awe supplied the context for ecstasy, that last emotional balm acting in double sense as transportation—the easing of the living past a profoundly unnerving moment, and the easing of the departing from time to eternity.

Late in 1838 John and Rachel Ricketts of Franklin County, Indiana, conveyed to a brother the details of the mother's death. With the letter went a lock of her hair, "some of the grave clothese," and the urging to "till all the purtikler about the death of our Old Mother." Surely, in this case, the "purtikler" were worth relating: "I feel gratified to inform you that she left the wourld in the triumfs of faith, in her dying moments Jesse and myself Sung a Cupple of favorite hyms and She Slapt her hands and shouted give glory to god and retained her senses while she had breath which gave us all a great deel of Satisfaction to See her happy. Such a great witness that she went happy out of the wourld."[60] "Happy" pertained particularly to things religious. It indicated spiritual transportation, in this case the salving ecstasy that allowed at least the Pyrrhic victory over death itself. For simple people accomplishments and victories came infrequently, and probably were prized the more when they did. Everyone, not just movers and shakers, was provided the chance for a final, illimitable conquest. "And to yield the ghost proudly," Melville mused, "and march out of your fortress with all the honors of war is not a thing of sinew and bone."[61] The weakest and lowest could do that. They could draw the fangs of the "grim monster" itself, the witnessing of which "triumphant" spectacle was a privilege" indeed.

Happiness and triumph involved foremost the intimation of a Christian hereafter. And it can hardly be doubted that this was the most compelling source of interest in the deathbed. Surely the scene of dying came under close scrutiny for earnests of felicitous immortality. However, undeniable as that may be, a striking thing about the deathly reflections is the almost total absence of explicit references to otherworldly rewards or even to the assurance that, whatever they were, a particular person would enjoy them. To be sure, people died "happy" in a prospect, or in the "triumph" of the faith, or with the consolation of a Christian hope. But these people, like Gray's paradigm, possessed only "trembling hope." However fraught with otherworldly implications and intimations, deathbed writings resolutely maintained a general, vague and allusive quality where the most profound matter was concerned. Even when a striking portent occurred, common people retained a caution in delving and construing. For example, when a Missouri man had been laid out in a back room, a dove lit in an open windowsill near where his body lay. That bird betokened things ultimate. "Pore John," a sister wrote, "could not talk to nun of us if he could he would have told us he was agowing home whare christains are at rest." But this letter stopped well short of heavenly visions; indeed it has an abrupt shift to immediacy and reality. Whatever "pore John's" immortal destiny, "that dove came to console us." In a world where "i have nothing to write to you but greaf and trouble" no more could be asked of the delicate harbinger on the windowsill. People with intense awareness of "the trouble in this world for humane beaings to gow through"[62] left eternal projections and certainties to those purporting to have greater discernment.

When 24-year old Halbert Stryker of Brownstown, Indiana, lay moments from eternity he informed his parents that "he was goeing to Jesus and Exhorted us all to try to meet him in haven." A burst of illumination allowed the dying man to say that the path "from Earth to Haven looked clear to him."[63] Characteristically, the path, not the destination became the manifest. Heavenly imagery entered humble writings almost not at all. Instead, the imagery regarding death and departure had a more prosaic, more immediate, less contestable and less sublime quality. It centered far more on what was to be escaped than on what was to be realized. Whatever "trembling hope" of heaven may have informed their deepest longings, these people spoke more often of death as a release from whatever had plagued them. Of course that human circumstance to which they sought an end took a myriad of forms. In 1848 the Thompsons of Mt. Meigs, Alabama, seem to have fallen on evil days. John killed his uncle Solomon; and Nancy, having been "to frindly" with someone, appeared to be in a "family way." In the midst of such unfoldings, Mary, another member of the family, took mortally ill and professed to be quite ready to go. "All she wanted," a neighbor wrote of her death, "was ease." With "the Devil . . . turned loose amongst the Thompsons," Mary may have felt the quite ample attraction of unadorned withdrawal.[64] In another letter which, like so many, gave generous reason for the sufficiency of the limited vision, an Indiana man told simply of a newly married person who had been "cald to try the realities of a better world."[65]

Only in an occasional instance regarding children did such people conjure any specific, rapturous images of the condition beyond the gates. Perhaps mankind has ever been quicker to conceive a heaven for children. In the spring of

1852 Charles Riddick of Yalobusha County, Mississippi, received the particulars regarding the death of a woman named Ginnie. Twelve months earlier she had lost a child, and now, following the birth of another, she took to her deathbed. The stricken woman was not, she averred, "affread" to die; and near the end she told of hearing children singing, among them her departed little Willie. Ginnie's husband, hoping perhaps to keep her to earth, suggested that she heard children in the yard; but the dying woman perceived what was beyond her spouse. A tear in the letter prevents exact rendering; but evidently Ginnie, with a "sweet smile" on her countenance, gently demurred.[66] As is the case here, about the only specific glimmering of the hereafter involved children, singing children. When Annis Pierce of New York State attempted the previously mentioned comforting of her daughter Emily, she did awkward rhapsody on the departed child's now singing "the song of Moses and the Saints."[67] Typically, about Ginnie who had divined something of the condition of a child who had preceded her, the glass now darkened. It was enough for the describer of her death to express the ritual trust that she was now beyond the cares and vexations with which mortality had burdened her. Or, as a Pennsylvania woman put it, there was the hope of a "wresting place . . . whare the wicked shall for ever ceace to trouble us."[68]

Thus, in a general, endlessly stated sentiment, death represented escape from the world's sadness, an end to the "pilgrimage" through spiritual and bodily hostility. In particular application of that, and in metaphor unexcelled in frequency, it meant the passage to that realm "where parting is no more." Years earlier Keziah Herrick and her sister Eunice parted on Lake Seneca's shores. Since then Keziah had neither seen nor heard from her westering sister. Now in 1854 any hope for reunion yet remaining centered on "fairer climes than these where the fears of parting will no more trouble us."[69] Therein resided the fullest tenable hope, the anticipation of an end to earthly separation and, as an Ogdensburg, New York, man put it, the place "where monster (death) will part us no more."[70] This involved a qualified, even a negative vision. But for people whose quotient of delight had had severe limitations, it seems to have been heaven enough. The headier divinations of limitless bliss and glory stayed in the condition of unused abstraction, perhaps humbly to be accepted should Providence see fit to bestow.

NOTES

1. *The Complete Works of Ralph Waldo Emerson,* Concord Edition (Boston: Houghton Mifflin, 1903), I, 143.
2. Michael Aaron Rockland, ed., *America in the Fifties and Sixties: Julián Marías on the United States,* trans. Blanche De Puy and Harold C. Raley (University Park: Pennsylvania State Univ. Press, 1972), p. 41.
3. (Berkeley, Calif.: Univ. of California Press, 1960), pp. 122, 193-94.
4. "Editor's Introduction," *Uncle Tom's Cabin or, Life Among the Lowly* (Cambridge, Mass.: Harvard Univ. Press, 1962), p. xi.
5. "The Pornography of Death," *Encounter* 5 (Oct. 1955), 50-51.
6. William Y. Sprague Diary, after the entry of Sept. 17, 1859 (Connecticut State Library).
7. Hiram Peck Diary, undated miscellany at beginning (New-York Historical Society). (This item is catalogued as the Henry Peck Diary, but it was kept by Henry's brother Hiram.)
8. Issac S. Barr Penmanship Book, Mrs. I.S. Barr Mss. (Mss. Div., Alabama Dept. of Archives and History).
9. Seth H. Willard Diary, Apr. 4, 1859 (Maine Historical Society).
10. P. 192.
11. *Consciousness in Concord; the text of Thoreau's hitherto "lost journal," 1840-1841, together with notes and a commentary by Perry Miller* (Boston: Houghton Mifflin, 1958), p. 75.
12. Robert W. Lovett, "Augustus Roundy's Cincinnati Sojourn," *Historical and Philosophical Society of Ohio Bulletin,* 19 (Oct. 1961), 260-61.
13. Sophronia C. Beebe to Jennie Akehurst, Feb. 4, 1858, Akehurst-Lines Collection (Div. of Special Collections, University of Georgia Libraries).

14. Annis Pierce to Caleb and Emily Carr, Nov. 6, 1856, Caleb M. Carr Letters (Collection of Regional History, Cornell University).

15. "On the Death of my 2 brothers & sister," Feb. 1851, Harris Family Papers (Indiana Historical Society).

16. Brigham Nims Diary, Feb. 11 and 12, 1846, Brigham Nims Family Papers (New Hampshire Historical Society).

17. Archibald B. Knode Diary, Sept. 30, Nov. 15, and Dec. 31, 1834, Archibald B. Knode Papers, Diaries and Account Books (Indiana Historical Society).

18. (Mrs. Oswald) to William Garland, Sept. 30, 1839, William Harris Garland Papers (Southern Historical Collection, University of North Carolina).

19. Julia Adams to Hannah Watrous, May 2, 1848, Phinehas Adams Papers (Huntington Library). By permission.

20. Charles Rich to Albina Rich, Dec. 5, 1853, Rich Family Papers (Maine Historical Society).

21. Albina Rich to Charles Rich, Dec. 7, 1853, Rich Family Papers.

22. *Unquiet Eagle: Memory and Desire in the Idea of American Freedom 1815-1860* (Ithaca, N.Y.: Cornell Univ. Press, 1967), pp. 40-41.

23. *The Gilded Age: A Tale of To-Day* (New York: Harper & Bros., 1915), I: 44-54.

24. Walter B. Foster Journal, July 24, 1842 (Missouri Historical Society).

25. A. P. Moss to Dear Emily, Sept. 18, 1853, Smith Collection (Six Vault, Ga., Dept. of Archives and History).

26. Josiah B. Chaney Diary, Sept. 17, 1845, Josiah B. Chaney Papers (Minnesota Historical Society).

27. Walter B. Foster Journal, Jan. 16, 1842.

28. Untitled poem apparently written by Mary Jane Crane, Feb. 9, 1841, Joel Crane and Eunice Fitch Family Correspondence (Indiana Historical Society).

29. *White Jacket or the World in a Man-of-War,* chap. 31.

30. *Pierre or, The Ambiguities,* Book 20, Pt. 1.

31. *The Complete Works of Ralph Waldo Emerson,* Centenary Ed. (Boston: Riverside Press, 1904), 6:5.

32. J.S. Brown to Ebenezer Brown, Sept. 20 and Oct. 9, 1850, Ebenezer Brown Papers (New Hampshire Historical Society).

33. Francis W. Squires Diaries, Mar. 1853 (Collection of Regional History, Cornell University).

34. Simeon Ives to Josiah Crosby, Sept. 8, 1847, Lyman Stuart

Collector. Stampless Covers (Collection of Regional History, Cornell University).

35. George and Fidelia Baldwin to Lawrence Parker, Oct. 2, 1847, Barbour-Parker Family Letters (Collection of Regional History, Cornell University).

36. R. Owen to brother and sister, April 22, 1836, Julia Bryce Lovelace Letters (Manuscripts Division, Alabama Department of Archives and History).

37. *Pierre,* Book 22, Pts 3 and 4.

38. *The American Pilgrimage: The Roots of American History, Religion and Culture* (New York: Collier Books, 1961), p. 105.

39. Francis W. Squires Diaries, Mar. 9, 1860.

40. Lucy Holcomb to Nahum Holcomb, May 10, 1837, Holcomb Family Letters (Connecticut State Library).

41. Fidelia and George Baldwin to Lawrence Parker, Nov. 2, 1845, Barbour-Parker Family Letters.

42. John Barber to Lawrence Parker, Nov. 2, 1845, Barbour-Parker Family Letters.

43. Quoted in Covey, *The American Pilgrimage,* p. 107.

44. Obadiah Ethelbert Baker Journal, Mar. 12, 1860, Obadiah Ethelbert Baker Collection (Huntington Library). By permission.

45. Henry Beeson Flanner Family Correspondence (Indiana Historical Society).

46. "The Present Dilemma in Philosophy," in *Pragmatism: A New Name for Some Old Ways of Thinking* (New York: Longman, Green, 1922), p. 16.

47. Elisha D. Perkins Diary, Jan. 8, 1850, HM 1547 (Huntington Library). By permission.

48. Mary and James Cole to brother (John Jones), Sept. 1, 1852, Morgan D. Jones letters (Mss. Div., Ala. Dept. of Archives and History).

49. Minerva Bacon to Lydia Barnhart, June 27, 1841, Lyman Stuart *Collector.*

50. L. Clark to Mrs. Ann Bromley, June 18, 1850, Lyman Stuart *Collector.*

51. *Mardi: and a Voyage Thither,* Chap. 9.

52. Mrs. Andrew W. Adams Diary, Apr. 12, 1856, Andrew W. Adams and Family Papers (Minnesota Historical Society).

53. A. J. Hayter to Sa. A. G. Hayter, June 14, 1855, Coleman-Hayter Letters, 1840-1900 (Western Historical Manuscript Collection, University of Missouri, Columbia).

54. *The Gilded Age,* 1:109-11.

55. Elizabeth and James Olin to Alfonso R. Peck, July 28, 1850, Peck Family Papers (Collection of Regional History, Cornell University).

56. Pauline H. Stratton Diary, Jan 12, 1855 (Western Historical Manuscripts Collection, University of Missouri, Columbia).

57. Lizzie Robbins to Julia Pelton, Sept. 8, 1858, Oliver Pelton Correspondence (Connecticut State Library).

58. Horatio N. Chandler Account Book, Jan. 15, 1841 (New Hampshire Historical Society). This item is both diary and account book.

59. C. S. Boardman to Homer Boardman, Oct. 9, 1839, Lyman Stuart Papers.

60. John and Rachel Ricketts to brother, Dec. 23, 1838 (Kentucky Historical Society).

61. *Mardi:and a Voyage Thither,* chap. 9.

62. Sarah Hayter and Elizabeth Coleman to C. J. Hayter, Oct. 9, 1844, Coleman-Hayter Letters, 1840-1900.

63. Aaron and Eliza Stryker to David Ireland, Sept. 7, 1859, James Ireland Family Correspondence (Indiana Historical Society).

64. Elizabeth Baskin to Miss N. J. Baskin, May 21, 1848, William Davis Boaz Papers (Manuscripts Division, Alabama Dept. of Archives and History).

65. Clark Sanderson to nephew, July 22, 1854, James Ireland Family Correspondence (Indiana Historical Society).

66. R. E. Riddick to Charles C. Riddick, Mar. 18, 1852, Charles C. Riddick Papers (Southern Historical Collection, University of North Carolina).

67. Annis Pierce to Caleb and Emily Carr, Nov. 6, 1856, Caleb M. Carr Letters.

68. Ann Woods to Aaron Nevius, Oct. 30, 1843, Orrin F. Smith and Family Papers, 1829-1932 (Minnesota Historical Society).

69. Keziah Herrick to Mary J. Bass, Feb. 10, 1854, Joel Crane and Eunice Fitch Family Correspondence.

70. Morgan Eastman to Lydia Barnhart, July 25, 1841, Lyman Stuart *Collector.*

Robert W. Habenstein and William M. Lamers

THE PATTERN OF LATE NINETEENTH-CENTURY FUNERALS

In major part the symbols of mourning during this period expressed the gloom and formality, the solemnity and lugubriousness of the feudal funeral of the late Middle Ages and Early Renaissance. That such a pattern of death-response should be incorporated into the mourning of a rapidly growing, ever increasingly industrialized American society is a puzzle for social and cultural historians. For decades Americans had been enthusiastically writing and reading romantic fiction; certainly the wave of Romanticism—a backward looking philosophy—would have supported such turning back from the simplicity and realism of American funeral customs of a century before. Whatever the basic reasons, the solemnity and gloom was obvious enough. The house in which the death had struck not only had its scarf or "crepe" on the door, but it was not unknown for the bereaved to drape the room in which the dead lay, or possibly, the whole downstairs of the house, in black or deep shades of grey. Deeply colored veils were often hung in the doorway; servants attired in mourning livery were stationed at the doorway to attend the callers. If the household contained a maid, she would wear black, with apron, collars and cuffs of white, with black

---

Reprinted from *The History of American Funeral Directing* by Robert W. Habenstein and William M. Lamers, copyright © 1955 by National Funeral Directors Association of the United States, Inc. By permission of the publisher.

ribbons attached to her white cap. For the bereaved, black was considered the color most suitable for the trappings of woe. Its sombre effect was reflected not only in the mourning garb but in the dress of the functionaries, the shroud, the hearse and its plumes, the pall spread over the casket, and even the horses used in the funeral cortege.[1]

Of the fabrics employed, funeral crepe was considered most effective; although black and blue-black bombazines, alpacas, black silks, black kid, and black cotton were used in the making of mourning garments and accessories. The combination of the shrouding folds of the major garment, the black mourning bonnet with streamers reaching "well below the waist line," and the black crepe of the widow's veil made her mourning garb the most distinctive and lugubrious of any. Following a death mourning wear was used to indicate not only degrees of kinship with the dead, but the several defined periods of mourning. The widow, for example, was clearly labeled by the white ruche that showed as an inner lining along the front of the bonnet. For the first year the widow was expected to wear everything with a dull black finish. Her gloves, purse, handkerchief border, ornaments and gown were to show no lustre, as if a lack of lustre in her appointments declared the lack of lustre brought into her entire being by death.

In the first six months of the second year of mourning the crepe gave way to less funereal materials, such as black silk or crepe-de-chine, and for the remainder of the year the use of both white and violet was permissible. After two years the widow again could wear ordinary clothes. Should a woman lose her husband late in life she might commonly wear mourning for the remainder of her days. As the 19th century drew to an end, the fashion of wearing all white for summer mourning made its appearance, although white never became a dominant mourning theme as it had been in classical antiquity. For women, the loss of a loved one—husband, child, boy or girl, or grown offspring, brother, sister, or parent, even grandparent—mourning garb was varied enough to indicate the nature of the bereavement.

The widower customarily wore a suit entirely of black

cloth with plain white linen. Any other coloring was prohibited. Shoes, gloves, cuff-links, and hat were all of dull black. A conspicuous crepe mourning band adorned the hat. For the widower, mourning might last for a year with a period of secondary mourning in which he was permitted to relieve his black garb by grey. The wearing of a mourning band on the sleeve of the coat was not generally approved, unless the ordinary costume was in the form of a uniform which might not be changed. With some latitude allowed for special cases of attachment, mourning was not generally prescribed or approved for kinfolk living apart from the immediate family, such as uncles, aunts, nephews, cousins and other collateral relatives.

In any event, the first six months after a death, commonly known as the period of "deep mourning," carried with it a proscription against participation in any social or recreational affairs. As the mourning colors during the mourning period grew progressively lighter, so in parallel fashion did the social and personal contacts of the mourners, and by the time all mourning garb was dispensed with, so were all restrictions as to movement and social contact. For the woman this was more definitely the case; for the man, social activity was resumed somewhat more quickly. Another phase of social contact, correspondence, fell under the regulation of mourning custom. Stationery was prescribed as to color: for the widow, white or grey with black border, a quarter inch wide for the first year of mourning, an eighth inch for the next six months, and a sixteenth for the remainder of the second year. Colored crests were prohibited, as was perfume. Simplicity in the lettering and even the containment of scrawling handwriting were advised.

Calling cards were likewise edged in black, the width of the edging indicating the degree of relationship to the deceased, the thinner the edge the more distant the relationship. Propriety and decorum were to be observed in all correspondence, as in all behavior involving other persons and in all actions, perceived or private, of the person in mourning. Post cards were decidedly not permissible.

Other classes of people participated in the symbolization

of the mourning gloom. Not only was the undertaker's garb of the traditional black, but so generally was the garb of all those who figured importantly in the funeral, minister, pall-bearers, drivers and other functionaries, as well as the bereaved. Friends would don either black or their darkest or most subdued dress to attend the ceremony. Other symbols were affected. It was still fashionable in 1880 to wear a funeral sash, or a linen scarf. These were worn along with gloves, ribbons and badges. An 1878 *The Casket* ad for badges lists "black, white or black-white combination lettered in gold or silver, 'Pall Bearer,' 'Bearer,' 'Undertaker,' or with Masonic, IOOF, Catholic or other society emblems as may be desired."

Music likewise symbolized solemnity, if not gloom. It was considered singularly appropriate at the time to have a brass band precede the funeral procession, and the strains of the "Dead March," from "Saul" with musicians marching in broken ranks, were as much in keeping with the tenor of the occasion as are the strains of "Lead Kindly Light" on the church organ for the funeral of today. The songs mentioned above were designed to be sung on such occasions. Other intensely religious songs, or, perhaps, the favorite numbers of the deceased might be included. In all cases, the emotional character of the situation was enhanced, reserves were further broken down, and feelings were given an opportunity to find full expression. The church bell tolling to mark the arrival of the funeral procession at the church has been a customary feature of village and city life in America since colonial days. In rural areas, the church bell played a communicative role in that by the different modes of tolling the age and sex of the deceased were indicated. In some sections of the country, a trombone choir was used to announce the death of a fellow member of the church. The musicians assembled in the belfry and played certain selections which were codes for the members. One piece was used for married adults and another for children.[2]

Despite the overwhelming tone of gloom, formality, and solemnity with which it was characterized, it would be a mistake to think of the late 19th-century funeral as entirely governed by the pattern of the feudal system of mourning behavior as developed in the late Middle Ages. The chapter on burial cases, coffins and caskets supplies us with an illustration of the breaking away from this pattern. Well before the Civil War, people were demanding that the receptacle for the dead should do more than indicate social status by its expensiveness—as was the case after the Revolutionary War—or serve as an object of mere utility. The very term "casket" signified box or container for something precious, and the preciousness of the human body was felt to be best expressed to the world *symbolically* by the aesthetic luxury of the casket, and *dramatically* to the world by the funeral ceremony. From about 1850 on, the casket found its meaning more and more in the realm of popular tastes where sweeps of fad and fashion played across the appetites and dispositions of the 19th century American mind. The appearance of the casket, its form and composition both subject to the prevailing canons of taste, signalized the beginnings of the breakdown of a system of mourning which was yet to reach its own peak several generations later.

By 1880 the enterprising town or city undertaker, selling caskets out of the catalogs of three or four large casket companies, could present a customer with at least a hundred different choices of casket styles, embracing such materials as wood, wood-cloth combination, metal, wood and metal, and metal and glass combinations. Colors ranged from the conventional black to varieties of silver, bronze, aniline blue and lavender, in many variations. Yet these caskets had a standard form, and came in a highly limited range of standard sizes. The discriminations in style which could be made covered a broad range, but the variations were minor; one chose from a great variety of styles, but seldom were the choices radically different.

The second major breakthrough of the funeral gloom of late 19th-century mourning came in the area of the setting, or backdrop for the casket. Just as the casket became more an object of beauty, or evocative of aesthetically pleasant feelings or imagery, so eventually did the setting change, and the heavy black folds of the casket drape were replaced by the colorful, warmer, or more striking colors of the casket lining, which by the end of the century had come to dominate the casket exterior, especially in the "couch" types.[3] With the remarkable changes in the burial receptacle and the increasing emphasis upon its aesthetic effect, the traditional "props" of the draped pedestal and, possibly the bedraped room, could only produce an ambiguous or disharmonious effect. A more appropriate setting commended itself in the form of the floral backdrop. Starting with the placing of a small bouquet on a table beside the casket—a custom lost in its origins—from the middle of the century on, there was a slowly increasing sentiment in favor of matching the color, beauty, and aesthetic appeal of the casket and its striking colored, or white lining, with the natural beauty and color of flowers. During the time when this new fashion was becoming popular or at least gaining acceptance, some question arose as to whether or not funeral flowers had pagan associations, and whether a wealth of floral tributes might not be an indefensible waste of money.

Although opposition to the use of flowers was never organized, church officials were not loath to criticize excesses in display as a departure from Christian custom. Another form of religious criticism appeared as early as 1878 when the Bishop of Rochester, New York, in a letter to the *Catholic Times* remarked that:

> Whatever of sentiment may have been in the use of flowers on and around a corpse when, at first, loving hands placed a few near it was killed by usage demanding that such tributes should be repaid on the first occasion available. Thus, in time, floral tributes for the house of mourning became a question of give and expect: a compliment to a friend with a marketable value attached. No wonder that some families deprecate the invasion of their homes with such tributes and cry out, "Omit the flowers."[4]

It is interesting to note that in the same city and in a catalogue dated the same year, the Stein Patent Burial Casket

Works advertised for order by funeral directors floral offerings, in fresh flowers or "immortelles" in twenty different designs, most of them carrying four or five sizes, and ranging in wholesale price from a dollar-and-a-half to twenty-five dollars. "Immortelles"—non-perishable, artificial, dried, or prepared natural flowers and leaves—generally were fifty-percent cheaper. Those wishing to order funeral decorations through their undertaker had a choice of set pieces: the Plain Wreath; Cross, flat or standing; Anchor, or Anchor Cross, flat or standing; Faith, Hope and Charity (anchor, cross and heart in one piece); Harp or Lyre, standing; Square and Compass; Crown, flat or standing; Star; Heart; Maltese Cross; monograms, sold by the letter; Three Links; Combinations of Wreath and Cross, Harp, Anchor, Crown, and Star; Crescent; Crescent and Star Combined; Broken Column; Monument; Shield; Sickle; and, finally, Lamb and Cross.

The fact that there was opposition to the use of flowers on the ground that they were pagan; to their extensive use on the score that it was wasteful; and to the sense of reciprocal necessity because it was worldly, indicates that the usage must have been growing. The broad choice of styles, forms, sizes and motifs, gives further proof, if such were needed, that a shift in popular taste was making heavy inroads upon the tradition of feudal gloom at the very time that the pompous and solemnly formal funeral seemed to be enjoying its greatest vogue.

• • • •

The effort to beautify the surroundings of death had further expression in the memorialization of the dead.

In their designs and materials, the gravestones themselves responded to the changing funeral mood of the day. Instead of the earlier simple marble or limestone slab, the sculptor went to work industriously to add cornices, fancy caps, arabesques, scrolls, imitation tree trunks, statuary. Sometimes he combined several types or shades of stone. The peculiar bad taste of the romantic period which produced Main Street mansions faintly reminiscent of German castles or Italian palaces, and furniture that looked to the jig-saw and lathe rather than to the carver's bench, filled cemeteries with a minor vertical forest of petrified and very indifferent art. But here again the impulse to create beauty even in death was strong, although the effect is not always happy to the modern eye which prefers simplicity and harmony. It has been well said however that with the passing of such ornateness, something has been lost as well as gained. The "uncouth lines and shapeless sculpture" of which Thomas Gray once spoke are no longer in fashion. The present tendency toward uniformity and simplicity may add a sense of dignity to cemeteries, but graveyards lack somewhat the intriguing personality of an earlier day.[5]

Something of the changing mood toward death and funerals can be learned from a reading of grave inscriptions. Wallis remarks:

> On these stone silhouettes of bygone days, we may read the hopes and despairs, the joys and frustrations of Everyman. The manner of expression may be ribald and ridiculous, pompous and lugubrious, eloquent, or serenely simple.
>
> The common grave slab probably originated as an effort to safeguard a new grave from wild beasts. Names and dates were inscribed for purposes of identification. An epitaph, representing pious sentiments consistent with a person's life, or words of advice or caution for the instruction of the living, later made one stone distinctive from another. Quotations from the Bible have long seemed singularly appropriate.[6]

Inscriptions and decorations on tombstones provide additional clues to popular attitudes toward life and death at any period. Early American epitaphs had minced no words, used no sweetened or softened expressions to veil or sugar the hard natural facts. Through the 18th century and before, and well into the 19th, they spelled out the reality of death. When they told biography it was unvarnished. They called sinners, sinners; saints, saints. They did not shun to tell what lay beneath them; not infrequently they spelled out the message with skull and cross-bones to illustrate the point. After having looked into the face of death, some survivors were not beyond making a crude jest or a merry pun. Although the endless variety tempts one to halt at length here, a few illustrations must suffice. There is the harsh New Hampshire epitaph, written in simplest imagery, which reads:

> This rose was sweet a while,
> But now is odour vile.[7]

Some forgotten necrophile uses an undated, nameless Massachusetts tombstone to express his frustration:

> Oh would that I could lift the lid and peer
> within the grave and watch the greedy worms
> that eat away the dead.[8]

Or the terse:

> Soon ripe
> Soon rotten
> Soon gone
> But not forgotten.[9]

Or the pathetic couplet to the eight-year-old boy who in 1795 was buried in Milford, Connecticut:

> Christ called at midnight as I lay
> In thirty hours was turned to clay.[10]

No one has ever written better "The short and simple annals" of a young wife and mother who died in childbirth:

> Eighteen years a maiden,
> One year a wife
> One day a mother
> Then I lost my life.[11]

Details concerning the manner of death were badly and boldly written:

> Killed by a kick of a colt
> in his bowells.[12]

When a four-year-old boy died of burns from an overturned coffee pot, his tombstone commented:

The boiling coffee on me did fall,
And by it I was slain
But Christ has brought my liberty
And in Him I'll rise again.[13]

Friends of Thomas Mulvaney were reminded:

Old Thomas Mulvaney lies here,
His mouth ran from ear to ear,
Reader, tread lightly on this wonder,
For if he yawns, you're going to thunder.[14]

In many old graveyards are found inscriptions and other reminders of the sicknesses that caused untimely and even timely deaths. Dropsy, heart disease, consumption, St. Vitus dance are not uncommonly mentioned. Nor are inscriptions wanting which describe the suffering brought on by the several maladies: "severest pains," "body affliction," "painful illness." Sermons in stone can be found on many an older monument in an old graveyard at the side of a church or next to the village green.

While there is no sharp cleavage, it is noticeable that after 1850 monument prose, verse and art more and more softened the hard facts, grew less didactic, less blunt, less inclined to roar with rude laughter. The skull and crossbones gave way to the winged cherub and to other symbols of faith and hope. By 1865 it was not deemed inappropriate as it would have been a half century before to write:

'Tis but the casket that lies here
The gem that fills it sparkles yet.[15]

And, by 1880 a wife would comment:

Stranger call this not a place
Of fear and gloom,
To me it is a pleasant spot
It is my husband's tomb.[16]

Sentiments such as those adorning tombstones in the 1880's conform in mood to that of the four-by-six-inch gilt-edged, gilt-printed "mourning" cards of the period. These were distributed to friends. The card of Thomas Ardron, who died April 19, 1891, at the age of 76 years, two months and eight days, has a dove at the top holding a streamer which bears the legend "In Loving Remembrance." Upon the outline of the Holy Bible are printed the Masonic symbols and the name of the departed. Below, on a scroll, is the elegiac verse:

How slender is life's silver cord.
How soon 'tis broken here!
Each moment brings a parting word,
And many a falling tear.

And though these years, to mortals given
Are filled with grief and pain,
There is a hope—the hope of heaven,
Where loved ones meet again.[17]

When James S. Pilling died on March 14, 1889, at the age of eight, his card, "In Loving Remembrance," carried two separate poems: the first reminded the bereaved that:

"There is no death." What seems so is transition;
This life of mortal breath
Is but the suburb of the life elysian,
Whose portal we call Death.[18]

The second dealt with the small boy himself:

Sleep on in thy beauty,
Thou sweet angel child,
By sorrow unslighted,
By sin undefiled.

Like the dove to the ark,
Thou hast flown to thy rest,
From the wild sea of strife,
To the home of the blest.[19]

The impulse to memorialize in verse and the willingness of verse makers to provide copy for such memorials have both persisted to our day. Even though mourning cards have long gone out of fashion, the reminders of death and anniversaries of death occasionally appear in the daily newspapers.

NOTES

1. See, for example, Marvin Dana, *The American Encyclopedia of Etiquette and Culture,* 1922, n.p., Part Six.
2. Frederick S. Frantz, "The Funeral Director in Grandpa's Time," in *Clinical Topics,* p. 6.
3. See George S. Herrick, "The Facts About Casket Textiles," *Casket and Sunnyside,* reprint contained in a brochure entitled *Casket Manufacturing,* n.d.
4. *The Casket,* July 1878.
5. Charles L. Wallis, *Stories on Stone* (New York: Oxford University Press, 1954), p. xv.
6. *Ibid.,* p. xi.
7. *Ibid.,* p. 185.
8. *Ibid.*
9. *Ibid.,* p. 181.
10. *Ibid.,* p. 182.
11. *Ibid.,* p. 173.
12. *Ibid.,* p. 116.
13. *Ibid.,* p. 119.
14. *The American Funeral Director;* loose clipping. Collection of the NFDA, Milwaukee, Wisconsin, n.p., n.d.
15. Wallis, *op. cit.,* p. 185.
16. Charles L. Wallis, "Their Last Words Had a Punch." *Saturday Evening Post,* April 17, 1954, p. 44.
17. Mourning card in Collection of NFDA, Milwaukee, Wisconsin.
18. *Ibid.*
19. *Ibid.*

Neil Harris

THE CEMETERY BEAUTIFUL

Until this era [1830s and 1840s], human burial was traditionally in crowded, nondescript churchyards, often surrounded by the bustle of growing cities; or, less happily, charnel houses were used. Interment was usually an austere, utilitarian procedure, relieved by religious services and sometimes by elaborate monuments. Few were concerned with the physical beauty of the body's final resting place; the dead would not care and the living—their eyes on a future life more glorious than any intimations of the terrestrial landscape—did not care either. It seemed futile, even vain, to worry about the situation of graves or the design of cemeteries.

But as hopes of future immortality grew less distinct, the living began to demand more certain means of communion with the dead. Anxiety produced a search for proof of an afterlife. This urge took one form in the spiritualist movement; its table-rappings and mediums enjoyed tremendous popularity in the middle third of the century. Another product of this concern was the greater physical interest in the dead. It was impossible to visit crowded and dirty churchyards with any sense of repose or beauty. Urban demands even made it necessary to move ancient bones from one

---

gravesite to another. Dank, depressing, overgrown graveyards conjured up images of despair and decay; the English variety provided Dickens with some of his most horrific descriptions.

The demands of the living soon took hold. College students and clergymen forecast the new interest. Rural cemeteries "are not for the dead. They are for the living," Henry Bellows orated at a Harvard Exhibition in 1831.[1] Theodore Dwight echoed the thought, as he proposed that gravesites be planned "with reference to the living as well as the dead."[2] One after another new cemeteries were built throughout the country; the first landscaped cemetery of importance was Mount Auburn, established in Cambridge during the 1830s. Shortly thereafter came Greenwood in Brooklyn, Green Mount in Baltimore, Laurel Hill, the Woodlands and the Monument Cemetery—all in Philadelphia—Mount Hope in Rochester, Harmony Grove in Salem and the Albany Rural Cemetery.[3] As their names implied, these institutions comprised unspoiled tracts of parkland; they ranged from fifty to two hundred acres in size. The cemetery corporations sold plots to lot holders, who would eventually become stockholders.[4] From the proceeds, grounds were landscaped and improved, gatehouses and chapels built, and careful maintenance established on a permanent basis. Rural cemeteries were to be places of beauty and tranquillity, secluded spots where bereaved relatives and friends could combine affectionate respect with a love of nature. There families could gather on sunny days, communing with the landscape to show their love for God and their remembrance of the dead. Called by one sponsor, "Rural Gardens for the Dead,"[5] these cemeteries were often managed by gardeners and landscapists; the major force behind Mount Auburn was Dr. Jacob Bigelow, an officer of the Massachusetts Horticultural Society. The tract had originally been purchased for botanical experiments.

The rural cemetery was envisioned as an open-air church where nature's hand alone would dominate. Some visitors may feel, wrote Nehemiah Cleaveland about Brooklyn's Greenwood Cemetery, that its entrance was too modest and small. But they would be wrong, he explained, for the cemetery owners did not want art to raise false expectations. "If the artificial portal be deficient in dignity," coming as it did from a sense of modesty, "not so will you find that of Nature. You are now in a vestibule of her own making. Its floor is a delicious greensward; its walls are the steep hill-side; lofty trees with their leafy capitals, form its colonnades . . . a great primeval temple."[6] Nature as the great architect was also the theme of another cemetery sponsor, J. H. B. Latrobe, who read his "Hymn" at the dedication of Green Mount in1839:

We meet not now where pillar'd aisles,
In long and dim perspective fade;
No dome, by human hands uprear'd,
Gives to this spot its solemn shade.
Our temple is the woody vale.
It shrines these grateful hearts of ours;
Our incense is the balmy gale,
Whose perfume is the spoil of flowers.[7]

Because nature, according to many contemporary theorists, inspired all architectural forms, it was appropriate for cemeteries to turn to her originals instead of to artificial imitations. Artistic delights, of course, could be added; Greenough, Thomas Crawford and Henry Kirke Brown were among the sculptors commissioned for monuments.[8] Philadelphia's Monumental Cemetery bore its name because of a Washington-Lafayette memorial, and Laurel Hill purchased some famous statuary by the English sculptor, Thom.[9] But nature's voice was loudest. The sections and avenues of the cemetery were forest retreats: Sylvan Pond, Willow Avenue, Indian Ridge. The pompous monuments of European cemeteries were condemned as effusions of vanity. Expense was not necessarily an evil, but florid elaborateness was. The cemetery testified to a hopeful love for God and creation; it symbolized a religion of joy. Nature was inherently beautiful, defying dreary churchyards by flowering even there. How much better it was to seek out such comforts deliberately, to enhance religious love and relieve doubts about God's benevolence.

Some of the cemeteries became so lovely that critics warned about excessive beauty; it was wrong to hide all the painful realities of death.[10] Awe and solemnity were necessary ingredients. Nonetheless, emphasis remained on nature's attractiveness and beauty. "My affection is for the country," cried John Pendleton Kennedy at Baltimore's Green Mount. He commended his fellow Marylanders for selecting beautiful sites for their own tombs, testimony to a "rational, reflecting piety; it tells of life unhaunted by the terrors of death."[11]

The rural cemetery movement displayed the characteristics of other artistic crusades. As in the monument movement, archaeology and history played their part; brochures for cemeteries were filled with references to the burial customs of Egyptians, Hebrews, Greeks and Indians, emphasizing that proper respect for the dead was an age-old, universal trait. Wilson Flagg's volume on Mount Auburn, one of the most elaborate of such works, included sections entitled, "Ancient and Modern Tombs," "Ancient Funeral Practices," "The Sepulchres of Thebes," "Ancient Interments in Great Britain," and a general history of human burial practices. The past not only validated the reform, but provided for its specific practices.[12]

The theme of art as a bridge to nature recurred in these campaigns as it had among the Transcendentalists and as it would for believers in landscape gardening and painting. Properly arranged, cemeteries can be "made subservient to some of the highest purposes of religion and human duty. They may preach lessons, to which none may refuse to listen, and which all that live must hear."[13] In a chapter entitled "The Moral Influence of Graves," Wilson Flagg remarked that "to a mourner who has never been inspired with a love of nature, the rural cemetery may present a new gospel of consolation."[14] The primary task remained "to combine the works of nature and art" in a manner conducive to solemnity and grandeur. Here "Taste and Art join with Nature herself," wrote Nehemiah Cleaveland, "in adorning the last home of the loved. . . . here the man of business . . . would often reassure his hesitating virtue."[15] "To the matchless beauties of nature," wrote another, "let us continue to add the skill of the sculptor . . . the florist . . . the architect."[16]

Cemetery publicists, like the Transcendentalists, considered nature superior to art as a symbol of Spirit. Religion had no more pleasing doctrine, wrote Flagg, than the faith which viewed "all material objects as the representations of something more beautiful and divine existing in the spiritual world."[17] Each part of nature bore an emblematic significance, particularly flowers, which symbolized immortality. It was even suggested that fine trees replace marble monuments as gravestones; as men advanced in civilization they prized "nature more and art less."[18]

Every detail fell into place in the scheme of a return to unspoiled nature. Wild flowers were preferable to domestic blooms, since the latter "always suggest the ideas of art, and of something that is to be bought and sold."[19] Violets, columbines and anemones should replace peonies and hydrangea bushes. The attempt to initiate spontaneity and cultivate wildness involved careful planning, but this paradox did not trouble cemetery promoters. Flagg even suggested that it might have been better if Sweet Auburn had had no trees when purchased; young ones could have been planted with room enough to allow for lateral expansion, and this would have presented a more naturally pleasing scene. Fences and hedges could be outlawed and wild birds encouraged to come and sing. Yet Flagg insisted that "affection, that loves to see the dead surrounded with images borrowed from nature and the skies, cannot . . . be cheated by its own artifices."[20] Of course this is essentially what was happening.

The same concern with man-made symbolism, the same simplification and concentration of allegorical forms linked the rural cemetery movement with the monument campaign. Too many emblems diluted the effect and destroyed the poetry. "Over a tomb we want a simple emblem, for a device, not an allegory; a sentiment, for an epitaph, not a sermon."[21] The Reverend Mr. Farley agreed, but he was one of many speaking out against Egyptian and Greek symbols—the inverted torch and the broken column—which from past associations were not appropriate to Christian burial.[22] George Templeton Strong was delighted that the "revised Pagan style" did not prevail at Greenwood. "I only noticed one pair of inverted torches and not a single urn or flying globe. . . . This recurrence to heathen taste and anti-Christian usage in architecture or art of any sort is or should be unreal and unnatural everywhere."[23] Even the principle of differentiation was introduced. Different ages, sexes and professions were distinguishable in life; distinctive monument forms could honor them in death: slender tablets for young girls, obelisks for public officials, pillars for those dying in old age.[24]

The note of self-congratulation at the selflessness of cemetery creators was another recurrent theme. "Little as the Christian Spirit is tied to outward form," wrote T. D. Woolsey, "it can not but rejoice to see ornaments of architecture in the house of His worship which it would not approve of elsewhere."[25] Cemeteries, like churches, were meant to be beautiful; human bodies were God's temples and it was appropriate that "a portion of the wealth which is lavished on palaces for the living" be appropriated to "adorn the habitations of the dead."[26] Decoration symbolized "our love of virtue." Like patriotic monuments, carefully tended gravesites testified to American morality and a willingness to spend money and energy glorifying revered ancestors. The dead made the living more virtuous by inspiring such acts of piety.

The rural cemetery also convinced doubters that Christianity could be allied to true beauty; appeals to the senses, as visitors to Europe and Transcendentalists had already discovered, were not necessarily the snares of Satan. Cemeteries were more than "delightful indications of a purer growth in our national character than politics and money-making."[27] They showed how close a connection existed "between taste and morals"; every "pure ideal of religion and virtue grows in beauty by the food upon which it feeds." The rural cemetery thus became "the means to a great end."[28]

NOTES

1. Henry W. Bellows, "Rural Cemeteries," Harvard Exhibition, October 18, 1831, Archives, Harvard University. Harvard Exhibitions in the early 1830s were replete with speeches about the improving arts. Joseph Stevens Buckminster Thacher spoke on "Respect for Public Monuments, whether Triumphal or for the Dead," at the 1832 Commencement, while others spoke on "The Comparative Influence of Natural Scenery, The Institutions of Society, and Individual Genius, on Taste."

2. Dwight, *Summer Tours,* p. 162.

3. There is no general work on the subject of American cemeteries. Hans Huth, *Nature and the American, Three Centuries of Changing Attitudes* (Berkeley, 1957), contains some helpful information, but this is confined to Mount Auburn. New England is particularly rich in rural cemeteries; besides the ones at Cambridge and Salem, by 1842 Worcester, Springfield, Lowell, Plymouth, New Haven, Portsmouth and Nashua all boasted rural cemeteries.

4. Laurel Hill was one of the smallest, containing originally only about twenty acres; by 1846 Greenwood, with one hundred and eighty acres, was a comparative giant. For statistics see *Greenwood Cemetery, Its Rules, Regulations, etc.* (New York, 1846), p. 3.

5. The phrase appeared in [Stephen Duncan Walker] *Rural Cemetery and Public Walk* (Baltimore, 1835), p. 20.

6. Nehemiah Cleaveland, *Green-Wood Illustrated . . . by James Smillie* (New York, 1847), p. 9. Many of the books about cemeteries served as vehicles for engravers like Smillie, mixing prints, poetry and sentimentality like the gift books of the era.

7. J. H. B. Latrobe, "The Hymn," *The Dedication of Green Mount*

Cemetery . . . (Baltimore, 1839), p. 15. Latrobe was the son of Benjamin Latrobe, the architect and engineer.

8. See Frederic A. Sharf, "The Garden Cemetery and American Sculpture: Mount Auburn," *Art Quarterly,* XXXIV (Spring, 1961), pp. 80-88. Crawford, E. A. Brackett, Ball Hughes, Horatio Greenough, Henry Kirke Brown and Henry Dexter were all represented in Mount Auburn. In time, cemetery promoters used the patronage of sculpture as a justification for the rural cemetery.

9. The monument to Washington and Lafayette, a superficially simple obelisk, was filled with hidden symbolism. See The Miscellaneous File (Sartain), NYPL; microfilms in AAA.

10. See the criticism of Mount Auburn and Laurel Hill in T. D. Woolsey, "Cemeteries and Monuments," *The New Englander,* VII (November, 1849), p. 489. See also, "Ornamental Cemeteries," *Yale Literary Magazine,* XXI (November 1855), pp. 45-50.

11. *The Dedication of Green Mount Cemetery* . . . (Baltimore, 1839), pp. 21, 32.

12. Enormous efforts went into the surveys of burial practices. See [John Brazer] "Burial of the Dead," *Christian Examiner,* XXI (November 1841; January 1842), pp. 137-163; 281-307.

13. *Dedication of Green Mount,* p. 3.

14. Wilson Flagg, *Mount Auburn: Its Scenes, Its Beauties, and Its Lessons* (Boston and Cambridge, 1861), p. 73.

15. Cleaveland, *Green-Wood Illustrated,* p. 3. The theme of uniting nature and art was a constant one in both the landscape garden campaign and the cemetery promotion.

16. *Guide to Laurel Hill Cemetery* . . . (Philadelphia, 1847), p. 22.

17. Flagg, *Mount Auburn,* p. 9.

18. *Ibid.,* p. 265.

19. *Ibid.,* p. 57.

20. *Ibid.,* p. 56.

21. *Ibid.,* p. 100.

22. Farley was speaking at a consecration for a congregation's burial plot. Cemetery proprietors encouraged churches to buy sections for ministers and their congregations. Presumably it would make things easier at the resurrection. Quoted in Cleaveland, *Green-Wood Illustrated,* p. 67.

23. *The Diary of George Templeton Strong,* Allan Nevins and Milton Halsey Thomas (eds.), (New York, 1952), I, p. 229.

24. Flagg, *Mount Auburn,* p. 100.

25. Woolsey, "Cemeteries and Monuments," p. 501.

26. Cleaveland, *Green-Wood Illustrated,* p. 67.

27. N. P. Willis, quoted in *Guide to Laurel Hill Cemetery,* p. 174.

28. Cornelia W. Walter, *Mount Auburn Illustrated . . . by James Smillie* (New York, 1847), p. 39. Like art galleries and parks, cemeteries would also teach refinement of manners. Americans "vie with Goth or Vandal in apparent hate of cultured arts, as painting, statuary, or relief, and deface all ornaments of skill," said one writer. Cemeteries would preach greater respect for beauty. See Campeador, *Rambling Reflections in Greenwood* (New York, 1853), p. 11.

Paul Carter

"IF A MAN DIE, SHALL HE LIVE AGAIN?"

Early in 1962, the year of John F. Kennedy's dramatic nuclear confrontation with Nikita Khrushchev, an editorial in an American theological monthly noted a strange paradox: contemporary man, more capriciously threatened by death than at any time since the Black Plague, seemed almost less concerned about it personally than he was about his professional status, his sex life, or the revolutionary disruption of his society. "Whether from cancer, cardiac causes, or nuclear attack, death tends to become a technical matter, representing more the issue of a struggle between the physician and the mortician than between life and death."[1] The writer may not have spoken for all of his contemporaries, in that era of the seat belt, of the warning on the cigarette package, and of the the movement to abolish capital punishment as "cruel and unusual." Still, it is possible that one reason why religious radicals of the day were able so comfortably to proclaim God's death was that man had come to think and feel differently about his own.

A class in philosophy at an American Catholic university, asked in 1968 to write "an essay on death: what they had been taught, and how much of it they now found convinc-

---

ing," expressed considerable hostility to the whole idea of life after death. "The day I was born I was given a command to *live* in this world, not sit around and wait in a church for the next," one student wrote. Another objected to the traditional imagery of *requiem aeternam dona eis domine,* repeated six times in the Burial Mass, whereby the believer came to think of the afterlife as rest, stasis, "the place where there are no more choices to be made—an intolerable idea for the activist existential consciousness of the youth-culture. "To the young, such a Heaven is precisely a Hell."[2]

Hostility to a religion of stasis and repose was of course no new thing in the United States. The Gilded Age in its own way had had an activist consciousness also. To affirm the continuity of human existence as a plausible and natural expectation, one popular preacher in that period felt he had also to affirm that "the world beyond Death will seem to be one with the life on this side of it," and, by inference from the pace of the life on this side, Phillips Brooks wrote in 1882, "the activity of the Eternal Life must be intense."[3] Yet even the most militant and "muscular" of Christians preached, usually, a gospel of activity in this world and of rest in the next. The same generation that wrote activist hymns like "Stand Up, Stand Up For Jesus" and "Work, For the Night Is Coming"[4] also wrote "We Are Going, We Are Going to a Home Beyond the Skies" and "In the Sweet By and By." Protestant Christians in America, if they were black, sang,

> Soon I will be done with the troubles of the world,
> Going home to God,

and if they were white, the sang "Softly and Tenderly Jesus Is Calling," with its echoing refrain,

> Come home, come home,
> Ye who are weary, come home,

or, in the somewhat more genteel environs of Lake Chautauqua, they sang,

Day is dying in the west,
Heav'n is touching earth with rest.[5]

The kinds of heavens men hope for can be taken as unconscious commentary on what they cherish or regret in this world. "We build heaven out of our joys, out of our sufferings, out of our griefs, out of our experiences, taking the best and noblest things, and arranging them so that they shall fill the imagination," Henry Ward Beecher declared. "Thus we construct our heaven to suit our personality."[6] Some of his contemporaries visualized heaven as a very "homey" place indeed; Washington Gladden for example looked forward to "landscapes like these we here look upon—hill and valley, . . . verdure and blossoms, sunny skies and smiling fields," and among these scenes Gladden envisioned songbirds, squirrels, crickets, cattle, and even "lambs skipping upon the hillside," a picture of heaven much like that of Elizabeth Stuart Phelps. Others were more cautious in their expectations. Preaching on Rev. 20:12, "And I saw the dead, small and great, stand before God," Phillips Brooks rejected the literalness of that text's image in favor of a metaphor: the dead stand before God in the same sense that "the poet stands before nature . . . the philosopher stands before . . . abstract truth . . . the artist stands before beauty."[7] But whether the promised Kingdom were to be taken literally or metaphorically, it was a hope that had to be consciously asserted against "a theory," as the novelist Miss Phelps put it, "which shuts us into our coffins, screws the lid down, and says, 'Now get out if you can!'"

Perhaps people burst into gospel songs in order to drown with music the doubts and disagreements they could not have harmonized by the exchange of words. Personal immortality, wrote Professor Charles Briggs in 1889, was an issue upon which "the consensus of Christendom is little, the dissensus is great, the questions undefined greater still." We have already noticed the wretched inability of many believing Americans to cope with Genesis in the light of evolution, and they seem to have been similarly helpless before this ultimate question. Elizabeth Phelps thought in 1886 that the tide was beginning to turn back toward hope for the world to come, but she conceded that "it has been the great effort of the time to establish a mathematical equation between an instructed mind and an abandoned faith."

> We learned that we were not men, but protoplasm. We learned that we were not spirits, but chemical combinations. We learned that we had laid up treasure in the wrong places. We learned that the drama of Hamlet and the Ode to Immortality were secretions of the gray matter of the brain.[8]

If Darwin seemed to be reducing man's soul to the caperings of a naked ape, Wundt seemed to be reducing it to the electrochemical discharges inside man's skull. In 1904 Sir William Osler somewhat regretfully summed up a half-century's research: "Modern psychological science dispenses altogether with the soul." Such phenomena as "the slow decay of mind with changes in the brain" gave pause to any scientific student trying to conceive of consciousness as existing without a corresponding material basis.[9] Long after the Gilded Age was over,[10] it remained possible to conclude from the physiological evidence that "clear-cut atheism and materialism" had become "the only tenable hypotheses" for modern rational man. As that tireless letter-writer Howard Phillips Lovecraft put it in 1921:

> You speak of immortality as if one's personality were something apart from his material structure, yet when we analyse personality we can trace every quality to the atoms and electrons of the body. Certainly, these electrons were never thus assembled until the body in question took form; and equally certainly they will never be thus assembled again. When a man dies, his body turns to liquids and gases whose molecules soon enter into an infinitude of new combinations—there is nothing left. Haeckel has dealt so clearly with this subject in *The Riddle of the Universe* that it is really superfluous for me to repeat the arguments here.[11]

When a distinguished philosopher like Paul Carus undertook to replace the old religion of "superstition" with a new "religion of science" he sometimes seemed to hold out the hope that science itself would vindicate man's belief in an afterlife. "The preservation of soul-life after the death of the individual is not an assumption, nor a probability, nor a mere hypothesis, but a scientific truth which can be proved by the surest facts of experience," Carus wrote in 1893. But upon examination this continuing soul-life turned out to be the evolutionary continuance of the individual's ideas, which in the monistic universe assumed by men like Carus would be interchangeable with those of anyone else, and of his actions, understood behavioristically: "Deeds live on, and what are we but the summation of our deeds!" In practice Carus's religion of science annihilated the individual ego as thoroughly as did Buddhism: "As soon as we rise above the pettiness of our individual being, the boundaries of birth and death vanish, and we breathe the air of immortality."

The dynamic sociologist Lester F. Ward played a similar game of words with the doctrine of an afterlife. "Science is not skeptical as to the immortality of the soul," Ward asserted, but he evidently did not mean the word "soul" in the Church's traditional sense: "Science postulates the immortality not of the human soul alone, but of the soul of the least atom of matter." Was this enough as a replacement for the age-old hope of religion? Ward believed so; "It is something to have learned that there exist, have always existed and will ever continue to exist, the indestructible and unchangeable elements and powers out of which, through similar processes, equal and perhaps far superior results may be accomplished." *As it was in the beginning, is now and ever shall be, world without end, Amen.*

It was a tremendous act of abnegation for a man who on the eve of the Civil War had sadly wondered whether he and his bride-to-be would ever be together in heaven. The mature Ward, like Carus, ended by concluding that all such desires as he had once confided to his diary were both illusory and egoistic.[12] His was the self-transcending ethic expressed in a poem by George Eliot, of which many thoughtful agnostics have been fond.

> Oh may I join the choir invisible
> Of those immortal dead who live again
> In minds made better by their presence: live
> . . . . .
> . . . in scorn
> For miserable aims that end with self,
> . . . . .
> So to live is heaven,
> To make undying music in the world.[13]

"When we attain the realization that death finishes the story, we know the worst," Corliss Lamont wrote in 1935. "And that worst is not really very bad." The author of *The Illusion of Immortality* was not the first American thus to depreciate the dread of personal cessation. Out of his experiences as a physician in a Confederate prison camp in the autumn of 1864, where men had perished in wartime misery at the rate of four hundred a week, Junius Henry Browne testified a quarter-century later that he could "not recall a single instance of a man who was troubled with doubt or alarm. . . . They were not concerned about the future, but about the past and present, leaving messages and mementos for the near and dear, and passing away gently and in peace." But what we can not know from such testimony is what proportion of these men were dying in calm certainty of the absoluteness of what was ending for them—and how many were letting go their hold on life while keeping a grip on the traditional comforts of religion. We do know that in the American Civil War the armies on both sides were periodically swept by religious revivals; that Robert E. Lee was not above dismounting from his horse and doffing his hat to pray with his men; and that an Ozark folksong celebrating one of the worst battles of that war ended with a prayer

> . . . to God my Saviour, consistent with His will,
> To save the souls of them brave men who fell on Shiloh's Hill.[14]

Radical anticlericals in the postbellum years sometimes conceded that belief in immortality was a great deterrent to the overthrow of orthodoxy. One such skeptic considered that particular doctrine "the great bulwark of the church, and the standing obstacle in the way of all organized movement against her." It was all very well for Emerson bravely to say "Of immortality, the soul, when well employed, is incurious," but testimony such as his would "not satisfy the mind of average humanity, which shudders at the thought of dissolution."[15] Moreover, were the survivors of all those young men fallen in battle expected stoically to affirm that the worst is not really very bad?

We have already heard the heartbroken cry that the Civil War wrung from Elizabeth Stuart Phelps, and in peacetime Phillips Brooks, that most serenely optimistic of men, spoke in one sermon of "the sadness, which no faith in immortality can dissipate, belonging to the death of those who die in youth, the sense of untimeliness which we cannot reason down." Brooks's Anglican colleague James DeKoven preached, "Beside some silent form, the quiet stillness of the dead, we stand and ask . . . where is he now? . . . Tell me not of physical laws and the workings of disease, of forces, and gases, and currents. Philosophy and science and culture have no words warm enough to comfort me. O Cross of Christ! Cast thou thy shadow on my breaking heart."[16]

The trouble with the consolations of science was that for many they were not really very consoling. A correspondent of the Providence *Journal* wrote sarcastically of the thin substitutes which science and philosophy were offering in place of the supreme hope of religion.

> Before long we shall become so scientific and so well-informed that when a person dies there will be no funeral services. Some one will read comforting passages from the Transactions of the American Scientific Association, and the mourners will go about with small hammers in their hands, chipping the rocks and assuaging their anguish by proving the antiquity of creation . . . . We have traded off all simple religious faiths for a few meagre scientific

facts; but there may come that day, when we think of bestowing our patronage on some undertaker, that we shall wish to trade back again, and in something of a hurry . . . . Darwin's greatest work is the last book we should want to read the last evening we spent on this earth.[17]

Charles Darwin himself was not happy with some of the comfortable words put forth in his name. "Believing as I do that man in the distant future will be a far more perfect creature than he now is, it is an intolerable thought that he and all other sentient beings are doomed to complete annihilation," Darwin wrote. "To those who fully admit the immortality of the human soul, the destruction of our world will not appear so dreadful." A distinguished survivor from the Gilded Age echoed these words of Darwin as recently as 1956: "With the planet's perishing, the last Robinson Crusoe on this wandering island in the sky will be finally dead, and nothing will be left, no value conserved, no purpose fulfilled from all that was endeavored and done on earth," wrote Harry Emerson Fosdick in his autobiography *The Living of These Days.* "My faith in immortality has been mainly a corollary from my faith that creation cannot be so utterly senseless and irrational."[18] Not all men of Fosdick's generation drew this corollary; compare the tragic naturalism of Bertrand Russell's *A Free Man's Worship.* But Russell and Fosdick would have agreed with Darwin that there is one fatal drawback in joining George Eliot's "choir invisible": one day, thanks to the Second Law of Thermodynamics, the chorus is going to have to stop singing. The poetess herself conceded the point:

> That better self shall live till human Time
> Shall fold its eyelids, and the human sky
> Be gathered like a scroll within the tomb
> Unread for ever.

Some contemporaries of Paul Carus and Lester Ward therefore considered their ethical conclusion that "the only worthy immortality is survival in the remembrance of one's fellow creatures" as little more than "a travesty and a trick." John Fiske cried, "If the world's long cherished beliefs are to fall, in God's name let them fall, but save us from the intellectual hypocrisy that goes about pretending we are none the poorer!" The argument that a person should be glad to lose his individual voice in the Choir Invisible because it is egoistic to desire the survival of one's own psyche is self-defeating, Theodore Munger added; if I cease to exist, I cease being able to give and serve. "It is one thing to see the difficulties in the way of immortality, but quite another thing to erect annihilation into morality, and . . . to claim for such morality a superiority over that of those who hope to live on."[19]

Some of those who hoped to live on may simply have been reviving Pascal's old argument for the necessity of the Wager: "If you gain, you gain all; if you lose, you lose nothing." If God and the afterlife are real, you gain immortality by gambling on their existence; if they are illusory, your consciousness will not survive to feel the humiliation of having been proved wrong. The skeptic's option, of refusing to call the toss of the coin at all, is not really available, since all men in their concrete decisions in life will act as if they believed in ultimate Being or in ultimate Nothingness. "And, thus," concluded that seventeenth-century mathematician and mystic, "when one is forced to play, he must renounce reason to preserve his life."[20]

Life is a narrow vale between the cold and barren peaks of two eternities. We strive in vain to look beyond the heights. We cry aloud, and the only answer is the echo of a wailing cry. From the voiceless lips of the unreplying dead there comes no word; but in the night of death hope sees a star and listening love can hear the rustle of a wing. He who sleeps here, when dying, mistaking the approach of death for the return of health, whispered with his latest breath, "I am better now." Let us believe, in spite of doubts and dogmas, and tears and fears, that these dear words are true of all the countless dead.[21]

It is not surprising that words like these were spoken at a funeral in the emotionally effusive Victorian Age, but on first reflection it is astonishing that they should have been spoken by Robert G. Ingersoll. Did the eloquent freethinker quail away from the courage of his convictions when he was burying his own brother? Admirers of Ingersoll have had trouble with this paragraph. One biographer, pondering the "rustle of a wing" passage, became convinced that these were no more than "the words of Ingersoll's agony. He may have found relief in the phantasm of the words but only while he said them."[22] But personal crisis was not the only occasion on which this crusading anticleric considered the ultimate question and came out with a tentatively affirmative answer. Ingersoll often delivered funeral orations, and they seem genuinely to have comforted the bereaved.

The comfort was sometimes ambiguous; "We do not know whether the grave is the end of this life or the door of another," Ingersoll admitted. Many of his beloved dead he commended, "without assurance, and without fear," to a half-personified Nature: "With morn, with noon, with night; with changing clouds and changeless stars; with grass and trees . . . with leaf and bud, with flower and blossoming vine . . . we leave our dead"—hinting perhaps at a Romantic pantheism, or perhaps at Spinoza's austere *natura sive deus;* or he may merely have meant that to mingle obliviously with the earth was better at any rate than consciously to endure the fatuous heavens or gross hells of tradition. He wrote with especial tenderness in 1885 to a bereaved mother, brought up in Calvinism and distraught to the point of insanity by the fear that her unconverted son was suffering in Hell, to tell her that if God existed her own heart, which "could never send your boy to endless pain," was the best revelation of Him.

After all, no one knows. The ministers know nothing. . . . Creeds are good for nothing except to break the hearts of the loving. . . . Listen to your heart, believe what it says, and wait with patience and without fear for whatever the future has for all. If we can get no comfort from what people know, let us avoid being driven to despair by what they do not know.[23]

Much of this was compatible with pure naturalistic humanism, but unlike most other naturalists Ingersoll always left a door open. The Great Infidel did not brush aside the notion of personal survival after death as egocentric fantasy; whatever else might be thought of the concept, it had for him at least the legitimacy of naturalness. "The idea of immortality . . . was not born of any book, nor of any creed, nor of any religion," Ingersoll said in one of his lectures. "It was born of human affection, and it will continue to ebb and flow beneath the mists and clouds of doubt and darkness as long as love kisses the lips of death."[24] In a letter to his wife in 1879, he voiced the hope that in the earth "my dust may mingle with yours. Even this hope gives a glow to the cheek of death. . . . We will keep to-gether until every passion dies, and then through the shadows of death, we will exchange dim looks of love."[25]

Was this sheer Victorian sentimentalism? Could one give full allegiance to the monistic world-view which typified the science of the Gilded Age and still indulge in a fancy as capriciously personal as this, except on what William James might have called a "moral holiday"? Only if personal hope could somehow be squared with impersonal conviction. Ingersoll was an orator, not a laboratory researcher, and his own answers to the question of immortality were expressed as platform or even graveside eloquence rather than as scientific reports (which is not to deny their intuitive integrity). But there were others who took a more theoretical and experimental approach to the problem.

"Immortality came under question simply because science could find no data for it," wrote Theodore T. Munger in 1885, but it was not thereby necessarily disproven. Personal immortality might therefore turn out to be not a mysterious disclosure of God's grace, to be accepted on faith, but a hitherto unrecognized natural phenomenon, to be measured like any other. Even in the matter-of-fact nineteenth century not all occult beliefs had turned out upon careful examination to be superstitions; hypnotism, wrote Minot J. Savage in 1889, had once been investigated and pronounced fraudulent, and clairvoyance and telepathy might now be going through the same process of rejection, examination, and eventual acceptance. "In a universe the size of this, a modest scientific man will hesitate about declaring as to what is or is not impossible."[26] Perhaps the persistence of personal identity after death is not, by the usual definition, "supernatural" at all.[27]

Some Victorian thinkers were already aware that the palpable material world upon which so much of their science seemed to rest was not so much a fact of experience as a mental construct. The quest for a tangible, measurable reality knowable by "common sense" had led unexpectedly instead to such notions as that of a "luminiferous ether," surely an idea as intangible, abstract, and contrary to common sense as Thomas Aquinas's angels dancing on the point of a pin. Noting as early as 1873 the overthrow of what had been classic textbook distinctions between "substances" that could be weighed and those more imponderable "substances" such as light, electricity, and magnetism, E. A. Sears wrote: "Matter has no ultimate units, but is divisible to the point where it vanishes from human perception." Hence, this religious apologist argued, "the best scientific research and progress do not tend downward toward a grosser materialism, but away from it." (Such reasoning has not been unknown in the twentieth century among theistic scientists, to the annoyance of many among their professional colleagues, as when Sir James Jeans concluded in 1931 that "the universe begins to look more like a great thought than like a great machine.")[28] If a dying God, or some semblance of Him, might be resuscitated by such argumentation, thought some in America's Gilded Age, so might man's own immortal soul.

Two lines of attack commended themselves to such inquirers. Assuming as many of them did a universe governed by natural causation rather than by miraculous fiat,[29] and knowable by empirical inquiry rather than by transempirical revelation, they had to locate human immortality within such a universe. The investigator might find it in space; if people do not go off at once to a "hell" or a "heaven" (which, as was seen earlier, raises the difficult question "Where?"[30]) then they may still be among us, engaging in activities which can be objectively measured. This was the method of "psychic research" and of Spiritualism. Or, he might find it in time; life after death is a natural inference from Darwinism. In his book *Old Faiths in New Light* (1879) Newman Smyth suggested that the human brain might not be the last step in evolution, but the first: "The brain may be only the embryonic condition of the matter of mind"—and the transition to an afterlife would then seem to be a natural process, "a conceivable and fitting termination of the whole course of nature."[31]

Going much further than this modest inference, Thomson Jay Hudson argued in *A Scientific Demonstration of the Future Life* (1895) that evolution did not merely permit immortality, it required it. Natural selection, by definition, never produces a physical or mental trait without some legitimate adaptive function, and yet there are depths of human consciousness which can in no sense be explained merely as a means for coping with man's natural environment. Therefore, Hudson reasoned, since the human psyche was endowed "with faculties that perform no function in this life," that fact constituted "demonstrative evidence that the subjective mind was created *ab initio,* with special reference to a future life."[32]

The British lecturer on evolution Henry Drummond, who was enough of a scientist to have gone on geological expeditions in the Rocky Mountains and enough of an evangelist to have traveled with Dwight L. Moody, took a somewhat different tack.[33] He believed that the partition between the watertight compartments labeled Science and Religion showed signs of giving way; that generalizations about natural phenomena, such as the theory of evolution, could be extended into the "supernatural," which would be shown eventually to be governed by the same kinds of laws that prevailed in the "natural" world; and therefore—a very long inference indeed!—that observed natural processes could be used by analogy to explain the Unseen. The organisms formerly limited to an ocean habitat which had evolved into air-breathing forms that conquered the land could thus become a metaphor for the transition from this world to the next: "Is the change from the earthly to the heavenly more mysterious than the change from the aquatic to the terrestrial mode of life?"[34]

This tempting, but logically shaky mode of reasoning was common among liberal theists in the Gilded Age. Contrast "the headless mollusk glued to rock in a world of water, and an antlered deer in a world of verdure"; contrast the dinosaur with man; these were transformations no more startling than the leap from death to the afterlife, Theodore Munger argued. "There is a reason why the reptile should become a mammal; it is more life. Is there no like reason for man? Shall he not have more life?" But there were hazards in this method of defending the faith. The trouble with "religious" Darwinism was that, like "social" Darwinism, it was equivocal; diametrically opposite conclusions could legitimately be drawn from the same scientific premises. The British agnostic Leslie Stephen warned hopeful believers that the fact of evolution could also be used as evidence against life after death.

> Does not the new theory make it difficult to believe in immortal souls? If we admit the difference between men and monkeys is merely a difference of degree, can we continue to hold that monkeys will disappear at their death like a bubble, and that men will rise from their ashes?

If, on the other hand, this difference between men and monkeys was one not of degree but of kind, so wide a gap would be a serious blow at the continuity inherent in a strict Darwinian view of the evolutionary process. To be consistent,

Stephen argued, we must either endow animals with "some kind of rudimentary souls," or deny the soul to man.[35]

Eventually, of course, the religious Darwinists could have answered arguments like Stephen's by citing further advances in evolutionary theory. Already scientists were beginning to doubt that Darwin's gradual and random "natural selection" was sufficient to account for the phenomena observed. By the mid-1880's Hugo DeVries was looking for a scientifically respectable way of viewing the development of life on earth as discontinuous, and in 1900 the rediscovery of Mendel's mutation theory gave this hypothesis empirical foundation.[36] It might then have been in order to interpret immortality as "discontinuous," that is, as a mutation which entered the natural order for the first time with man. Developments in physics as well as in genetics seemed to permit the same general conclusion: "With every new form of force, with every new birth of the universal energy into a higher plane, there appear new, unexpected, and, previous to experience, wholly unimaginable properties and powers," Joseph LeConte asserted. "Why may not immortality be one of these new properties?"[37]

This would still have left unanswered the question of which "men" first acquired this new power. Did Neanderthal Man, who was physically more primitive than modern man but who laid out his dead with their tools and other possessions (an act having clearly religious implications) possess a soul, whereas the primeval hominid in Kenya who initially stumbled upon the use of tools lacked one? In any case, such an approach compromised the integrity of the religious apologist's entire position. Impelled toward skepticism by what seemed on inescapable inference from science (continuity, in the classic Darwinist version of the evolutionary hypothesis), and then propelled toward faith by what seemed another (genetic discontinuity, as in the mutation theory), he would have been forced to measure the validity of his doctrines by their scientific plausibility rather than by their intrinsic merit as religious ideas—exactly as positivists like E. L. Youmans were demanding that he do.

Furthermore, to have claimed that man's immortal soul was a mutation rather than an adaptive progression would have been only a temporary victory for religion. Just around the corner as the Gilded Age ended was the science of Dirac and Heisenberg and Bohr, which one after another would overthrow the traditional dichotomous pairs—"space/time," "matter/energy," "wave/particle," "mind/body"; perhaps one day the "life/death" antithesis might also have to be discarded. Such an outcome would hardly have satisfied the conventional wisdom of the Gilded Age, although it might have pleased Mary Baker Eddy, whose *Science and Health* (first published in 1875) did seem to argue that whether an individual be considered "living" or "dead" is largely a matter of one's point of view. More congenial to the kind of vision in that period that has been described as "matter-of-fact" or "opaque" would have been the approach to immortality which sought for the afterlife neither in the temporal unfolding of evolution nor in a Heaven above our heads, but in opaque and matter-of-fact phenomena such as tables, trumpets, slates, noises, and voices.[38]

"It is twenty-five years since the tiny raps at Hydesville, New York, ushered in the grandest movement of all the centuries," President Victoria Claflin Woodhull told the American Association of Spiritualists as she took the chair at their 1873 annual convention. "Led by heartless science, the world was fast declining into the blank of Atheism, but the dawning of the light of Spiritualism has driven doubt back . . ."[39] Stimulated by the religious ferment of the 1840's, particularly by universalism whose denial of the doctrine of eternal punishment opened the way to a revolutionary new concept of the hereafter, and by Swedenborgianism with its unorthodox portrayal of the invisible world, Spiritualism attracted a respectable following in the United States; Adin Ballou became a convert, and William Lloyd Garrison and Horace Greeley both flirted with the movement. In the Fifties the cult spread to England, where it attracted attention both among the credulous and among the more cautious—men, for example, like the mathematician Augustus De Morgan, co-founder (with Boole) of symbolic logic and modern algebra; Sir William Crookes, a pioneer in experimental physics; and Alfred Russell Wallace, co-discoverer with Darwin of the principle of natural selection.[40] From time to time revelations of fraud checked the growth of the movement,[41] but faith has often outlived fraud.

NOTES

1. [F. Bruce Morgan] "Is This the Post-Christian Era?" lead editorial, *Theology Today,* XVIII (January 1962), pp. 399-405.

From either an historical or sociological point of view all such judgments are impressionistic and to some degree subjective: "Despite the importance of the topic, empirical studies of the individual's relationship to death have been comparatively few and recent. Great obstacles to research are posed by people's reluctance to discuss so private a matter, as well as by their underlying ambivalence toward death itself." John W. Riley, Jr., "Death," in David L. Sills, ed., *International Encyclopedia of the Social Sciences* (New York, 1968), Vol. IV, p. 23. If people are in fact more willing to talk to investigators in personal terms about sexual matters than they are about death, considering that both of these subjects were taboo areas in polite society not so long ago, we may be less "emancipated" in our attitude toward personal extinction than Professor Morgan's essay implies.

2. John J. McMahon, "Catholic Students Look at Death," *Commonweal,* LXXXVIII (January 26, 1968), pp. 491-494. By 1968 the only surprising feature of such testimony was its occurrence in a church-controlled classroom. Half a century earlier, questionnaires on the belief in God and in personal immortality among American college students and among natural and social scientists had shown what was coming. See James H. Leuba, *The Belief in God and Immortality: a Psychological, Anthropological and Statistical Study* (Boston, 1916), esp pp. 185-213.

3. A. V. G. Allen, *Life and Letters of Phillips Brooks* (New York, 1901), Vol. II, p. 481. Conversely, there remained many in the "activist" 1960's who thought of life after death not as activity but as repose. "In a public lecture I once remarked, quite incidentally, that Christ did not promise us eternal rest by *eternal life* and that the concept of 'life' is scarcely synonymous with 'rest.' Many in

the audience were troubled and did not understand." Ignace Lepp, *Death and its Mysteries* (New York, 1968), p. 183.

4. Sidney E. Mead has a penetrating comment on America's Protestant folk-hymns (such as this one, which he quotes) in his seminal essay "The American People: Their Space, Time, and Religion," Chapter I of *The Lively Experiment: the Shaping of Christianity in America* (New York, 1963), esp. p. 12.

5. For the dating of the composition of these hymns I am indebted to a study by Evelyn Hubbard, "A Survey of the Hymnary of the Gilded Age," unpublished seminar paper, Northern Illinois University, 1967.

6. Henry Ward Beecher, *Yale Lectures on Preaching* (three volumes in one, New York, 1887), Third Series, Chapter XII, p. 320. Perhaps Beecher was unaware of the Feuerbachian implications of that last line!

7. Washington Gladden, *How Much Is Left of the Old Doctrines?* (Boston, 1899), pp. 314, 316; William Scarlett, ed., *Phillips Brooks: Selected Sermons* (New York, 1949), p. 369.

8. Charles A. Briggs, *Whither? A Theological Question for the Times* (New York, 1889), p. 285; Elizabeth Stuart Phelps, "The Psychical Wave," *The Forum,* I (June, 1886), pp. 380, 381, 388.

9. William Osler, *Science and Immortality* [The Ingersoll Lecture, 1904] Boston, 1904, p. 25. For a characteristic contemporary statement of this position, see the quotation from E. Duhring's *Der Werth des Lebens* in William James, *Human Immortality: Two Supposed Objections to the Doctrine* [The Ingersoll Lecture, 1898], 2nd edition, Boston, 1899, p. 11, n. 2.

10. In 1932, contemplating a new wave of discoveries in neurophysiology (popularly expressed in books with titles like *The Wisdom of the Body* and *The Physical Basis of Mind*) which seemed to overthrow completely any dualistic concept of "mind" and "body" as separate entities, the philosopher Roy Wood Sellars commented: "It is upon this rock that all theories of immortality break to pieces." Sellars, *The Philosophy of Physical Realism* (New York, 1932), p. 304, as quoted in Ashley Montagu, *Immortality* (New York, 1955), p. 25. See also the discussion of the destructive monistic implications of physiology and medicine for the concept of survival after death in Corliss Lamont, *The Illusion of Immortality* (London, [1935] 1936), pp. 58-112.

11. Lovecraft to Frank Belknap Long, July 17, 1921, in H. P. Lovecraft, *Selected Letters,* Vol. I, *1911-1924* (Sauk City, Wis., 1965), p. 141.

12. Paul Carus, *The Religion of Science* (Chicago, [1893] 1896), pp. 48, 39, 56: Samuel Chugerman, *Lester F. Ward, the American Aristotle* (Durham, N.C., 1939), pp. 249f.

13. Quoted in Ashley Montagu, *op. cit.,* p. 67, and in Philip S. Moxom, *The Argument for Immortality* (Cambridge, Mass., 1894), p. 4. Montagu's and Moxom's own comments upon this widely-anthologized poem may be read as a debate in miniature on the merits of George Eliot's position on the immortality question. Moxom's paper is more readily available to the modern reader in John Henry Barrows, ed., *The World's Parliament of Religions* (Chicago, 1893), pp. 466-479.

14. Corliss Lamont, *op. cit.,* p. 239; Junius Henry Browne, "The Dread of Death," *The Forum,* VI (October 1888), p. 220; Alan Lomax, ed., *The Folk Songs of North America* (Garden City, 1960), p. 350.

15. "Confessions of a Skeptic," *The Forum,* II (November 1886), p. 290.

16. A. V. G. Allen, *op. cit.,* Vol. III, p. 370; James DeKoven, "The Christian Struggle," Sermon XIX in *Sermons Preached on Various Occasions . . .* (New York, 1880), p. 203.

17. Quoted in "Editor's Easy Chair," *Harper's New Monthly Magazine,* LII (March 1876), pp. 612f.

18. Francis Darwin, ed., *Life and Letters of Charles Darwin* (London, 1888), Vol.I, p. 312; Harry Emerson Fosdick, *The Living of These Days: an Autobiography* (New York, 1956), p. 241. Compare the very similar argument of Lyman Abbott in *The Theology of an Evolutionist* (Boston, 1897), pp. 170f.

19. John Fiske, *Through Nature to God* (Boston, [1899] 1900), p. 170; Theodore T. Munger, "Immortality and Modern Thought," *Century Magazine,* XXX [n. s., VIII] (May 1885), p. 76.

20. Blaise Pascal, *Pensées,* tr. by W.F. Trotter (New York, 1941), pp. 81, 82, and *passim* in Section III, "On the Necessity of the Wager."

21. Robert G. Ingersoll, "Address at the Funeral of His Brother," as reprinted in Ingersoll, *The House of Death, Being Funeral Orations and Addresses, etc.* (London, 1897), pp. 72f.

22. Orvin Larson, *American Infidel: Robert G. Ingersoll* (New York, 1962), p. 143.

23. Robert G. Ingersoll, *The House of Death,* pp. 36, 64, 87f.

24. Ingersoll, *The Ghosts, and Other Lectures* (Washington, 1878), p. 14.

25. Quoted in C. H. Cramer, *Royal Bob: the Life of Robert G. Ingersoll* (Indianapolis, 1952), p. 264.

26. Munger, "Immortality and Modern Thought," as cited in n. 19, above, p. 68; Minot J. Savage, "Experiences with Spiritualism," *The Forum,* VIII (December 1889), p. 451. Compare Alexander Winchell, *Sketches of Creation* (New York, 1870), p. 371: "There must be a substratum that has not yet been sounded lying beneath the confused and apparently capricious phenomena of clairvoyance, mesmerism, dreams, and spiritual manifestations. With much imposition, there is much which can not be scientifically ignored. It remains to resolve the mystery of these sporadic phenomena—to reduce them to law . . . ."

27. More recently it has been possible for at least one well known and highly articulate American clergyman to combine the most radical skepticism toward all the traditional doctrines of the Church with a heightened belief in immortality. James A. Pike, "Why I'm Leaving the Church," *Look,* April 29, 1969, pp. 54-58; James A. Pike with Diane Kennedy, *The Other Side: an Account of My Experiences with Psychic Phenomena* (New York, 1969).

28. E. A. Sears, "The Transparencies of Nature," New York *Christian Advocate,* XLIX (January 1, 1874), p. 1; Sir James Jeans, *The Mysterious Universe,* new rev. ed. (New York and Cambridge, [1932] 1935), p. 186.

29. "Miracle, in the sense of violation of law, is simply impossible. . . . It is as impossible for God to perform a miracle in this sense as it is for him to lie. . . . In what sense, then, is a miracle possible? I answer, only as an occurrence or a phenomenon *according to a law higher than any we yet know."* Joseph LeConte, *Evolution: its Nature, its Evidences, and its Relation to Religious Thought,* 2nd rev. ed. (New York, [1891] 1899), p. 356. Italics in the original.

30. For an example of the speculative difficulties people got themselves into in their efforts to answer this question literally, see Andrew Jackson Davis, *Views of our Heavenly Home* (Rochester, N.Y., [1878] 1910), pp. 64-87, and esp. p. 165, where Davis attempted an estimate of the distance between Earth and Heaven in miles.

31. Newman Smyth, *Old Faiths in New Light* (New York, 1879), pp. 377, 375. See the expansion of this idea in the same author's *The Place of Death in Evolution* (New York, 1897).

32. Thomson Jay Hudson, *A Scientific Demonstration of the Future Life* (1895; 8th edition, Chicago, 1904), p. 255. But for a powerful contemporary rebuttal to this reasoning, see Chauncey Wright, "Evolution of Self-Consciousness," an abridgment of which appears in Perry Miller, ed., *American Thought: Civil War to*

World War I (New York and Toronto, 1954), pp. 28-45. Wright argued that those aspects of man's psyche which he had been pleased to think of as peculiarly his own can be accounted for by natural evolutionary processes; see esp. pp. 31-38.

33. Drummond's work with Moody went so far as helping in the personal ministry to those who came to the "inquiry-room" after Moody's sermons; Ernst Benz, *Evolution and Christian Hope: Man's Concept of the Future, from the Early Fathers to Teilhard de Chardin* (New York, 1966), p. 156. For an example of Drummond's public lectures on evolution, see *The Ascent of Man* (New York, 1894); for an example of his more purely devotional writing—the kind that would have made him congenial to Dwight L. Moody, in spite of the latter's rejection of the theory of evolution—see Drummond's often-reprinted essay on I Corinthians 13, *The Greatest Thing in the World.*

34. Henry Drummond, *Natural Law in the Spiritual World* (Philadelphia, 1893), p. 218.

35. Munger, "Immortality and Modern Thought," as cited in notes 19 and 26, above, pp. 72, 74;"L. S." [Leslie Stephen], "Darwinism and Divinity," *Popular Science Monthly,* I (June 1872), pp. 199, 200. Evolutionary theists really could elect neither option, for to have granted souls to "lower" animals would have undermined their denial of man's basically animal nature, so crucial to their optimism about his future potential. Nevertheless at least one of them, who had affirmatively answered the question of whether animals had souls, proceeded to the logical next question "Are they immortal?" and, after a bit of verbal hemming and hawing, concluded with a tentative "yes"; if ours persist after death, so in all fairness ought theirs. James Freeman Clarke, "Have Animals Souls?" *Atlantic Monthly,* XXXIV (October 1874), p. 421.

36. H. T. Pledge, *Science Since 1500* (London, [1939] 1947), p. 222. A readable and still fairly accurate popular account of DeVries's work is in Willy Ley, *The Days of Creation* (New York, 1941), pp. 97-102.

37. Joseph LeConte, *op. cit.,* p. 318. A variant on this hypothesis of immortality as "emergent" is that of Henri Bergson, in his *Creative Evolution* (New York, 1937); another, popular among twentieth-century immortalists who have read Freud, posits a "death-trauma" comparable to the "birth-trauma" of psychoanalytic theory, thereby neatly resolving the paradox that man should suffer anxiety at the prospect of moving on to a world which by definition is better than this one. Ignace Lepp, as cited in n. 3, above, pp. 168f.

38. An argument against the usual liberal-theist concept of human immortality as being in violation of the unity of the space-time continuum is in Arthur S. Eddington, *The Nature of the Physical World* (Cambridge, 1928; Ann Arbor, 1958), p. 351.

39. *Proceedings of the Tenth Annual Convention of the American Association of Spiritualists, held at Grow's Opera Hall, Chicago, on Tuesday, September 16* [1873], p. 35.

40. Robert W. Delp, "Andrew Jackson Davis: Prophet of American Spiritualism," *Journal of American History,* LIV (June 1967), p. 44; Joseph McCabe, *Spiritualism: a Popular History from 1847* (London, 1920), p. 105. The 1890 U. S. Census listed 334 organized Spiritualist congregations, with 45,000 (living) communicants; in short, there were a few more Spiritualists in the United States than there were Mennonites (41,541, divided into twelve bodies), and a few less than there were Universalists (49,194). There were three times that many Mormons and Jews, twelve times that many Episcopalians, and thirty times that many Colored Baptists. Henry King Carroll, *The Religious Forces of the United States, Enumerated, Classified, and Described on the Basis of the Government Census of 1890* ["American Church History Series," I] (New York, 1893), General Statistical Summaries, Table II, pp. 390f., and Table IV, p. 394.

41. The confession in 1888 by one of the original Fox sisters of Hydesville that the "spirit rappings" which had made her famous were no more than the cracking of her own knuckle bones was a particularly crushing blow. New York *Herald,* September 24 and October 10, 1888, as quoted in McCabe, *op. cit.,* pp. 44 and 45.

Elizabeth Stuart Phelps

THE GATES AJAR

We have been over tonight to the grave.

She proposed to go by herself, thinking, I saw, with the delicacy with which she always thinks, that I would rather not be there with another. Nor should I, nor could I, with any other than this woman. It is strange. I wished to go there with her. I had a vague, unreasoning feeling that she would take away some of the bitterness of it, as she has taken the bitterness of much else.

It is looking very pleasant there now. The turf has grown fine and smooth. The low arbor-vitae hedge and knots of Norway spruce, that father planted long ago for mother, drop cool, green shadows that stir with the wind. My English ivy has crept about and about the cross. Roy used to say that he should fancy a cross to mark the spot where he might lie; I think he would like this pure, unveined marble. May-flowers cover the grave now, and steal out among the clover-leaves with a flush like sunrise. By and by there will be roses, and, in August, August's own white lilies.

We went silently over, and sat silently down on the grass, the field-path stretching away to the little church behind us, and beyond, in front, the slope, the flats, the river, the hills cut in purple distance melting far into the east. The air was thick with perfume. Golden bees hung giddily over the blush in the grass. In the low branches that swept the grave a little bird had built her nest.

Reprinted from *The Gates Ajar* by Elizabeth Stuart Phelps. Published by Fields, Osgood, and Co., 1869, pp. 84-88, 133-48.

Aunt Winifred did not speak to me for a time, nor watch my face. Presently she laid her hand upon my lap, and I put mine to it.

"It is very pleasant here," she said then, in her very pleasant voice.

"I meant that it should be," I answered, trying not to let her see my lips quiver. "At least it must not look neglected. I don't suppose it makes any difference to *him.*"

"I do not feel sure of that."

"What do you mean?"

"I do not feel sure that anything he has left makes no 'difference' to him."

"But I don't understand. He is in heaven. He would be too happy to care for anything that is going on in this woful world."

"Perhaps that is so," she said, smiling a sweet contradiction to her words, "but I don't believe it."

"What do you believe?"

"Many things that I have to say to you, but you cannot bear them now."

"I have sometimes wondered, for I cannot help it," I said, "whether he is shut off from all knowledge of me for all these years till I can go to him. It will be a great while. It seems hard. Roy would want to know something, if it were only a little, about me."

"I believe that he wants to know, and that he knows, Mary; though, since the belief must rest on analogy and conjecture, you need not accept it as demonstrated mathematics," she answered, with another smile.

"Roy never forgot me here!" I said, not meaning to sob.

"That is just it. He was not constituted so that he, remaining himself, Roy, could forget you. If he goes out into his other life forgetting, he becomes another than himself. That is a far more unnatural way of creeping out of the difficulty than to assume that he loves and remembers. Why not assume that? In fact, why assume anything else? Neither reason, nor the Bible, nor common sense, forbids it. Instead of starting with it as an hypothesis to be proved if we can, I lay it down as one of those probabilities for which Butler would say, 'the presumption amounts nearly to certainty'; and if any one can disprove it, I will hear what he has to say. There!" she broke off, laughing softly, "that is a sufficient dose of metaphysics for such a simple thing. It seems to me to lie just here: Roy loved you. Our Father, for some tender, hidden reason, took him out of your sight for a while. Though changed much, he can have forgotten nothing. Being *only out of sight,* you remember, not lost, nor asleep, nor annihilated, he goes on loving. To love must mean to think of, to care for, to hope for, to pray for, not less out of a body than in it."

"But that must mean—why, that must mean—"

"That he is near you. I do not doubt it."

The sunshine quivered in among the ivy-leaves, and I turned to watch it, thinking.

"I do not doubt," she went on, speaking low,—"I cannot doubt that our absent dead are very present with us. He said, 'I am with you always,' knowing the need we have of him, even to the end of the world. He must understand the need we have of them. I cannot doubt it."

• • • •

20th

"I thank thee, my God, the river of Lethe may indeed flow through the Elysian Fields,—it does not water the Christian's Paradise."

Aunt Winifred was saying that over to herself in a dreamy undertone this morning, and I happened to hear her.

"Just a quotation, dear," she said, smiling, in answer to my look of inquiry, "I couldn't originate so pretty a thing. *Isn't* it pretty?"

"Very; but I am not sure that I understand it."

"You thought that forgetfulness would be necessary to happiness?"

"Why,—yes; as far as I had ever thought about it; that is, after our last ties with this world are broken. It does not seem to me that I could be happy to remember all that I have suffered and all that I have sinned here."

"But the last of all the sins will be as if it had never been. Christ takes care of that. No shadow of a sense of guilt can dog you, or affect your relations to Him or your other friends. The last pain borne, the last tear, the last sigh, the last lonely hour, the last unsatisfied dream, forever gone by; why should not the dead past bury its dead?"

"Then why remember it?"

" 'Save but to swell the sense of being blest.' Besides, forgetfulness of the disagreeable things of this life implies forgetfulness of the pleasant ones. They are all tangled together."

"To be sure. I don't know that I should like that."

"Of course you wouldn't. Imagine yourself in a state of being where you and Roy had lost your past; all that you had borne and enjoyed, and hoped and feared, together; the pretty little memories of your babyhood, and first 'half-days' at school, when he used to trudge along beside you,—little fellow! how many times I have watched him!—holding you tight by the apron-sleeve or hat-string, or bits of fat fingers, lest you should run away or fall. Then the old Academy pranks, out of which you used to help each other; his little chivalry and elder-brother advice; the mischief in his eyes; some of the 'Sunday-night talks', the first novel that you read and dreamed over together; the college stories; the chats over the corn-popper by firelight; the earliest, earnest looking-on into life together, its temptations conquered, its lessons learned, its disappointments faced together,—always you two,—would you like to, are you *likely* to, forget all this?

"Roy might as well be not Roy, but a strange angel, if you should. Heaven will be not less heaven, but more, for this pleasant remembering. So many other and greater and happier memories will fill up the time then, that after years these things may—probably will—seem smaller than it seems to us now they can ever be; but they will, I think, be always dear; just as we look back to our baby-selves with a pitying sort of fondness, and, though the little creatures are of small enough use to us now, yet we like to keep good friends with them for old times' sake.

"I have no doubt that you and I shall sit down some summer afternoon in heaven and talk over what we have been saying to-day, and laugh perhaps at all the poor little dreams we have been dreaming of what has not entered into the heart of man. You see it is certain to be so much *better* than anything that I can think of; which is the comfort of it. And Roy—"

"Yes; some more about Roy, please."

"Supposing he were to come right into the room now,—and I slipped out,—and you had him all to yourself again—Now, dear, don't cry, but wait a minute!" Her caressing hand fell on my hair. "I did not mean to hurt you, but to say that your first talk with him, after you stand face to face, may be like that.

"Remembering this life is going to help us amazingly, I fancy, to appreciate the next," she added, by way of period. "Christ seems to have thought so, when he called to the minds of those happy people what, in that unconscious ministering of lowly faith which may never reap its sheaf in the field where the seed was sown, they had not had the comfort of finding out before,—'I was sick and in prison, and ye visited me.' And to come again to Abraham in the parable, did he not say, 'Son, *remember* that thou in thy lifetime hadst good things and Lazarus evil'?"

"I wonder what it is going to look like," I said, as soon as I could put poor Dives out of my mind.

"Heaven? Eye has not seen, but I have my fancies. I think I want some mountains, and very many trees."

"Mountains and trees!"

"Yes; mountains as we see them at sunset and sunrise, or when the maples are on fire and there are clouds enough to make great purple shadows chase each other into lakes of light, over the tops and down the sides,—the *ideal* of mountains which we catch in rare glimpses, as we catch the ideal of everything. Trees as they look when the wind cooes through them on a June afternoon; elms or lindens or pines as cool as frost, and yellow sunshine trickling through on moss. Trees in a forest so thick that it shuts out the world, and you walk like one in a sanctuary. Trees pierced by stars, and trees in a bath of summer moons to which the thrill of

'Love's young dream' shall cling forever—but there is no end to one's fancies. Some water, too, I would like."

"There shall be no more sea."

"Perhaps not; though, as the sea is the great type of separation and of destruction, that may be only figurative. But I'm not particular about the sea, if I can have rivers and little brooks, and fountains of just the right sort; the fountains of this world don't please me generally. I want a little brook to sit and sing to Faith by. O, I forgot! she will be a large girl probably, won't she?"

"Never too large to like to hear your mother sing, will you, Faith?"

"O no," said Faith, who bobbed in and out again like a canary, just then,—"not unless I'm *dreadful* big, with long dresses and a waterfall, you know. I s'pose, maybe, I'd have to have little girls myself to sing to, then. I hope they'll behave better'n Mary Ann does. She's lost her other arm, and all her sawdust is just running out. Besides, Kitty thought she was a mouse, and ran down cellar with her, and she's all shooken up, somehow. She don't look very pretty."

"Flowers, too," her mother went on, after the interruption. "*Not* all amaranth and asphodel, but a variety and color and beauty unimagined; glorified lilies of the valley, heavenly tea-rose buds, and spiritual harebells among them. O, how your poor mother used to say,—you know flowers were her poetry,—coming in weak and worn from her garden in the early part of her sickness, hands and lap and basket full: 'Winifred, if I only supposed I *could* have some flowers in heaven I shouldn't be half so afraid to go!' I had not thought as much about these things then as I have now, or I should have known better how to answer her. I should like, if I had my choice, to have day-lilies and carnations fresh under my windows all the time."

"Under your windows?"

"Yes. I hope to have a home of my own."

"Not a house?"

"Something not unlike it. In the Father's house are many mansions. Sometimes I fancy that those words have a literal meaning which the simple men who heard them may have understood better than we, and that Christ is truly 'preparing' my home for me. He must be there, too, you see,—I mean John."

I believe that gave me some thoughts that I ought not to have, and so I made no reply.

"If we have trees and mountains and flowers and books," she went on, smiling, "I don't see why not houses as well. Indeed, they seem to me as supposable as anything can be which is guess-work at the best; for what a homeless, desolate sort of sensation it gives one to think of people wandering over the 'sweet fields beyond the flood' without a local habitation and a name. What could be done with the millions who, from the time of Adam, have been gathering there, unless they lived under the conditions of organized society? Organized society involves homes, not unlike the homes of this world.

"What other arrangement could be as pleasant, or could be pleasant at all? Robertson's definition of a church exactly fits. 'More united in each other, because more united in God.' A happy home is the happiest thing in the world. I do not see why it should not be in any world. I do not believe that all the little tendernesses of family ties are thrown by and lost with this life. In fact, Mary, I cannot think that anything which has in it the elements of permanency is to be lost, but sin. Eternity cannot be the great blank ocean which most of us have somehow or other been brought up to feel that it is, which shall swallow up, in a pitiless, glorified way, all the little brooks of our delight. So I expect to have my beautiful home, and my husband, and Faith, as I had them here; with many differences and great ones, but *mine* just the same. Unless Faith goes into a home of her own,—the little creature! I suppose she can't always be a baby.

"Do you remember what a pretty little wistful way Charles Lamb has of wondering about all this?

" 'Shall I enjoy friendships there, wanting the smiling indications which point me to them here,—the "sweet assurance of a look"? Sun, and sky, and breeze, and solitary walks, and summer holidays, and the greenness of fields, and the delicious juices of meats and fish, and society, . . .

and candle-light and fireside conversations, and innocent vanities, and jests, and *irony itself,*—do these things go out with life?' "

"Now, Aunt Winifred!" I said, sitting up straight, "what am I to do with these beautiful heresies? If Deacon Quirk *should* hear!"

"I do not see where the heresy lies. As I hold fast by the Bible, I cannot be in much danger."

"But you don't glean your conjectures from the Bible."

"I conjecture nothing that the Bible contradicts. I do not believe as truth indisputable anything that the Bible does not give me. But I reason from analogy about this, as we all do about other matters. Why should we not have pretty things in heaven? If this 'bright and beautiful economy' of skies and rivers, of grass and sunshine, of hills and valleys, is not too good for such a place as this world, will there be any less variety of the bright and beautiful in the next? There is no reason for supposing that the voice of God will speak to us in thunder-claps, or that it will not take to itself the thousand gentle, suggestive tongues of a nature built on the ruins of this, an unmarred system of beneficence.

"There is a pretty argument in the fact that such sunrises, such opening of buds, such fragrant dropping of fruit, such bells in the brooks, such dreams at twilight, and such hush of stars, were fit for Adam and Eve, made holy man and woman. How do we know that the abstract idea of a heaven needs imply anything very much unlike Eden? There is some reason as well as poetry in the conception of a 'Paradise Regained.' A 'new earth wherein dwelleth righteousness.' "

"But how far is it safe to trust to this kind of argument?"

"Bishop Butler will answer you better than I. Let me see, —Isaac Taylor says something about that."

She went into the bookcase for his "Physical Theory of Another Life," and, finding her place, showed me this passage:—

"If this often repeated argument from analogy is to be termed, as to the conclusions it involves, a conjecture merely, we ought then to abandon altogether every kind of abstract reasoning; nor will it be easy afterwards to make good any principle of natural theology. In truth, the very basis of reasoning is shaken by a scepticism so sweeping as this."

And in another place:—

"None need fear the consequences of such endeavors who have well learned the prime principle of sound philosophy, namely, not to allow the most plausible and pleasing conjectures to unsettle our convictions of truth . . . resting upon positive evidence. If there be any who frown upon all such attempts, . . . they would do well to consider, that although individually, and from the constitution of their minds, they may find it very easy to abstain from every path of excursive meditation, it is not so with others who almost irresistibly are borne forward to the vast field of universal contemplation,—a field from which the human mind is not to be barred, and which is better taken possession of by those who reverently bow to the authority of Christianity, than left open to impiety."

"Very good," I said, laying down the book. "But about those trees and houses, and the rest of your 'pretty things'? Are they to be like these?"

"I don't suppose that the houses will be made of oak and pine and nailed together, for instance. But I hope for heavenly types of nature and art. *Something that will be to us then what these are now.* That is the amount of it. They may be as 'spiritual' as you please; they will answer all the purpose to us. As we are not spiritual beings yet, however, I am under the necessity of calling them by their earthly names. You remember Plato's old theory, that the ideal of everything exists eternally in the mind of God. If that is so,—and I do not see how it can be otherwise,—then whatever of God is expressed to us in this world by flower, or blade of grass, or human face, why should not that be expressed forever in heaven by something corresponding to flower, or grass, or human face? I do not mean that the heavenly creation will be less real than these, but more so. Their 'spirituality' is of such a sort that our gardens and forests and homes are but shadows of them.

"You don't know how I amuse myself at night thinking

this all over before I go to sleep; wondering what one thing will be like, and another thing; planning what I should like; thinking that John has seen it all, and wondering if he is laughing at me because I know so little about it! I tell you, Mary, there's a 'deal o' comfort in 't,' as Phoebe says about her cup of tea."

July 5

Aunt Winifred has been hunting up a Sunday school class for herself and one for me; which is a venture that I never was persuaded into undertaking before. She herself is fast becoming acquainted with the poorer people of the town.

I find that she is a thoroughly busy Christian, with a certain "week-day holiness" that is strong and refreshing, like a west wind. Church-going, and conversations on heaven, by no means exhaust her vitality.

She told me a pretty thing about her class; it happened the first Sabbath that she took it. Her scholars are young girls of from fourteen to eighteen years of age, children of church-members, most of them. She seemed to have taken their hearts by storm. *She* says, "They treated me very prettily, and made me love them at once."

Clo Bentley is in the class; Clo is a pretty, soft-eyed little creature, with a shrinking mouth, and an absorbing passion for music, which she has always been too poor to gratify. I suspect that her teacher will make a pet of her. She says that in the course of her lesson, or, in her words,—

"While we were all talking together, somebody pulled my sleeve, and there was Clo in the corner, with her great brown eyes fixed on me. 'See here!' she said in a whisper, 'I can't be good! I would be good if I could *only* just have a piano!' 'Well, Clo,' I said, 'if you will be a good girl, and go to heaven, I think you will have a piano there, and play just as much as you care to.'

"You ought to have seen the look the child gave me! Delight and fear and incredulous bewilderment tumbled over each other, as if I had proposed taking her into a forbidden fairy-land.

"'Why, Mrs. Forceythe! Why, they won't let anybody have a piano up there! not in *heaven?'*

"I laid down the question-book, and asked what kind of place she supposed that heaven was going to be.

" 'O,' she said with a dreary sigh, 'I never think about it when I can help it. I suppose we *shall all just stand there!'*

"And you?" I asked of the next, a bright girl with snapping eyes.

" 'Do you want me to talk good, or tell the truth?' she answered me. Having been given to understand that she was not expected to 'talk good' in my class, she said, with an approving, decided nod: 'Well, then! I don't think its going to be *anything nice* anyway. No I don't! I told my last teacher so, and she looked just as shocked, and said I never should go there as long as I felt so. That made me so mad, and I told her I didn't see but I should be as well off in one place as another, except for the fire.'

"A silent girl in the corner began at this point to look interested. 'I always supposed,' said she, 'that you just floated round in heaven—you know—all together—something like ju-jube paste!'

"Whereupon I shut the question-book entirely, and took to talking to myself for a while.

" 'But I never thought it was anything like that,' interrupted little Clo, presently, her cheeks flushed with excitement. 'Why, I should like to go, if it is like that! I never supposed people talked, unless it was about converting people, and saying your prayers, and all that.'

"Now, weren't those ideas (facts) alluring and comforting for young girls in the blossom of warm human life? They were trying with all their little hearts to 'be good,' too, some of them, and had all of them been to church and Sunday school all their lives. Never, never, if Jesus Christ had been Teacher and Preacher to them, would He have pictured their blessed endless years with Him in such bleak colors. They are not the hues of His Bible."

PART THREE

"Death Shall Have No Dominion"

The Twentieth Century

A dramatic reversal in perception of relationship between life and death has taken place in this century. The social visibility of natural death in American society has been drastically reduced. Indeed, that topic has become a taboo and dying an alien event. In part, declining visible presence of death has been a consequence of decreasing mortality rates. As earlier noted, that rate stands presently at approximately nine per 1,000 population, which represents a striking 47 percent reduction over the seventeen per 1,000 rate at the opening of this century.

There are other factors, however, which have been equally significant in forming the modern perception of and response to death. In the first selection of Part III, historian Philippe Ariès describes the historical evolution of death as a taboo topic. While he contends in a later section of his volume that this "interdiction of death" has been carried farther in Western Europe than in the United States, the pattern described in the excerpted passage does apply to the latter.

A second basic matter in the present relationship of death to life has been the dynamic process of urbanization. That process rendered old funerary forms ineffective and encouraged the growth of the funeral industry through which relatives and friends of the deceased transferred their active role in last rites activity to the hands of the specialist. In the second selection of this section Leroy Bowman analyzes the consequences of "city civilization" for the funeral and for the social impact of death. Rather surprisingly he ultimately declines to accept the "bitter deduction" inherent in the analysis, namely that the death of a single individual is no longer so important as it would have been previously to the community in which he lived. The deduction is sound, however. In a related essay Robert Blauner considers the social impact of mortality on contemporary society. He concludes that the present social organization of death, helped along by demographic changes, has gone far to diminish the visibility of death.

Medical progress in the present century has also had profound result for living and dying. One consequence is that life expectancy at birth stands now in excess of seventy years. The number of fatalities from essentially all infectious diseases has been drastically reduced. Death from most major killers of the nineteenth century, such as tuberculosis, have been all but eradicated. Physical suffering among the sick is more subject to human control than ever before. On the other hand, current care practices have had certain questionable consequences as well. Thus, the emergence of the hospital as the socially accepted location for dying may have worked to support the cultural taboo surrounding death and made the dying process all the more alien. Both Ariès and Blauner examine certain aspects of death in the hospital setting. In the next selection Dr. Elisabeth Kubler-Ross discusses the interrelation of death fear, social taboo, and modern treatment patterns.

Finally, it should be noted also that trends in cemetery construction reflect the changed perception of death in this century. The cemetery no longer functions as a bridge between the dead and the living world. The personal relationship between the living and the dead envisioned in the nineteenth-century rural cemetery was lost with the so-called memorial park movement clearly underway by the 1920's. The old rhetoric of "garden" or "park" continued but the presence of death and the dead was minimized. As Herbert Blaney's 1917 essay indicates, the "modern park cemetery" had little use for personalized headstones or other "freakish" adornments of the past. Its promise was careful and "perpetual" care by promoters, a commitment which has meant a steady diminution in vegetative and other "obstacles" to easy maintenance. Its emphasis was on efficient use of land, not promotion of continued association with the deceased. If the colonial graveyard functioned as a place for body disposal and as a warning to the living, the memorial park provided a socially inconspicuous location where the dead could be made to disappear from the world of the living, a very different matter. Significantly, Blaney observes that in the new cemetery there was no need for stones because exact location of burial would be established in well-kept records, corruptible—if anyone wishes to find it. The popularity of such cemeteries offers graphic commentary on the changing relationship of death to life in the present century.

Philippe Ariès

FORBIDDEN DEATH

During the long period we have covered, from the Early Middle Ages until the mid-nineteenth century, the attitude toward death changed, but so slowly that contemporaries did not even notice. In our day, in approximately a third of a century, we have witnessed a brutal revolution in traditional ideas and feelings, a revolution so brutal that social observers have not failed to be struck by it. It is really an absolutely unheard-of phenomenon. Death, so omnipresent in the past that it was familiar, would be effaced, would disappear. It would become shameful and forbidden.[1]

This revolution occurred in a well defined cultural area, where in the nineteenth century the cult of the dead and of cemeteries did not experience the great development noted in France, Italy, and Spain. It even seems that this revolution began in the United States and spread to England, to the Netherlands, to industrialized Europe; and we can see it today, before our very eyes, reaching France and leaving oil smudges wherever the wave passes.

At its beginning doubtlessly lies a sentiment already expressed during the second half of the nineteenth century: those surrounding the dying person had a tendency to spare him and to hide from him the gravity of his condition. Yet

---

they admitted that this dissimulation could not last too long, except in such extraordinary cases as those described by Mark Twain in 1902 in "Was it Heaven or Hell?" The dying person must one day know, but the relatives no longer had the cruel courage to tell the truth themselves.

In short, at this point the truth was beginning to be challenged.

The first motivation for the lie was the desire to spare the sick person, to assume the burden of his ordeal. But this sentiment, whose origin we know (the intolerance of another's death and the confidence shown by the dying person in those about him) very rapidly was covered over by a different sentiment, a new sentiment characteristic of modernity: one must avoid—no longer for the sake of the dying person, but for society's sake, for the sake of those close to the dying person—the disturbance and the overly strong and unbearable emotion caused by the ugliness of dying and by the very presence of death in the midst of a happy life, for it is henceforth given that life is always happy or should always seem to be so. Nothing had yet changed in the rituals of death, which were preserved at least in appearance, and no one had yet had the idea of changing them. But people had already begun to empty them of their dramatic impact; the procedure of hushing-up had begun. This is very noticeable in Tolstoy's stories about death.

Between 1930 and 1950 the evolution accelerated markedly. This was due to an important physical phenomenon: the displacement of the site of death. One no longer died at home in the bosom of one's family, but in the hospital, alone.

One dies in the hospital because the hospital has become the place to receive care which can no longer be given at home. Previously the hospital had been a shelter for the poor, for pigrims; then it became a medical center where people were healed, where one struggled against death. It still has that curative function, but people are also beginning to consider a certain type of hospital as the designated spot for dying. One dies in the hospital because the doctor did not succeed in healing. One no longer goes to or will go to the hospital to be healed, but for the specific purpose of dying. American sociologists have observed that there are today two types of seriously ill persons to be found in hospitals.[2] The most archaic are recent immigrants who are still attached to the traditions of death, who try to snatch the dying person from the hospital so he can die at home, *more majorum;* the others are those more involved in modernity who come to die in the hospital because it has become inconvenient to die at home.

Death in the hospital is no longer the occasion of a ritual ceremony, over which the dying person presides amidst his assembled relatives and friends. Death is a technical phenomenon obtained by a cessation of care, a cessation determined in a more or less avowed way by a decision of the doctor and the hospital team. Indeed, in the majority of cases the dying person has already lost consciousness. Death has been dissected, cut to bits by a series of little steps, which finally makes it impossible to know which step was the real death, the one in which consciousness was lost, or the one in which breathing stopped. All these little silent deaths have replaced and erased the great dramatic act of death, and no one any longer has the strength or patience to wait over a period of weeks for a moment which has lost a part of its meaning.

From the end of the eighteenth century we had been impressed by a sentimental landslide which was causing the initiative to pass from the dying man himself to his family—a family in which henceforth he would have complete confidence. Today the initiative has passed from the family, as much an outsider as the dying person, to the doctor and the hospital team. They are masters of death—of the moment as well as of the circumstances of death—and it has been observed that they try to obtain from their patient "an acceptable style of living while dying." The accent has been placed on "acceptable." An acceptable death is a death which can be accepted or tolerated by the survivors. It has its antithesis: "the embarrassingly graceless dying," which embarrasses the survivors because it causes too strong an emotion to burst forth; and emotions must be avoided both in the hospital and everywhere in society. One does not have the right to become emotional other than in private, that is to say, secretly. Here, then, is what has happened to the great death scene, which had changed so little over the centuries, if not the millennia.

• • • •

The point has even been reached at which, according to [Geoffrey] Gorer's observations, the choking back of sorrow, the forbidding of its public manifestation, the obligation to suffer alone and secretly, has aggravated the trauma stemming from the loss of a dear one. In a family in which sentiment is given an important place and in which premature death is becoming increasingly rare (save in the event of an automobile accident), the death of a relative is always deeply felt, as it was in the Romantic era.

A single person is missing for you, and the whole world is empty. But one no longer has the right to say so aloud.

The combination of phenomena which we have just analyzed is nothing other than the imposition of an interdict. What was once required is henceforth forbidden.

The merit of having been the first to define this unwritten law of our civilization goes to the English sociologist, Geoffrey Gorer.[3] He has shown clearly how death has become a taboo and how in the twentieth century it has replaced sex as the principal forbidden subject. Formerly children were told that they were brought by the stork, but they were admitted to the great farewell scene about the bed of the dying person. Today they are initiated in their early years to the physiology of love; but when they no longer see their grandfather and express astonishment, they are told that he is resting in a beautiful garden among the flowers. Such is "The Pornography of Death"—the title of a pioneering article by Gorer, published in 1955—and the more society was liberated from the Victorian constraints concerning sex, the more it rejected things having to do with death. Along with the interdict appears the transgression: the mixture of eroticism and death so sought after from the sixteenth to the eighteenth century reappears in our sadistic literature and in violent death in our daily life.

This establishment of an interdict has profound meaning. It is already difficult to isolate the meaning of the interdict on sex which was precipitated by the Christian confusion between sin and sexuality (though, as in the nineteenth century, this interdict was never imposed). But the interdict on death suddenly follows upon the heels of a very long period —several centuries—in which death was a public spectacle from which no one would have thought of hiding and which was even sought after at times.

The cause of the interdict is at once apparent: the need for happiness—the moral duty and the social obligation to contribute to the collective happiness by avoiding any cause for sadness or boredom, by appearing to be always happy, even if in the depths of despair. By showing the least sign of sadness, one sins against happiness, threatens it, and society then risks losing its *raison d'être.*

NOTES

1. P. Ariès, "La mort inversee," *Archives européennes de sociologie,* Vol. VIII (1967), pp. 169-95.

2. B. G. Glasser and A. L. Strauss, *Awareness of Dying* (Chicago, 1965).

3. G. Gorer, *Death, Grief, and Mourning in Contemporary Britain* (New York, 1965), a key work.

Leroy Bowman

THE EFFECTS OF CITY CIVILIZATION

The present factory and city civilization in the United States differs from the farm and small community civilization of a few generations ago. As scientific and technological discoveries resulted in machines, and machines in factories, the factories drew men and their families to jobs in growing cities and to a kind of life that was new to them. Old habits had to be changed when prescribed work at a machine during stipulated hours took the place of hard but family-determined tasks and hours on the farm. The pace of life quickened, the spaciousness of the old gave way to the crowdedness of the new. The time-honored traditions which every one knew, did not work so well in the city, some of them not at all. Most particularly, the ways of relaxing together that characterized rural life were not appropriate in the city. In many other ways city life demanded change in the thought and action of the new comers.

Among the large scale developments within the population of cities that changed the social atmosphere was the influx of greater numbers of immigrants brought by opportunities for jobs in factories. The peoples who came were from countries whose ways of life differed in large measure from that of the North European countries of earlier immigration. Ethnic and religious differences were sharper and

---

more numerous; and, in the proximity of diverse customs and faiths, a further cause arose to bring into question the old convictions, habits and assurances. Life in cities was not merely a shift from habits, usages and routines; it involved a strain on the sense of adequacy of city dwellers to face the more intangible problems. Most devastating was the break in the ways in which individuals associated with each other, in family relations, in social gatherings, in the mutual interests or separation of youth from their elders. The strain of adjustment made itself felt, then, both in superficial and material ways, also on social and psychic levels.

It was not alone the cities which felt the impact of industrialism or even of urbanism. The city, invaded from the small towns and the open country, developed the seeds of a new culture, and with them, in turn invaded the rural areas from which its inhabitants had come. Science flourished in the concentrations of people, and so also did the centers of art and culture. For these the non-city folk were as eager as their urban cousins. Science and technology along with other advances made transportation and communication rapid, easy, and extensively available. Railroads, highways, automobiles, airplanes, telegraph, telephone, radio, television, motion pictures, brought the words, actions, problems and strains of the city to the rural areas. Today the latter are "citified," only in less degree than the cities. Urbanism is at present not a matter of city as over against the country side, but a matter rather of degree, with its most intense concentration in metropolises, its least in the out of the way places.

All this is not only pertinent to the study of modern funerals; it is basic. The remainder of this chapter explains the effects of the industrial and social changes of the last century on the form and meaning of the funeral.

Misfit of Old Funeral Forms to Urban Conditions

As towns in America grew in size and number the part played in funerals by the undertaker increased in scope and responsibility. In the earliest colonial days, and until considerably later in isolated rural or cultural communities, members of the family and neighbors performed all the tasks consequent to death. The washing of the body and its "laying out" were the first tasks usually done by a member of the intimate family group but not infrequently by a friendly neighbor. The male members of the family dug the grave, if it was to be located in a family plot on the farm, or the sexton did, if the body was to be interred in the churchyard. The coffin containing the body was carried by family members, neighbors and friends to the church; and those closest to the deceased, or the sexton, filled the grave after the coffin had been lowered. The funeral was a family and neighborhood affair, taking place in the home.

Increasingly thereafter family conditions developed that made the home funeral less suitable and the role of the family somewhat different from that of the 1860's and '70's. Housing quarters for the family were, by and large, much more limited in space; stairways and foyers created problems for the moving of caskets; parlors or living rooms were too small to accommodate the visitors at the wake and funeral assemblages. In such restricted quarters to keep the body in the living rooms for two or three days created serious problems. Families became smaller decade by decade, and near dwellers less neighborly. Consequently there were fewer whose daily personal relations were disturbed by the death, fewer to take part in the duties of the funeral according to the former custom. Relatives, even those of close connection with the immediate family, were scattered, and either could not come long distances, or found living accommodations difficult or expensive. In another sense the home became less suitable for the funeral gatherings: the family's circle of acquaintances was increasingly made up of persons met in a number of various relationships, relatively few of whom were familiar with the home. The funeral assemblage became a wider, more ephemeral group of acquaintances. To meet these several difficulties the funeral home became more and more the place of preparation of the body, for holding the wake, and in a fraction of cases, for the final ritual.

The metamorphosis in the community brought about by the growth of cities has affected the funeral as much as or more than has the change in the family. In the earliest days the funeral was as much a community as a family matter, when the community consisted of a closely knit, geographically isolated group of families. Occupations were less diverse than later, and unusual events were treated as community responsibilities. Death of an individual was a deprivation of customary social give and take to a large proportion of the total group, and a matter of common knowledge and discussion of all. The loss of one life was a distinctly felt diminution of the total community. In cities, the family found itself in a much more limited relationship to nearby families; neighborhood activities and neighborly relations became less and less real.

In a small community, particularly one which is centered around agricultural vocations and interests, attendance at funerals can be decided by individuals. In cities, factory and office workers are subject to comparatively inflexible rules regulating working hours, and attendance at a funeral of any one but a relative is forbidden or is granted only at the expense of a day's pay. One result has been greater emphasis on the wake to which workers may go in the evening. The country over, it is estimated that there is a larger attendance at wakes than at funeral services. The funeral home, having more of a public and less of an intimate flavor, fits into the pattern of community relationships better than does the family home.

Of more importance, however, for the conduct of the funeral, is the loss of person to person communication of information about the death and the funeral. It becomes known in much larger measure through the obituary notices in the daily papers. However, because of the cost, not every funeral is advertised in the papers and many are noted in only one or a few such daily periodicals. The news articles of deaths cover a very few of all the deaths, since the large number are of little news value. As a consequence, as city culture becomes more prevalent, a smaller proportion of friends and acquaintances learn of the occurrence of death before the funeral takes place. This is true in general even when individual notices are sent out by the family, since the trend is toward smaller lists of notices. From these, as well as other causes, the community aspect that looms so large in funerals of the past, especially those in small centers, has very greatly diminished.

The Jewish funeral, like all others, originally was communal. Every one was expected to come. The transition to the more urban allocation of responsibilities and pattern of attendance has resulted in a special group, the Hevrah Kadisha, representing the community. It assumes some of the roles enacted in former days by relatives and neighbors; in some communities it performs certain phases of preparation of the body; in other communities it functions only in the charitable provision of appropriate funerals for needy persons within the group.

The settlement of minority groups in cities has brought about an uncertainty in the minds of many citizens concerning the proprieties to be followed. Each cultural group has had its own peculiarites of mortuary practices, adapting in time to a more "American" pattern. In the process not only the members of these groups but all citizens have become less certain of the proper procedures to follow. Older Americans in the closely knit smaller communities were familiar with the roles that relatives, friends and neighbors formerly played; but as the knowledge proved inadequate in cities, uncertainty succeeded assurance. In consequence the funeral director, more than willing to instruct, became a feature more essential than before.

Urbanization has taken its toll from the churches also, through the influence of high mobility which has characterized an industrialized, urban civilization. In a rural economy families remain for years, and even generations, rooted in one locality, often retaining an old homestead for many decades. In cities factory jobs, commercial and professional positions, coupled with the compulsion of shifting neighborhoods, compel frequent changes of residence. As families move, church affiliations are broken, and connections in new locations delayed or neglected. Thus it happens that the church, which with the family and the community formed the combination of institutions that made the funeral an important event, has lost much of its influence over the ritual for a large number of people. The multiplicity of organizations in urban areas has indirectly worked toward that end in smaller measure. A fraternal or patriotic order, while not in any sense opposed to church-conducted funerals, may take charge of the service. In some cases in which conflict on the selection of minister arises between members of the family affiliated with different faiths, compromise is made by agreeing upon a ceremony under a fraternal order to which the deceased belonged.

Adaptations Made by the Funeral Industry

The folkways which governed the roles of the attendants and the procedures to be followed in rural areas and small towns in the United States were inapplicable in the industrialized culture of the cities. In the new conditions in the cities, in the heterogeneous mass of people and the number and variety of national origins, there was no common cultural background on which to base a new set of practices applicable to all. There was something of a vacuum, into which the burial entrepreneur moved and began to formulate custom to his own liking.

The funeral business is the last to appear in a growing community among the economic services. In a study of 101 cities: "Coefficients of correlation were calculated between population and the number of each kind of economic service in the community . . . on the basis of frequency of persons per single economic service one might predict the probable order of appearance of each kind of economic service in a small, growing community. According to the present study, the economic services that would be among the first to appear are the food stores, doctor and filling station. The economic service of dry goods store and funeral director would be the last to appear." (1, pp. 60-62) Because, in part, undertaking as a business came late to developing and changing communities, it was unhindered by tradition from rapid adaptation to urban conditions.

Funeral directing, itself a product of urban development, has adapted its practices to make the most of the opportunity to mold a mass culture for funerals. As a full-time vocation of any considerable number of practitioners it is something less than one hundred years old, having grown out of vocations in which occasional services directly related to funerals were given. Among them were the trade of the carpenter who made the early coffins for the family, the cabinet maker, the livery man, the sexton. For many years undertaking was combined with one or more other types of business to furnish a living and an outlet for all the skills of the proprietor. During the Civil War the greatest impetus to undertaking was provided in the need to preserve the remains of those killed in combat until they could be delivered to their families and buried. Concoction of embalming fluids and experiments in embalming had been pursued for years prior to that time and by several individuals. The war gave the opportunity for further experimentation, a measure of perfection in the process, and a foothold for a full-time vocation. From the time of its close the leadership in the development of embalming passed from chemists and physicians to embalming companies and undertakers. (2) This has become increasingly evident.

Embalming laid the basis for the continued and increasing emphasis on the body at the funeral. Through its effects, the body could be retained above ground longer and more safely than through the use of ice to preserve it. Embalming afforded also the opportunity for, and basic method of, "restoring" the facial features of the dead to a likeness to the living face. "Beautification" and elaboration of accessories to the laid-out body developed rapidly from that historic point on. Embalming, itself an inexpensive operation, opened the way for the development and expansion of the methods that in part have resulted in increasingly costly funerals.

A second technical development that helped materially to pave the way for an expanded industry was the adoption, at about the end of the first decade of the century, of motorized hearses and cars. Motor hearses were expensive, especially as changes in style necessitated repeated replacements. Nevertheless, use of them lessened the burden of the procession to the cemetery which had to cover long distances as the city cemeteries were moved from central areas to outskirts, and even beyond city limits.

Pride of bereaved families in following out the folkways surrounding the funeral, and the satisfaction of friends and neighbors in their roles on such occasion had increasingly to be relinquished in city environments. As a substitute funeral attendants were offered passive participation in an event, or series of events, the arrangements of which were largely in the hands of a specialist. Passive observation nearly always leads to expectations of more spectacular performance than does active participation. The commercial drive of the funeral director for more elegance and display therefore fitted the need for a substitute for the folk habits involving active participation of previous years. In one other way transition to city life made the modern funeral acceptable to families. In cities they became accustomed to paying for services they previously had performed themselves. And with the rise in their standard of living they had money to pay for the services.

The funeral establishment, too, has followed a pattern of adaptation to city conditions. At first, especially in the east, stores were used. Later large residences were taken over as they became available in changing residential areas and finally, new buildings were erected as funeral establishments. Variations in the stages at which the sequence begins, occur in different parts of the country, but the progression has been consistently toward the elegant, costly and stylish building.

Equipment for funerals has steadily increased in mechanical excellence and coverage of detailed needs. Materials, mechanisms and specific services have multiplied along with the decline in the control over the conduct of funerals by family, church and community. The funeral director has succeeded in filling with material and pecuniary values the gap made by the social values expressed in neighborly concern and active complementary roles.

Cremation as a means of disposing of the remains is one adaptation to urban conditions that is utilized in a minority of instances. The cremation movement has not been fostered by the funeral directors' association nor the trade journals, but has been independently led. It arose out of the concern for the problem of increasing space needed for burial plots as cities grew in size. In the early stages of the movement its proponents were disturbed also by the problem of sanitation, presenting itself as an accumulation of dead human bodies a few feet underground in the enlarging cemeteries. Following its first consideration in England discussion of the question in the United States became most active during the last three quarters of the nineteenth century and the early years of the twentieth.

The two aspects of the problem have never been met completely. The question of space has been solved temporarily, and in part only, by the conversion of tracts at the periphery or outside city limits to cemetery use. The problem of sanitation involved in numerous burials has been met partially by the same action, but more particularly by modern sanitary provisions.

However, the chief significance of cremation is of a different nature. It is the one technical development that serves to redress the imbalance of bargaining power between undertaker and customer, by counteracting the emphasis on the body and allowing for a more wholesome attitude toward the funeral on the part of the family. Logically resort to cremation eliminates the need of embalming, "restoration," and lavish expenditures for casket and all funeral "goods," but allows for all the social and spiritual aspects of the funeral period. The only objection to its use, and it is a formidable one, is its failure to satisfy the religious requirements of Catholics and Orthodox Jews. One obstacle to its use, gradually being overcome, is the inaccessibility of crematories in certain cities in the country.

Because of the ease, dispatch and thoroughness of the process, it is favored by a large majority of the intellectual group in the population, with the exception of those whose religious commitments prohibit its use. The undertaking industry opposes or discourages its use for obvious reasons, going to the unfair and ridiculous limit, as we have seen, of successful advocacy of state laws to require that cremation take place only when the body is enclosed in a casket. Nevertheless the utilization of cremation is steadily increasing throughout the country.

Functions of the Funeral in Small and Large Communities

The subject of the adequacy of the conduct of funerals and the values involved in it which help meet the needs of present-day society leads directly to considerations of function. What results does it achieve for individuals, the family, groups, the community? What effects are actually experienced by the participants? The most universal feature of all funerals, excepting only the disposal of the body and the religious ceremony, is the assembling of relatives, friends and neighbors of the deceased, or in strongly coherent groups, the assembling of all the members. It has been said by social scientists that in societies less developed than our own, there is a desire, stimulated by the death, to reexperience total group association. The same desire in modified forms is to be found in modern society. To bring the whole group together is the accepted tradition in this country when death comes to a member.

The function performed by the gatherings in small communities—i. e., the strengthening of the sense of community solidarity—is real, not great. Persons of various faiths, of various vocations and economic levels come together in the wake or at the religious service. They have an experience that, from all the evidence, is fraught more with a recognition of participation in a total network of community relations, than is felt by attendants in cities.

The larger the town the more the gatherings at wakes and rituals lose significance for the community as a whole to become occasions on which groups may derive a modicum of added coherence. In this respect much depends on the strength of the already existing bond between the members, and on the relative isolation from the larger community. Among certain minority groups, for example, a funeral brings together representatives of all the organizations and societies, and a very large number of all the adults of the ethnic community. As in the case of the village or small town, there is seldom any tangible result other than a slightly intensified sense of coherence of the nationality group. This result is to be observed even among a people who may be scattered in several pockets of population throughout a metropolis.

It is impossible, in the face of all the evidence, to ascribe to the funeral any but a small effect in knitting communities or groups together, an effect seen at its maximum in small communities and isolated groups. For the most part, even in these social segments, it serves merely to reassert momentarily an existing solidarity. The effect upon the family is not as fugitive. The funeral serves in many cases in which the immediate family or near relatives are scattered to bring them together and to renew and strengthen the family tie.

The result most frequently mentioned as intended or desired by the family from the series of events before burial, is status or prestige for itself, achieved supposedly through display of costly casket, flowers and other features of the funeral. To evaluate this function, or to measure it by comparison of instances occurring under diverse circumstances is difficult. Many persons take great pride in the elegance of funerals for which they have been responsible. If the pride or other satisfaction is great and enduring enough to balance the loss of returns from money that might have been used for other purposes, then clearly costly types of funerals are justified from their standpoint. It is a matter of the values that are to be associated with a "fine" as opposed to a modest showing.

There is at least this much of the undertaker's point of view on the matter of costs that cannot be gainsaid: it is not extravagance on the part of the client to follow the course that in the end gives greatest returns to him. Nor is it exploitation on the part of the seller to persuade him to choose the style of funeral if he, the seller, is certain it will provide the greatest satisfaction. There is, however, a great preponderance of evidence that he cannot be sure that the funeral he provides does answer the need of the family in any deep sense. The brief period of the burial procedures, the unusual state of mind and consequent temporarily twisted set of values of the client family during that period, and the pressures bearing on them during the moments of choice, render their judgments at the time less reliable than at other times.

Many complain bitterly later that they would have decided on more modest funerals if they had been given unfettered choice. Many who have had to lower their standard of living because of a lavish funeral have discovered that their decisions have not been based on rational assessment of the lasting value of funerals to the family. There is very serious question that the lasting returns from the expensive funeral are commensurate with the outlay in any but a limited number of instances.

The wished-for result of large expenditures is the elevation of the status of the family in the community of acquaintances. But rarely is the status of a family raised in the opinion of neighbors and friends by ostentation at a funeral. Almost invariably it is recognized as conspicuous display, whether it is approved or not. Occasionally acquaintances predict a lowering in the standard of living of a family and with it a somewhat lower status. Or, even though the participants enjoy an elaborate wake and funeral, in their eyes the standing of the family may be lowered, if to furnish it the family has had to accept charity from some source.

There are circumstances, however, in which lavish, costly funerals bring to the family much attention from fellow members of the group or "set" of which they are a part. For a brief span of time the surviving family members become the center of social activity, as happens in some immigrant groups at certain stages of assimilation. Nevertheless, even in these cases judgment concerning the family's permanent status must be exercised with caution. In the first place the funeral may be looked upon as just another show and "party," the like of which any one of a large number of families is expected to put on under similar circumstances. In the second place, among certain minority groups, a substantial portion of the cost of the affair is contributed by those who take part, and they therefore have less feeling of being outclassed than might otherwise be the case.

Unusual circumstances may result in isolated instances in which the neighbors have come to a realization for the first time of the worth of a family through the medium of a funeral, especially in the case of a very retiring household. Except in small communities, however, the funeral held by an obscure family usually goes unnoticed. The smaller the community the more will be known about the status to be ascribed to any family funeral.

Under certain circumstances a funeral may bring a great deal of prestige to a family, sometimes with a measure of permanence. Such is the case when the funeral of a member of an organization is used for the aggrandizement of the whole group. For example, the funeral of a relative of an official in a religious denomination may be the occasion to have outstanding leaders attend; and in other ways to make the wake and ceremony notable. More often, a political organization may demonstrate its strength by directing the attendance of hundreds of government officials who owe their positions to it. In cases of this kind it cannot be said that the funeral achieves status for the deceased, or for the family, but rather that the organization confers status on the funeral. It is also true that the status acquired is not due to costly and elaborate materials but to group action. If, then, achievement of status is a function of the funeral, it is at best a thin and brittle blessing.

The third and only other important social or functional value of the funeral is that of strengthening the basic rules of life in the convictions and habits of the persons assembled at the wake and ceremony. There is no questioning the fact that at a funeral largely attended by loyal members of a church or other group, or by the residents of long standing in a small town, there is a focusing of emphasis on the old, established ideals. The group turns back to the older norms of group living. The group, as a whole, does not turn to the more problematical areas of need for formulation of ideals for a changing situation. It is reaffirmation of faith, sacred and secular, that they experience.

In a situation, however, in which the majority in the group, or the dominant leaders, are engaged in a struggle to elevate the status of the group or to correct a social injustice that oppresses them, or in other ways to conduct a campaign for change in government, labor relations, religion, education or any other field, the group turns at a funeral to a reaffirmation of the new faith. In such situations, aside from its identifying purpose, the members of the group are often more heterogeneous than in funerals of the kind described. In both cases, far more than in other funerals, the size of the group enhances the intensity of group reaction.

The third function of the funeral, then, the strengthening of devotion to group ideals, operates in those cases in which the ideals are accepted. In a very large number of funerals of individuals neither devoutly orthodox nor socially progressive, little group sense of ideals is to be met. In such cases probing reveals a variety of individual reactions. Not infrequently, however, doubts and arguments come forth. In the car, on the way to or from the cemetery, or later in informal groups, conflicting opinions on an individual basis are expressed about the advantage of living a righteous life. In such cases it would seem that the death had raised the question of ideals, but the group had come up with no convincing answers. At times like these, however, the discussants often express a sense of "release" following their remarks about moral and ethical convictions.

Two other items are mentioned from time to time as functions of the funeral. One is purging of an emotional kind through wailing or other public expression of grief. It is a practice surviving in very few cultural groups. It is certain that some individuals, especially members of the immediate family, find satisfaction in wailing when it is the expected thing to do. That it lessens grief at all is not so certain. In the groups in which it has been the custom many of the younger generation, who look on it as mere role playing, are irritated by it. It is not universal enough to regard it seriously as a main function of the funeral. Nor is there sufficient evidence to say that any positive results come from it. At best, it befits a closely knit cultural group into which has not yet permeated the tradition of restraining emotion in public.

In certain Pentecostal groups in cities and in some out of the way communities, outbursts of revelry are stimulated by a funeral in which the whole group finds occasion to indulge in riotous activity, sometimes for days. (3, pp. 650-654) In the urban groups, at least, the experience is very similar to those stimulated by happenings other than death, except that emotional expressions reach a higher peak than they do at Sunday or mid-week outbursts. They may also last for a longer period.

A fifth function observed occasionally, especially by ministers, is the public pronouncement of the end of a life and the stamping of all former relations with the deceased with the "seal of finality." It is true that witnessing the lowering of the casket and the filling of the grave over it leaves a clear impression of finality. However its importance is lessened by the fact that an ever diminishing number witness the rite. That the committal service is of consequence, even to family or friends is questionable, except where it is essential in the religious ritual. A much more useful instrumentality to impress the finality of death on the community is the obituary notice in the newspaper. In the small, well knit group or community no ceremonial marking of the end is needed. Lastly it is questionable if a ritualistic assertion that relations with the deceased are at an end is important under modern urban conditions. City dwellers have learned the art of making and breaking, or at least taking lightly in their stride, the multiplicity of ephemeral relationships.

As size of the community is one variable that determines in part the effectiveness of the funeral, another is the relative prominence of the deceased within the group or in the community. The death of a leader affects the members partly because it influences the achievements of the group as a whole, but mostly because it disrupts the continuing responses to him. In consequence the funeral becomes a total group affair in the measure in which the dead leader was felt to be important in group affairs and in the degree he was known by the members.

Prominence of the deceased in the community or the larger society greatly affects the attendance at the funeral. At the lower end of the scale of prominence is the young child whose funeral is planned very simply, costs relatively little and is attended by few. Its effect in the community is small. At the upper end of the scale is the person whose name is known to all, and whose acts have been watched by thousands. He may be a statesman, artist, prize fighter, baseball player or gangster. According to the measure of his fame or notoriety his funeral will be attended by masses of persons, and descriptions of it will be read widely.

The nature of his life activities determines the type of individuals who make up the bulk of the attendants at his funeral. However, curiosity and the excitement of the crowd usually dominate the demonstration attending the funerals of the notorious, the appeal of whose lives has been to the most primitive ideas and practices. Sometimes the mass attendance is used by an organized group for its own aggrandizement, as is sometimes exemplified in the conduct of one or another branch of gangsterism when one of its leaders is buried. The funeral of a statesman, on the other hand, serves to magnify the ideals and basic purposes of the total society.

Whenever the funeral celebrates the life and work of a person in a group too large to encompass the reliving of face to face collective experiences, it assumes a character different from the usual funeral. That it has a function cannot be gainsaid; but that function is so different in emphasis as to alter its fundamental nature. It becomes a public ceremonial, leaving to the family and close friends the need of the more intimate get together that the usual funeral answers. It may be a mass demonstration approximating the characteristics of a mob, and possessing little but very momentary effect. Paradoxically, the effect of the mass demonstration is almost invariably restricted, giving a certain release of a strictly emotional nature. The ideal funeral influences individuals in a contrary fashion.

One type of misfortune demonstrates the failure of large-city culture to provide a ritual to alleviate the suddenly aroused apprehension of large numbers of persons. The misfortune may come to an individual or to a group, and always involves the revelation of a danger that may befall any one who habitually follows the course of action in which the victim, or victims, met their crisis. Examples include the tragedy of a kidnapped child, the drowning of a child in waters under public jurisdiction, the death of a number of children in a cave-in of earth thrown up in the process of construction, an unsolved murder of a citizen engaged in a laudable pursuit. Through the press, radio and television the fears of masses of people are aroused, and often kept alive for days. Invariably the question of responsibility becomes acute, and investigations are started by private and public agencies.

The funeral in such a case usually becomes a focus of public attention, and may attract an unusually large attendance. Nevertheless, the many thousands, or even millions, who have been disturbed by the death and whose assurance in certain of the collective processes is shaken, are afforded only the slight satisfaction of expressing themselves in a small circle of friends and listening to their fears in reply. True, the tragedy may increase public pressure eventually to correct wholly or in part the defect in provisions for the common safety. And yet the need of interaction between affected individuals which the funeral provides in small groups, is not, and cannot be furnished on a large scale.

The possibility of devising a mass ritual is always present, but its processes and effects are not of the kind to perform the function of a constructive ritual, valuable though they may be in other ways. The main defect in them, from the standpoint of human interaction, lies in the fact that action in masses takes only one direction. People are talked to, and not heard, in meetings, in the press and over the radio. Interpersonal or intergroup discourse is difficult if not impossible, as is member-leader interaction.

The funeral of a prominent person may involve little or no re-experiencing of group association. As a matter of fact, it is a new experience for many of the participants. It may in certain cases such as that of a person long retired, bring renewed recognition of status to one or more members of the family. It usually brings out in greater simplicity the purposes and ideals to which the person devoted his public life.

Theory of the Functioning of Funerals

A concise statement of the principles governing the influence of the funeral on the family, the group and the community is given below to bring into perspective the points that have been made at greater length in this chapter. It will serve to make clearer the measure in which the stimulus for the funeral operates in various situations, and the social factors that limit the significance of funerals. It will serve also to lay the foundation for the treatment of the effect of death and the funeral on the individual.

It is the sense of interruption that provides the stimulus to hold the funeral, interruption of the interaction of individuals within the family, or within a group, or interruption of activity of the whole community. The larger the group or the community, the less actual interruption occurs because of the loss of a member. The more intimate, continuous and vital the interaction between the individuals has been, and the more the group activity has been regarded as vital to the welfare of the members, the greater the need to provide for some sort of group experience to bring about a new equilibrium.

This need is met by a repetition of group association at a meeting in which the social aspect is the predominant feature. On a higher level the need for reassurance is met in a ritual at which the group contemplates the common underlying ideals of the society, as well as philosophical and spiritual assurance that life is worthwhile. In the degree to which the death has disturbed interaction or activity will the disturbance shift the concern of those affected from the habitual prosecution of daily tasks to the problem of reestablishing reliance both on the beneficent working of the community or society, and on its guiding principles.

On the family of the deceased devolves the responsibility to carry through a series of gatherings providing the community with the means of reassuring itself. The family is hard pressed and distraught, and needs the sense of a supportive community around it. From this feeling arises an enhanced desire to be regarded in the community as worthy of sympathy, and hence the family seeks from the funeral a heightened status.

The three social effects to be hoped for of the funeral, a sense of solidarity in the group, reassurance of the validity of the ideals and guiding principles commonly accepted, and a heightened rapport of the family with the community, are actually realized when the community of interacting individuals is small enough in numbers and coherent enough for the individuals in it to know each other.

The question that obtrudes itself, in view of the foregoing analysis is: what factors prevent a fuller functioning of the modern funeral, especially in urban areas? There are three partial answers. First, for a re-experiencing of group association and a consequent augmenting of group solidarity, it is essential that the dead person should have been an integral part of an interacting number of individuals. That situation is found only in small measures, if association with all the residents of a city neighborhood, or association with one group of persons in all activities, is meant. The growing multiplicity of organizations in modern urban society has steadily whittled away the significance of the funeral.

A second partial answer to the question concerning the lack of significance of many funerals lies both in the diversity of ideals held by various segments of the population and in the impoverishment of social ideals in a changing society.

The third answer to the fundamental question lies in the relation of the family to the rest of the community. It is the members of the family who act for the deceased at the funeral; it is they who appeal through the wake and the religious service for public recognition of his life and accomplishments. When the family is connected only with a number of unrelated organizations and with a widespread net of casual individual acquaintances, there exists no practical opportunity to make an effective appeal for recognition. Even if all the connections of a person could be brought together, there frequently is no one basis in the moral, ethical or spiritual areas, on which to make an appeal. As a consequence, in many funerals the family accepts "an ounce of dross for its ounce of gold," and pours out its longing for recognition in extravagant display.

A bitter deduction from this line of thought could be drawn, namely, that the death of one person is not so important as once it would have been, at least to the community in which he has lived. To state the conclusion is almost to refute it; for the death of any one represents a universal tragedy only made more dreadful by the growth of population. The trouble lies in the persistent effort to make the old form of the funeral serve in a situation in which it functions poorly. There is as great a need as ever for a recognition of the sorrows of bereavement; there is even greater need for unity on basic values and high ideals for this generation. Individuals, groups and communities cannot afford to ignore the stimulus that arises from a death to assay the kinds and amount of vital interaction between persons and groups, nor the incentive to get a perspective on the lives of close associates, and through it a deeper understanding of the meaning of their own lives.

REFERENCES

1. Clarence Schettler, "Relation of City-Size to Economic Services," *American Sociological Review,* 8, 1 (February 1943).
2. Robert W. Habenstein and William M. Lamers, *The History of American Funeral Directing,* Milwaukee, Bulfin Printers, 1955.
3. Joseph H. Douglass, "The Funeral of 'Sister President,'" in T. M. Newcomb and E. L. Hartley, *Readings in Social Psychology,* (New York: Henry Holt and Company, 1947).

Robert Blauner

DEATH AND SOCIAL STRUCTURE

Mortality and its impact are not constants. In general, the demographic structure of the preindustrial societies results in an exposure to death that appears enormous by the standards of modern Western life. Malinowski, writing of the Trobriand Islanders and other natives of Eastern New Guinea, states that "death . . . causes a great and permanent disturbance in the equilibrium of tribal life."[1] The great impact of mortality and the vividness of death as a theme in life emerge clearly from Goody's account of the LoDagaa of West Africa.[2] Jules Henry's study of the Kaingang "Jungle People" of the Brazil highlands depicts a tribe whose members are in daily contact with death and greatly obsessed with it.[3] Kingsley Davis speculates that many characteristics of Indian life, such as the high birth rate, the stress on kinship and joint households, and the religious emphasis, may be attributed to the nearness to death that follows from the conditions of that subcontinent.[4] The relatively small scale of communities in most preindustrial societies compounds death's impact. Its regular occurrence—especially through the not infrequent catastrophes of war, famine and epidemics—involves more serious losses to a society of small scale, a point that has been made forcibly by Krzywicki:

"Death and Social Structure" by Robert Blauner, *Psychiatry: Journal for the Study of Interpersonal Processes,* Vol. 29, November 1966, pp. 378-94. Reprinted by special permission of The William Alanson White Psychiatric Foundation, Inc.

> Let us take, for instance, one of the average Australian tribes (usually numbering 300-600 members). The simultaneous loss of 10 persons is there an event which quantitatively considered, would have the same significance as the simultaneous death of 630,000 to 850,000 inhabitants in the present Polish state. And such catastrophes, diminishing an Australian tribe by some 10 persons, might, of course occur not infrequently. An unfortunate war-expedition, a victorious night attack by an enemy, a sudden flood, or any of a host of other events might easily cause the death of such a number of tribesmen: in addition, there were famines, such as that which forced the Birria, for instance, to devour all their children, or the epidemics which probably occurred from time to time even in primitive communities. And what is most important, conditions of primitive life sometimes created such situations that there was a simultaneous loss of about a dozen or a score of persons of the same sex and approximately the same age. Then such a misfortune affecting a community assumed the dimensions of a tribal disaster.[5]

This is not to suggest that a continuous encounter with mortality is equally prevalent in all preindustrial societies. Variations among primitive and peasant societies are as impressive as common patterns; I simply want to make the point that *many* nonmodern societies must organize themselves around death's recurrent presence. Modern societies, on the other hand, have largely succeeded in containing mortality and its social disruptiveness. Yet the impact of mortality on a society is not a simple matter of such demographic considerations as death rates and the size of the group. Also central is the manner in which a society is organized, the way it manages the death crisis, and how its death practices and mortuary institutions are linked to the social structure.

Life-Expectancy, Engagement, and the Social Relevance of the Dead

Death disrupts the dynamic equilibrium of social life because a number of its actual or potential consequences create problems for a society. One of these potential consequences is a social vacuum. A member of society and its constituent groups and relationships is lost, and some kind of gap in institutional functioning results. The extent of this vacuum depends upon how deeply engaged the deceased has been in the life of the society and its groups. The system is more disrupted by the death of a leader than by that of a common man; families and work groups are typically more affected by the loss of those in middle years than by the death of children or old people. Thus a key determinant of the impact of mortality is the age and social situation of those who die, since death will be more disruptive when it frequently strikes those who are most relevant for the functional activities and the moral outlook of the social order.

In modern Western societies, mortality statistics are more and more made up of the very old. The causes are obvious: The virtual elimination of infant and child mortality and the increasing control over the diseases of youth and middle life. Almost one million American males died in 1960. Eight percent were younger than 15 years. Fifty-five percent were 65 or older (29 percent were past 75), and another 18 percent were between 55 and 64. The middle years, between 15 and 54, claimed the remaining 19 percent of the deaths.[6] As death in modern society becomes increasingly a phenomenon of the old, who are usually retired from work and finished with their parental responsibilities, mortality in modern society rarely interrupts the business of life. Death is uncommon during the highly engaged middle years, and the elderly are more and more segregated into communities and institutions for their age group.

Although accurate vital statistics for contemporary preindustrial societies are rare, the available data indicates that the primary concentration of death is at the opposite end of the life-span, in the years of infancy and childhood. For example, among the Sakai of the Malay Peninsula, approximately 50 percent of the babies born die before the age of three; among the Kurnai tribe of Australia 40 to 50 percent die before the age of 10.[7] Fifty-nine percent of the 1956 male deaths in Nigeria among the "indigenous" blacks were children who had not reached their fifth birthday. Thirty-five percent of an Indian male cohort born in the 1940's died before the age of 10.[8] The same concentration of mortality in the early years was apparently also true of historical preindustrial societies.

Aside from this high infant and child mortality, there is no common pattern in the age composition of death in preindustrial societies. In some, there appears to be a secondary concentration in old age, suggesting that when mortality in the early years is very high, the majority of those who survive may be hardy enough to withstand the perils of middle life and reach old age. This seems to be the situation with the Tikopia, according to the limited demographic data. Thirty-six percent of the deaths in one period studied were those of people over 58, almost equaling the proportion who died in the first seven years.[9]

In other societies and historical periods, conditions are such that mortality remains heavy in the middle years, and few people reach the end of a normal lifespan. Thus calculations of age at death taken from gravestones erected during the early Roman empire (this method is notoriously unreliable, but the figures are suggestive) typically find that 30 to 40 percent of the deceased were in their twenties and thirties; the proportion who died past the age of 50 was only about 20 percent.[10] The life-table of the primitive Cocos also illustrates this pattern. Only 16 percent of the deaths are in the old-age group (past 55 years), since mortality continues high for that minority of the population which survives childhood.[11] The contrast in death frequency during the middle years is suggested by the data shown in Table 1 on mortality rates for specific age periods for four countries.

The demographic pattern where mortality is high in the middle years probably results in the most disruption of ongoing life. Procedures for the reallocation of the socially necessary roles, rights, and responsibilities of the deceased must be institutionalized. This is most essential when the roles and responsibilities are deemed important and when there is a tight integration of the society's groups and institutions. Such is the situation among the LoDagaa of West Africa, where many men die who are young and middle-aged.

TABLE 1
*NUMBER OF DEATHS DURING SPECIFIED YEAR OF AGE PER 1,000 MALES ALIVE AT BEGINNING OF AGE PERIOD**

	Age				
Country	*20-25*	*25-30*	*30-35*	*35-40*	*40-45*
Congo, 1950-52	54	49	68	82	96
Mexico, 1940	46	53	62	71	84
U.S.A., 1959	9	9	10	14	23
Canada, 1950-52	2	2	2	2	3

*From United Nations, *Demographic Yearbook*, 13th Edition; New York, Department of Economic and Social Affairs, 1961; p. 360. Decimals have been rounded off to the nearest integer.

Since the kinship structure is highly elaborated, these deaths implicate the whole community, particularly the kinship group of the bereaved spouses. The future rights of these now unattached women, still sexually active and capable of child-bearing, emerge as an issue which must be worked out in the funeral ceremonies through a transfer to new husbands.[12] In contrast, in modern Western societies, the death of a husband typically involves only the fragmented conjugal family; from the point of view of the social order as a whole, it makes little difference whether a widow replaces her deceased husband, because of the loose integration of the nuclear family into wider kinship, economic, and political spheres.

Another way of containing the impact of mortality is to reduce the real or ideal importance of those who die. Primitive societies, hard hit by infant and child mortality, characteristically do not recognize infants and children as people; until a certain age they are considered as still belonging to the spirit world from which they came, and therefore their death is often not accorded ritual recognition—no funeral is held.[13] Ariès has noted that French children were neither valued nor recognized in terms of their individuality during the long period of high infant mortality:

> No one thought of keeping a picture of a child if that child had . . . died in infancy . . . it was thought that the little thing which had disappeared so soon in life was not worthy of remembrance. . . . . Nobody thought, as we ordinarily think today, that every child already contained a man's personality. Too many of them died.[14]

One of the consequences of the devaluation of the old in modern society is the minimization of the disruption and moral shock death ordinarily brings about.

But when people die who are engaged in the vital functions of society—socializing the young, producing sustenance, and maintaining ceremonies and rituals—their importance cannot be easily reduced. Dying before they have done their full complement of work and before they have seen their children off toward adulthood and their own parenthood, they die with *unfinished business.* I suggest that the almost universal belief in ghosts in preindustrial societies[15] can be understood as an effect of this demographic pattern on systems of interpersonal interaction, and not simply as a function of naive, magical and other "unsophisticated" world views. Ghosts are reifications of this unfinished business, and belief in their existence may permit some continuation of relationships broken off before their natural terminus. Perhaps the primitive Manus have constructed the most elaborate belief system which illustrates this point:

> Each man worships a spirit who is called the Sir-Ghost, usually the spirit of his father, though sometimes it may be the son, or brother, or one who stood in the mother's brother-sister relationship. The concrete manifestation of this Sir-Ghost is the dead person's skull which is placed in a bowl above the inside of the front entry of the house. Any male can speak to his Sir-Ghost and receive communications from him. The Sir-Ghost acts as a ward, protecting his son from accidents, supervising his morals, and hopefully bringing him wealth. The relationship between the Sir-Ghost and his ward is a close parallel to that between father and son. With some changed emphases, it continues the relationship that existed in life and was broken by death. Since Manus die early, the tenure of

a Sir-Ghost is typically only one generation. When the ward, the son, dies, this is seen as proof of the ghost's ineffectiveness, and the son's son casts him out, installing his own newly deceased father as Sir-Ghost. The same spirit, however, is not a Sir-Ghost to other families, but only a regular ghost and as such thought to be malicious.[16]

More common in primitive societies is an ambivalent attitude toward the ghost. Fear exists because of the belief that the dead man, frustrated in his exclusion from a life in which he was recently involved, wants back in, and, failing this, may attempt to restore his former personal ties by taking others along with him on his journey to the spirit world. The elaborate, ritually appropriate funeral is believed to keep the spirit of the dead away from the haunts of the living,[17] and the feasts and gifts given for the dead are attempts to appease them through partial inclusion in their life. It would appear that the dead who were most engaged in the life of society have the strongest motives for restoring their ties, and the most feared ghosts tend to be those whose business has been the least completed. Ghosts of the murdered, the suicide, and others who have met a violent end are especially feared because they have generally died young, with considerable strength and energy remaining. Ghosts of women dying in childbirth and of the unmarried and childless are considered particularly malignant because these souls have been robbed of life's major purpose; at the funeral the unmarried are often given mock marriages to other dead souls. Ghosts of dead husbands or wives are dangerous to their spouses, especially when the latter have remarried.[18] The spirit of the grandparent who has seen his children grow up and procreate is, on the other hand, the least feared; among the LoDagaa only the grandparent's death is conceded to be a natural rather than a magical or malignant event, and in many societies there is only a perfunctory funeral for grandparents, since their spirits are not considered to be in conflict with the living.[19]

The relative absence of ghosts in modern society is not simply a result of the routing of superstition by science and rational thought, but also reflects the disengaged social situation of the majority of the deceased. In a society where the young and middle-aged have largely liberated themselves from the authority of and emotional dependence upon old people by the time of the latter's death, there is little social-psychological need for a vivid community of the dead. Whereas in high-mortality societies, the person who dies often literally abandons children, spouses, and other relatives to whom he is owing affection and care, the deceased in advanced societies has typically completed his obligations to the living; he does not owe anything. Rather, the death is more likely to remind survivors of the social and psychological debts they have incurred toward him—debts that they may have been intending to pay in the coins of attention, affection, care, appreciation, or achievement. In modern societies the living use the funeral and sometimes a memorial to attempt to "make up for" some of these debts that can no longer be paid in terms of the ordinary give and take of social life.

The disengagement of the aged in modern societies enhances the continuous functioning of social institutions and is a corallary of social structure and mortality patterns. Disengagement, the transition period between the end of institutional functioning and death, permits the changeover of personnel in a planned and careful manner, without the inevitably disruptive crises of disorganization and succession that would occur if people worked to the end and died on the job. The unsettling character of the Kennedy assassination for our nation suggests the chaos that would exist if a bureaucratic social structure were combined with high mortality in the middle years.[20]

For the older person, disengagement may bring on great psychological stress if his ties to work and family are severed more abruptly and completely than he desires. Yet it may also have positive consequences. As Robert Butler has described, isolation and unoccupied time during the later years permit reviewing one's past life.[21] There is at least the potential (not always realized) to better integrate the manifold achievements and disappointments of a lifetime, and doing so, to die better. Under favorable circumstances, disengagement can permit a person to complete his unfinished business before death: To right old wrongs, to reconcile longstanding hostile relations with relatives or former friends; to take the trip, write the play, or paint the picture that he was always planning. Of course, often the finances and health of the aged do not permit such a course, and it is also possible that the general status of the aged in a secular, youth-and-life oriented society is a basic obstacle to a firm sense of identity and self-worth during the terminal years.

Bureaucratization of Modern Death Control

Since there is no death without a body—except in mystery thrillers—the corpse is another consequence of mortality that contributes to its disruptiveness, tending to produce fear, generalized anxiety, and disgust.[22] Since families and work groups must eventually return to some kind of normal life, the time they are exposed to corpses must be limited. Some form of disposal (earth or sea burial, cremation, exposure to the elements) is the core of mortuary institutions everywhere. A disaster that brings about massive and unregulated exposure to the dead, such as that experienced by the survivors of Hiroshima and also at various times by survivors of great plagues, famines, and death-camps, appears to produce a profound identification with the dead and a consequent depressive state.[23]

The disruptive impact of a death is greater to the extent that its consequences spill over onto the larger social territory and affect large numbers of people. This depends not only on the frequency and massiveness of mortality, but also on the physical and social settings of death. These vary in different societies, as does also the specialization of responsibility for the care of the dying and the preparation of the body for disposal. In premodern societies, many deaths take place amid the hubbub of life, in the central social territory of the tribe, clan, or other familial group. In modern societies, where the majority of deaths are now predictably in the older age brackets, disengagement from family and economic function has permitted the segregation of death settings from the more workaday social territory. Probably in small towns and rural communities, more people die at home than do so in urban areas. But the proportion of people who die at home, on the job, and in public places must have declined consistently over the past generations with the growing importance of specialized dying institutions—hospitals, old people's homes, and nursing homes.[24]

Modern societies control death through bureaucratization, our characteristic form of social structure. Max Weber has described how bureaucratization in the West proceeded by removing social functions from the family and the household and implanting them in specialized institutions autonomous of kinship considerations. Early manufacturing and entrepreneurship took place in or close to the home; modern industry and corporate bureaucracies are based on the separation of the workplace from the household.[25] Similarly, only a few generations ago most people in the United States either died at home, or were brought into the home if they had died elsewhere. It was the responsibility of the family to lay out the corpse—that is, to prepare the body for the funeral.[26] Today, of course, the hospital cares for the terminally ill and manages the crisis of dying; the mortuary industry (whose establishments are usually called "homes" in deference to past tradition) prepares the body for burial and makes many of the funeral arrangements. A study in Philadelphia found that about ninety percent of funerals started out from the funeral parlor, rather than from the home, as was customary in the past.[27] This separation of the handling of illness and death from the family minimizes the average person's exposure to death and its disruption of the social process. When the dying are segregated among specialists for whom contact with death has become routine and even somewhat impersonal, neither their presence while alive nor as corpses interferes greatly with the mainstream of life.

Another principle of bureaucracy is the ordering of regularly occurring as well as extraordinary events into predictable and routinized procedures. In addition to treating the ill and isolating them from the rest of society, the modern hospital as an organization is committed to the routinization of the handling of death. Its distinctive competence is to contain through isolation, and reduce through orderly procedures, the disturbance and disruption that are associated with the death crisis. The decline in the authority of religion as well as shifts in the functions of the family underlies this fact. With the growth of the secular and rational outlook, hegemony in the affairs of death has been transferred from the church to science and its representatives, the medical profession and the rationally organized hospital.

Death in the modern hospital has been the subject of two recent sociological studies: Sudnow has focused on the handling of death and the dead in a county hospital catering to charity patients; and Glaser and Strauss have concentrated on the dying situation in a number of hospitals of varying status.[28] The county hospital well illustrates various trends in modern death. Three-quarters of its patients are over 60 years old. Of the 250 deaths Sudnow observed, only a handful involved people younger than 40.[29] This hospital is a setting for the concentration of death. There are 1,000 deaths a year; thus approximately three die daily, of the 330 patients typically in residence. But death is even more concentrated in the four wards of the critically ill; here roughly 75 percent of all mortality occurs, and one in 25 persons will die each day.[30]

Hospitals are organized to hide the facts of dying and death from patients as well as visitors. Sudnow quotes a major text in hospital administration: "The hospital morgue is best located on the ground floor and placed in an area inaccessible to the general public. It is important that the unit have a suitable exit leading onto a private loading platform which is concealed from hospital patients and the public."[31] Personnel in the high-mortality wards use a number of techniques to render death invisible. To protect relatives, bodies are not to be removed during visiting hours. To protect other inmates, the patient is moved to a private room when the end is foreseen. But some deaths are unexpected and may be noticed by roommates before the hospital staff is aware of them. These are considered troublesome because elaborate procedures are required to remove the corpse without offending the living.

The rationalization of death in the hospital takes place through standard procedures of covering the corpse, removing the body, identifying the deceased, informing relatives, and completing the death certificate and autopsy permit. Within the value hierarchy of the hospital, handling the corpse is "dirty work," and when possible attendants will leave a body to be processed by the next work shift. As with so many of the unpleasant jobs in our society, hospital morgue attendants and orderlies are often Negroes. Personnel become routinized to death and are easily able to pass from mention of the daily toll to other topics; new staff members stop counting after the first half-dozen deaths witnessed.[32]

Standard operating procedures have even routinized the most charismatic and personal of relations, that between the priest and the dying patient. It is not that the church neglects charity patients. The chaplain at the county hospital daily goes through a file of the critically ill for the names of all known Catholic patients, then enters their rooms and administers extreme unction. After completing his round of each ward, he stamps the index card of the patient with a rubber stamp which reads: "Last Rites Administered. Date ______ Clergyman ________." Each day he consults the files to see if new patients have been admitted or put on the critical list. As Sudnow notes, this rubber stamp prevents him from performing the rites twice on the same patient.[33]

This example highlights the trend toward the depersonalization of modern death, and is certainly the antithesis of the historic Catholic notion of "the good death."

In the hospitals studied by Glaser and Strauss, depersonalization is less advanced. Fewer of the dying are comatose, and as paying patients with higher social status they are in a better position to negotiate certain aspects of their terminal situation. Yet nurses and doctors view death as an inconvenience, and manage interaction so as to minimize emotional reactions and fuss. They attempt to avoid announcing unexpected deaths because relatives break down too emotionally; they prefer to let the family members know that the patient has taken "a turn for the worse," so that they will be able to modulate their response in keeping with the hospital's need for order.[34] And drugs are sometimes administered to a dying patient to minimize the disruptiveness of his passing—even when there is no reason for this in terms of treatment of the reduction of pain.

The dying patient in the hospital is subject to the kinds of alienation experienced by persons in other situations in bureaucratic organizations. Because doctors avoid the terminally ill, and nurses and relatives are rarely able to talk about death, he suffers psychic isolation.[35] He experiences a sense of meaninglessness because he is typically kept unaware of the course of his disease and his impending fate, and is not in a position to understand the medical and other routines carried out in his behalf.[36] He is powerless in that the medical staff and the hospital organization tend to program his death in keeping with their organizational and professional needs; control over one's death seems to be even more difficult to achieve than control over one's life in our society.[37] Thus the modern hospital, devoted to the preservation of life and the reduction of pain, tends to become a "mass reduction" system, undermining the subjecthood of its dying patients.

The rationalization of modern death control cannot be fully achieved, however, because of an inevitable tension between death—as an event, a crisis, an experience laden with great emotionality—and bureaucracy, which must deal with routines rather than events and is committed to the smoothing out of affect and emotion. Although there was almost no interaction between dying patients and the staff in the county hospital studied by Sudnow, many nurses in the other hospitals became personally involved with their patients and experienced grief when they died. Despite these limits to the general trend, our society has gone far in containing the disruptive possibilities of mortality through its bureaucratized death control.

The Decline of the Funeral in Modern Society

Death creates a further problem because of the contradiction between society's need to push the dead away and its need "to keep the dead alive."[38] The social distance between the living and the dead must be increased after death, so that the group first, and the most affected grievers later, can reestablish their normal activity without a paralyzing attachment to the corpse. Yet the deceased cannot simply be buried as a dead body: the prospect of total exclusion from the social world would be too anxiety-laden for the living, aware of their own eventual fate. The need to keep the dead alive directs societies to construct rituals that celebrate and insure a transition to a new social status, that of spirit, a being now believed to participate in a different realm.[39] Thus, a funeral that combines this status transformation with the act of physical disposal is universal to all societies, and has justly been considered one of the crucial *rites de passage.*[40]

Because the funeral has been typically employed to handle death's manifold disruptions, its character, importance, and frequency may be viewed as indicators of the place of mortality in society. The contrasting impact of death in primitive and modern societies, and the diversity in their modes of control, is suggested by the striking difference in the centrality of mortuary ceremonies in the collective life. Because death is so disruptive in simple societies, much "work" must be done to restore the social system's functioning. Funerals are not "mere rituals," but significant adaptive structures, as can be seen by considering the tasks that make up the funeral work among the LoDagaa of West Africa. The dead body must be buried with the appropriate ritual so as to give the dead man a new status that separates him from the living; he must be given the material goods and symbolic invocations that will help guarantee his safe journey to the final destination and at the same time protect the survivors against his potentially dangerous intervention in their affairs (such as appearing in dreams, "walking," or attempting to drag others with him); his qualities, lifework, and accomplishments must be summed up and given appropriate recognition; his property, roles, rights, and privileges must be distributed so that social and economic life can continue; and, finally, the social units—family, clan, and community as a whole—whose very existence and functioning his death has threatened, must have a chance to vigorously reaffirm their identity and solidarity through participation in ritual ceremony.[41]

Such complicated readjustments take time, and therefore the death of a mature person in many primitive societies is followed by not one, but a series of funerals (usually two or three) that may take place over a period ranging from a few months to two years, and in which the entire society, rather than just relatives and friends, participates.[42] The duration of the funeral and the fine elaboration of its ceremonies suggest the great destructive possibilities of death in these societies. Mortuary institutions loom large in the daily life of the community, and the frequent occurrence of funerals may be no small element in maintaining societal continuity under the precarious conditions of high mortality.[43]

In Western antiquity and the middle ages, funerals were important events in the life of city-states and rural communities.[44] Though not so central as in high-mortality and sacred primitive cultures (reductions in mortality rates and secularism both antedate the industrial revolution in the West), they were still frequent and meaningful ceremonies in the life of small-town, agrarian America several generations ago. But in the modern context they have become relatively unimportant events for the life of the larger society. Formal mortuary observances are completed in a short time. Because of the segregation and disengagement of the aged and the gap between generations, much of the social distance to which funerals generally contribute has already been created before death. The deceased rarely have important roles or rights that the society must be concerned about allocating, and the transfer of property has become the responsibility of individuals in cooperation with legal functionaries. With the weakening of beliefs in the existence and malignancy of ghosts, the absence of "realistic" concern about the dead man's trials in his initiation to spirithood, and the lowered intensity of conventional beliefs in an afterlife, there is less demand for both magical precautions and religious ritual. In a society where disbelief or doubt is more common than a firm acceptance of the reality of a life after death,[45] the funeral's classic function of status transformation becomes attenuated.

The recent attacks on modern funeral practices by social critics focus on alleged commercial exploitation by the mortuary industry and the vulgar ostentatiousness of its service. But at bottom this criticism reflects this crisis in the function of the funeral as a social institution. On the one hand, the religious and ritual meanings of the ceremony have lost significance for many people. But the crisis is not only due to the erosion of the sacred spirit by rational, scientific world views.[46] The social substructure of the funeral is weakened when those who die tend to be irrelevant for the ongoing social life of the community and when the disruptive potentials of death are already controlled by compartmentalization into isolated spheres where bureaucratic routinization is the rule. Thus participation and interest in funerals are restricted to family members and friends rather than involving the larger community, unless an important leader has died.[47] Since only individuals and families are affected, adaptation and bereavement have become their private responsibility, and there is little need for a transition period to permit society as a whole to adjust to the fact of a single death. Karl Marx was proved wrong about "the withering away of the state," but with the near disappearance of death as a public event in modern society, the withering away of the funeral may become a reality.

In modern societies, the bereaved person suffers from a paucity of ritualistic conventions in the mourning period. He experiences grief less frequently, but more intensely, since his emotional involvements are not diffused over an entire community, but are usually concentrated on one or a few people.[48] Since mourning and a sense of loss are not widely shared, as in premodern communities, the individualization and deritualization of bereavement make for serious problems in adjustment. There are many who never fully recover and "get back to normal," in contrast to the frequently observed capacity of the bereaved in primitive societies to smile, laugh, and go about their ordinary pursuits the moment the official mourning period is ended.[49] The lack of conventionalized stages in the mourning process results in an ambiguity as to when the bereaved person has grieved enough and thus can legitimately and guiltlessly feel free for new attachments and interests.[50] Thus at the same time that death becomes less disruptive to the society, its prospects and consequences become more serious for the bereaved individual.

Some Consequences of Modern Death Control

I shall now consider some larger consequences that appear to follow from the demographic, organizational, and cultural trends in modern society that have diminished the presence of death in public life and have reduced most persons' experience of mortality to a minimum through the middle years.[51]

The Place of the Dead in Modern Society

With the diminished visibility of death, the perceived reality and the effective status and power of the dead have also declined in modern societies. A central factor here is the rise of science: Eissler suggests that "the intensity of service to the dead and the proneness for scientific discovery are in reverse proportion."[52] But the weakening of religious imagery is not the sole cause; there is again a functional sociological basis. When those who die are not important to the life of society, the dead as a collective category will not be of major significance in the concerns of the living.

Compare the situation in high-mortality primitive and peasant societies. The living have not liberated themselves emotionally from many of the recently deceased and therefore need to maintain symbolic interpersonal relations with them. This can take place only when the life of the spirits and their world is conceived in well-structured form, and so, as Goode has phrased it, "practically every primitive religious system imputes both power and interest to the dead."[53]

Their spheres of influence in preindustrial societies are many: Spirits watch over and guide economic activities and may determine the fate of trading exchanges, hunting and fishing expeditions, and harvests. Their most important realm of authority is probably that of social control: They are concerned with the general morality of society and the specific actions of individuals (usually kin or clansmen) under their jurisdiction. It is generally believed that the dead have the power to bring about both economic and personal misfortunes (including illness and death) to serve their own interests, to express their general capriciousness, or to specifically punish the sins and errors of the living. The fact that a man as spirit often receives more deference from, and exerts greater power over, people than while living may explain the apparent absence of the fear of death that has been observed in some primitive and ancestor-worship societies.[54]

In modern societies the influence of the dead is indirect and is rarely experienced in personified form. Every cultural heritage is in the main the contribution of dead generations to the present society,[55] and the living are confronted with problems that come from the sins of the past (for example, our heritage of Negro slavery). There are people who extend their control over others after death through wills, trust funds, and other arrangements. Certain exceptional figures such as John Kennedy and Malcolm X become legendary or almost sainted and retain influence as national symbols or role models. But, for the most part, the dead have little status or power in modern society, and the living tend to be liberated from their direct, personified influence.[56] We do not attribute to the dead the range of material and ideal interests that adheres to their symbolic existence in other societies, such as property and possessions, the desire to recreate networks of close personal relationships, the concern for tradition and the morality of the society. Our concept of the inner life of spirits is most shadowy. In primitive societies a full range of attitudes and feelings is imputed to them, whereas a scientific culture has emptied out specific mental and emotional contents from its vague image of spirit life.[57]

Generational Continuity and the Status of the Aged

The decline in the authority of the dead, and the widening social distance between them and the living, are both conditions and consequences of the youthful orientation, receptivity to innovation, and dynamic social change that characterize modern society. In most preindustrial societies, symbolic contacts with the spirits and ghosts of the dead were frequent, intimate, and often long-lasting. Such communion in modern society is associated with spiritualism and other deviant belief-systems; "normal" relations with the dead seem to have come under increasing discipline and control. Except for observing Catholics perhaps, contact is limited to very specific spatial boundaries, primarily cemeteries, and is restricted to a brief time period following a death and possibly a periodic memorial.[58] Otherwise the dead and their concerns are simply not relevant to the living in a society that feels liberated from the authority of the past and orients its energies toward immediate preoccupations and future possibilities.

Perhaps it is the irrelevance of the dead that is the clue to the status of old people in modern industrial societies. In a low-mortality society, most deaths occur in old age, and since the aged predominate among those who die, the association between old age and death is intensified.[59] Industrial societies value people in terms of their present functions and their future prospects; the aged have not only become disengaged from significant family, economic, and community responsibilities in the present, but their future status (politely never referred to in our humane culture) is among the company of the powerless, anonymous, and virtually ignored dead.[60] In societies where the dead continue to play an influential role in the community of the living, there is no period of the lifespan that marks the end of a person's connection to society and the aged before death begin to receive some of the awe and authority that is conferred on the spirit world.

The social costs of these developments fall most heavily on our old people, but they also affect the integrity of the larger culture and the interests of the young and middle-aged. The traditional values that the dead and older generations represent lose significance, and the result is a fragmentation of each generation from a sense of belonging to and identity with a lineal stream of kinship and community. In modern societies where mobility and social change have eliminated the age-old sense of closeness to "roots," this alienation from the past—expressed in the distance between living and dead generations—may be an important source of tenuous personal identities.

These tendencies help to produce another contradiction. The very society that has so greatly controlled death has made it more difficult to die with dignity. The irrelevance of the dead, as well as other social and cultural trends, brings about a crisis in our sense of what is an appropriate death. Most societies, including our own past, have a notion of the ideal conditions under which the good man leaves the life of this world: For some primitives it is the influential grandfather; for classical antiquity, the hero's death in battle; in the middle ages, the Catholic idea of "holy dying." There is a clear relationship between the notion of appropriate death and the basic value emphases of the society, whether familial, warlike, or religious. I suggest that American culture is faced with a crisis of death because the changed demographic and structural conditions do not fit the traditional concepts of appropriate death, and no new ideal has arisen to take their place. Our nineteenth-century ideal was that of the patriarch, dying in his own home in ripe old age but in the full possession of his faculties, surrounded by family, heirs, and material symbols of a life of hard work and acquisition. Death was additionally appropriate because of the power of religious belief, which did not regard the event as a final ending. Today people characteristically die at an age when their physical, social, and mental powers are at an ebb, or even absent, typically in the hospital, and often separated from family and other meaningful surroundings. Thus "dying alone" is not only a symbolic theme of existential philosophers; it more and more epitomizes the inappropriateness of how people die under modern conditions.

I have said little about another modern prototype of mortality, mass violence. Despite its statistical infrequency in "normal times," violent death cannot be dismissed as an unimportant theme, since it looms so large in our recent past and in our anxieties about the future. The major forms, prosaic and bizarre, in which violent death occurs, or has occurred, in the present period are: (1) Automobile and airplane accidents; (2) the concentration camp; and (3) nuclear disaster. All these expressions of modern violence result in a most inappropriate way of dying. In a brilliant treatment of the preponderance of death by violence in modern literature, Frederick Hoffman points out its inherent ambiguities. The fact that many people die at once, in most of these situations, makes it impossible to mitigate the effects on the survivors through ceremonies of respect. While these deaths are caused by human agents, the impersonality of the assailant, and the distance between him and his victim, makes it impossible to assign responsibility to understandable causes. Because of the suddenness of impact, the death that is died cannot be fitted into the life that has been lived. And finally, society experiences a crisis of meaning when the threat of death pervades the atmosphere, yet cannot be incorporated into a religious or philosophical context.[61]

A Final Theoretical Note: Death and Social Institutions

Mortality implies that population is in a constant (though usually a gradual) state of turnover. Society's groups are fractured by the deaths of their members and must therefore maintain their identities through symbols that are external to and outlast individual persons. The social roles through which the functions of major societal institutions are carried out cannot be limited to particular individuals and their unique interpretations of the needs of social action; they must partake of general and transferable prescriptions and expectations. The order and stability required by a social system are threatened by the eventual deaths of members of small units such as families, as well as political, religious, and economic leaders. There is, therefore, a need for more permanent institutions embedding "impersonal" social roles, universal norms, and transcendent values.

The frequent presence of death in high-mortality societies is important in shaping their characteristic institutional structure. To the extent that death imperils the continuity of a society, its major institutions will be occupied with providing that sense of identity and integrity made precarious by its severity. In societies with high death rates, the kinship system and religion tend to be the major social institutions.

Kinship systems organized around the clan or the extended family are well suited to high-mortality societies because they provide a relative permanence and stability lacking in the smaller nuclear group. Both the totem of the clan and the extended family's ties to the past and the future are institutionalized representations of continuity. Thus, the differential impact of mortality on social structure explains the apparent paradox that the smaller the scale of a community, the larger in general is its ideal family unit.[62] The very size of these kinship units provides a protection against the disintegrating potential of mortality, making possible within the family the varied resources in relational ties, age-statuses, and cultural experience that guarantee the socialization of all its young, even if their natural parents should die before they have become adults.

In primitive and peasant societies the centrality of magic and religion are related to the dominant presence of death. If the extended family provides for the society's physical survival, magic and counter-magic are weapons used by individuals to protect themselves from death's uncontrolled and erratic occurrence. And religion makes possible the moral survival of the society and the individual in an environment fraught with fear, anxiety, and uncertainty. As Malinowski and others have shown, religion owes its persistence and power (if not necessarily its origin) to its unique capacity to solve the societal and personal problems that death calls forth.[63] Its rituals and beliefs impart to the funeral ceremonies those qualities of the sacred and the serious that help the stricken group reestablish and reintegrate itself through the collective reaffirmation of shared cultural assumptions. In all known societies it serves to reassure the individual against possible anxieties concerning destruction, nonbeing, and finitude by providing beliefs that make death meaningful, afterlife plausible, and the miseries and injustices of earthly existence endurable.

In complex modern societies there is a proliferation and differentiation of social institutions that have become autonomous in relationship to kinship and religion, as Durkheim pointed out.[64] In a sense these institutions take on a permanence and autonomy that makes them effectively independent of the individuals who carry out the roles within them. The economic corporation is the prototype of a modern institution. Sociologically it is a bureaucracy and therefore relatively unconnected to family and kinship; constitutionally it has been graced with the legal fiction of immortality. Thus the major agencies that organize productive work (as well as other activities) are relatively invulnerable to the depletion of their personnel by death, for their offices and functions are impersonal and transferable from one role-incumbent to another. The situation is very different in traditional societies. There family ties and kinship groups tend to be the basis of economic, religious, and other activities; social institutions interpenetrate one another around the kinship core. Deaths that strike the family therefore reverberate through the entire social structure. This type of social integration (which Durkheim termed "mechanical solidarity,") makes premodern societies additionally vulnerable to death's disruptive potential—regardless of its quantitative frequency and age distribution.

On the broadest level, the relationship between death and society is a dialectic one. Mortality threatens the continuity of society and in so doing contributes to the strengthening of social structure and the development of culture. Death weakens the social group and calls forth personal anxieties; in response, members of a society cling closer together. Specific deaths disrupt the functioning of the social system and thereby encourage responses in the group that restore social equilibrium and become customary practices that strengthen the social fabric. Death's sword in time cuts down each individual, but with respect to the social order it is double-edged. The very sharpness of its disintegrating potential demands adaptations that can bring higher levels of cohesion and continuity. In the developmental course of an individual life, death always conquers; but, as I have attempted to demonstrate throughout this essay, the social system seems to have greatly contained mortality in the broad span of societal and historical development.

NOTES

*I am grateful to the Equitable Life Assurance Society and its Director of Social Research, John W. Riley, Jr., for support of this project. Aid was also provided by the Institute of Social Science,

University of California, Berkeley. I thank Fred Deyo for his research assistance, and David Matza, Norman Ryder, and Sheldon Messinger for their especially helpful comments.

1. Bronislaw Malinowski, *Argonauts of the Western Pacific;* London, Routledge, 1922; p. 490; cited in Lucien Levy-Bruhl, *The "Soul" of the Primitive;* London, Allen and Unwin, 1928; p. 226.

2. Jack Goody, *Death, Property and the Ancestors;* Stanford, Stanford Univ. Press, 1962. This is the most thorough investigation in the literature of the relationships between the mortuary institutions of a society and its social structure; I am indebted to Goody for many ideas and insights.

3. Jules Henry, *Jungle People;* Richmond, Va., William Byrd Press, 1941.

4. Kingsley Davis, *The Population of India and Pakistan;* Princeton, Princeton Univ. Press, 1951; p. 64.

5. Ludwik Krzywicki, *Primitive Society and Its Vital Statistics;* London, Macmillan, 1934; p. 292. The very scale of modern societies is thus an important element of their control of mortality; unlike the situation in a remote village of India or the jungle highlands of Brazil, it would require the ultimate in catastrophic mortality, all-out nuclear war, for death to threaten societal survival.

6. United Nations, *Demographic Yearbook,* 1961, 13th Edition; New York, Department of Economic and Social Affairs, 1961; see Table 15. A very similar age distribution results when a cohort of 100,000 born in 1929 is tabulated in terms of the proportions who die in each age period. See Louis I Dublin and Alfred J. Lotka, *Length of Life;* New York, Ronald, 1936; p. 12. The outlook for the future is suggested by a more recent life-table for females in Canada. Of 100,000 babies born in the late 1950's, only 15 percent will die before age 60. Seventy percent will be 70 years old or more at death; 42 percent will die past 80. See United Nations, *Demographic Yearbook;* pp. 622-676.

7. See footnote 5; pp. 148, 271. A more recent demographic study of the Cocos-Keeling Islands in the Malay Peninsula found that 59 percent die before age five. See T. E. Smith, "The Cocos-Keeling Islands: A Demographic Laboratory," *Population Studies* (1960) 14: 94-130. Among 89 deaths recorded in 1952-1953 among the Tikopia, 39 percent were of infants and children below age eight. See W. D. Borrie, Raymond Firth, and James Spillius, "The Population of Tikopia, 1929 and 1952," *Population Studies* (1957) 10: 229-252. The Rungus Dusun, "a primitive, pagan agricultural"

village community in North Borneo, lose 20 percent of their females in the first year of life, and another 50 percent die between the first birthday and motherhood. See P. J. Koblenzer and N. H. Carrier, "The Fertility, Mortality and Nuptiality of the Rungus Dusun," *Population Studies* (1960) 13: 266-277.

8. United Nations, *Demographic Yearbook,* in footnote 6; pp. 622-676.

9. See Borrie, Firth, and Spillius, in footnote 7; p. 238.

10. Calculated from tables in J. C. Russell, "Late Ancient and Medieval Population," *Transactions of the Amer. Philosophical Soc.,* Vol. 48, Part 3, pp. 25-29.

11. See Smith, in footnote 7. In Nigeria during 1956, only 13 percent of male deaths recorded were of men older than 55 years. Twenty-eight percent occurred among males between 5 and 54. Similarly, in Algeria during the same year, 30 percent of all male deaths among the Moslem population took people during the middle years of life (between 15 and 49). Only 13 percent were old men past 60. See United Nations, *Demographic Yearbook,* in footnote 6; Table 15.

12. See Goody, in footnote 2; pp. 30, 73 *ff.* In some high-mortality societies, such as traditional India, remarriage is not prescribed for the affected widows. Perhaps this difference may be related to the much greater population density of India as compared to West Africa.

13. Robert Hertz, "The Collective Representation of Death," in Hertz, *Death and the Right Hand,* translated by Rodney and Claudia Needham; Aberdeen, Cohen and West, 1960; pp. 84-85. See also Goody, in footnote 2; pp. 208 *ff.*

14. Philippe Ariès, *Centuries of Childhood: A Social History of Family Life,* translated by Robert Baldick; New York, Knopf, 1962; pp. 38 *ff.*

15. After studying 71 tribes from the human area files, Leo Simmons generalizes that the belief in ghosts is "about as universal in primitive societies as any trait could be." See Simmons, *The Role of the Aged in Primitive Society;* New Haven, Yale Univ. Press, 1945; pp. 223 *ff.* Another student of death customs reports that "the fear of a malignant ghost governs much of the activity of primitive tribes." See Norman L. Egger, "Contrasting Attitudes Toward Death Among Veterans With and Without Battle Experience and Non-Veterans," unpublished M. A. Thesis, Dept. of Psychology, Univ. of Calif., Berkeley, 1948; p. 33.

16. Adapted from William Goode, *Religion Among the Primitives;* Glencoe, Ill., Free Press, 1951; pp. 64 *ff.,* 194 *ff.* The former Sir-Ghost, neglected after his forced retirement, is thought to wander on the sea between the villages, endangering sea voyages. Eventually he becomes a sea-slug. A similar phenomenon is reported with respect to the shades of ancient Rome; a deceased husband began as a shade with a distinct personality, but was degraded to the rank of the undifferentiated shades that haunt the world of the dead after time passed and the widow remarried. Thus the unfinished business had been completed by someone else. See James H. Leuba, *The Belief in God and Immortality;* Boston, Sherman, French, 1916; pp. 95-96.

17. The most complete materials on ambivalence toward ghosts are found in James G. Frazer, *The Fear of the Dead in Primitive Religion,* 3 vols.; London, Macmillan, 1933, 1934, and 1936. Volume II is devoted to various methods of keeping dead spirits away.

The connection between the ambivalent attitude toward the ghost and the neomort's uncompleted working out of his obligations on earth is clear in Henry's description of the Kaingang: "The ghost-soul loves and pities the living whom it has deserted, but the latter fear and abhor the ghost-soul. The ghost-soul longs for those it has left behind, but they remain cold to its longings. 'One pities one's children, and therefore goes with them (that is, takes them when one dies). One loves (literally, lives in) one's children, and dies and goes with one's children, and one (the child) dies.' The dead pity those they have left alone with no one to care for them. They have left behind parts of themselves, for their children are those 'in whom they live.' But to the pity, love and longing of the ghost-soul, the children return a cry of 'Mother, leave me and go!' as she lies on the funeral pyre. The Kaingang oscillate between a feeling of attachment for the dead and a desire never to see them again." See Henry, in footnote 3; p. 67.

Eissler suggests that an envy of the living who continue on is one of the universal pains of dying. Such an attitude would be understandably stronger for those who die in middle life. See Kurt R. Eissler, *The Psychiatrist and the Dying Patient;* New York, Internat. Univ. Press, 1955; pp. 149-150.

18. See Frazer, in footnote 17; Vol III, pp. 103-260.

19. See Goody, in footnote 2, pp. 208-209; Levy-Bruhl, in footnote 1, p. 219; and Hertz, in footnote 13, p. 84.

20. See Elaine Cumming and William E. Henry, *Growing Old*

(New York, Basic Books, 1961) for a theoretical discussion and empirical data on the disengagement of the old in American society. In a more recent statement, Cumming notes that disengagement "frees the old to die without disrupting vital affairs," and that "the depth and breadth of a man's engagement can be measured by the degree of potential disruption that would follow his sudden death." See "New Thoughts on the Theory of Disengagement," in *New Thoughts on Old Age,* edited by Robert Kastenbaum; New York, Springer, 1964; pp. 11, 4.

21. Robert N. Butler, "The Life Review: An Interpretation of Reminiscence in the Aged," PSYCHIATRY (1963) 26:65-76; see p. 67.

22. Many early anthropologists, including Malinowski, attributed human funerary customs to an alleged instinctive aversion to the corpse. Although there is no evidence for such an instinct, aversion to the corpse remains a widespread, if not universal, human reaction. See the extended discussion of the early theories in Goody, in footnote 2; pp. 20-30; and for some exceptions to the general rule, Robert W. Habenstein, "The Social Organization of Death," *International Encyclopedia of the Social Sciences,* forthcoming.

23. Robert J. Lifton, "Psychological Effects of the Atomic Bomb in Hiroshima: The Theme of Death," *Daedalus,* (1963) 92: 462-497. Among other things, the dead body is too stark a reminder of man's mortal condition. Although man is the one species that knows he will eventually die, most people in most societies cannot live too successfully when constantly reminded of this truth. On the other hand, the exposure to the corpse has positive consequences for psychic functioning, as it contributes to the acceptance of the reality of a death on the part of the survivors. A study of deaths in military action during World War II found that the bereaved kin had particularly great difficulty in believing in and accepting the reality of their loss because they did not see the body and witness its disposal. T. D. Eliot, "Of the Shadow of Death," *Annals Amer. Academy of Political and Social Science* (1943) 229: 87-99.

24. Statistics on the settings of death are not readily available. Robert Fulton reports that 53 percent of all deaths in the United States take place in hospitals, but he does not give any source for this figure. See Fulton, *Death and Identity;* New York, Wiley, 1965; pp. 81-82. Two recent English studies are also suggestive. In the case of the deaths of 72 working-class husbands, primarily in the middle years, 46 died in the hospital; 22 at home; and 4 at work or

in the street. See Peter Marris, *Widows and Their Families;* London, Routledge and Kegan Paul, 1958; p. 146. Of 359 Britishers who had experienced a recent bereavement, 50 percent report that the death took place in a hospital; 44 percent at home; and 6 percent elsewhere. See Geoffrey Gorer, *Death, Grief, and Mourning;* London, Cresset, 1965; p. 149.

25. Max Weber, *Essays in Sociology,* translated and edited by H. H. Gerth and C. Wright Mills; New York, Oxford Univ. Press, 1953; pp. 196-198. See also Max Weber, *General Economic History,* translated by Frank H. Knight; Glencoe, Ill., Free Press, 1950.

26. Leroy Bowman reports that aversion to the corpse made this preparation an unpleasant task. Although sometimes farmed out to experienced relatives or neighbors, the task was still considered the family's responsibility. See Bowman, *The American Funeral: A Study in Guilt, Extravagance and Sublimity;* Washington, D.C., Public Affairs Press, 1959; p. 71.

27. William K. Kephart, "Status After Death," *Amer. Sociol. Review* (1950) 15:635-643.

28. David N. Sudnow, "Passing On: The Social Organization of Dying in the County Hospital," unpublished Ph.D. Thesis, Univ. of Calif., Berkeley, 1965. Sudnow also includes comparative materials from a more well-to-do Jewish-sponsored hospital where he did additional fieldwork, but most of his statements are based on the county institution. Barney G. Glaser and Anselm L. Strauss, *Awareness of Dying;* Chicago, Aldine, 1965.

29. See Sudnow, in footnote 28; pp. 107, 109. This is even fewer than would be expected by the age-composition of mortality, because children's and teaching hospitals in the city were likely to care for many terminally ill children and younger adults.

30. See Sudnow, in footnote 28; pp. 49, 50.

31. J. K. Owen, *Modern Concepts of Hospital Administration;* Philadelphia, Saunders, 1962; p. 304; cited in Sudnow, in footnote 28; p. 80. Such practice attests to the accuracy of Edgar Morin's rather melodramatic statement: "Man hides his death as he hides his sex, as he hides his excrements." See E. Morin, *L'Homme et La Mort dans L'Histoire;* Paris, Correa, 1951; p. 331.

32. See Sudnow, in footnote 28; pp. 20-40, 49-50.

33. See Sudnow, in footnote 28; p. 114.

34. See Glaser and Strauss, in footnote 28; pp. 142-143, 151-152.

35. On the doctor's attitudes towards death and the dying, see August M. Kasper, "The Doctor and Death," pp. 259-270, in *The*

Meaning of Death, edited by Herman Feifel; New York, McGraw-Hill, 1959. Many writers have commented on the tendency of relatives to avoid the subject of death with the terminally ill; see, for example, Herman Feifel's "Attitudes toward Death in Some Normal and Mentally Ill Populations," pp. 114-132 in *The Meaning of Death.*

36. The most favorable situation for reducing isolation and meaninglessness would seem to be "where personnel and patient both are aware that he is dying, and where they act on this awareness relatively openly." This atmosphere, which Glaser and Strauss term an "open awareness context," did not typically predominate in the hospitals they studied. More common were one of three other awareness contexts they distinguished: "the situation where the patient does not recognize his impending death even though everyone else does" (close awareness); "the situation where the patient suspects what the others know and therefore attempts to confirm or invalidate his suspicion" (suspected awareness); and "the situation where each party defines the patient as dying, but each pretends that the other has not done so" (mutual pretense awareness). See Glaser and Strauss, in footnote 28; p. 11.

37. See Glaser and Strauss, in footnote 28; p. 129. Some patients however, put up a struggle to control the pace and style of their dying, and some prefer to leave the hospital and end their days at home for this reason (see Glaser and Strauss, in footnote 28; pp. 95, 181-183). For a classic and moving account of a cancer victim who struggled to achieve control over the conditions of his death, see Lael T. Wertenbaker, *Death of a Man;* New York, Random House, 1957.

For discussions of isolation, meaninglessness, and powerlessness as dimensions of alienation, see Melvin Seeman, "On the Meaning of Alienation." *Amer. Sociol. Review* (1959) 24:783-791; and Robert Blauner, *Alienation and Freedom: The Factory Worker and His Industry;* Chicago, Univ. of Chicago Press, 1964.

38. Franz Borkenau, "The Concept of Death," *The Twentieth Century* (1955) 157: 313-329; reprinted in *Death and Identity,* pp. 42-56 (see footnote 24).

39. The need to redefine the status of the departed is intensified because of tendencies to act toward him as if he were alive. There is a status discongruity inherent in the often abrupt change from a more or less responsive person to an inactive, nonresponding one. This confusion makes it difficult for the living to shift their mode of interaction toward the neomort. Glaser and Strauss report that

relatives in the hospital often speak to the newly deceased and caress him as if he were alive; they act as if he knows what they are saying and doing. Nurses who had become emotionally involved with the patient sometimes back away from postmortem care because of a "mystic illusion" that the deceased is still sentient. See Glaser and Strauss, in footnote 28; pp. 113-114. We are all familiar with the expression of "doing the right thing" *for the deceased,* probably the most common conscious motivation underlying the bereaved's funeral preparations. This whole situation is sensitively depicted in Jules Romain's novel, *The Death of a Nobody;* New York, Knopf, 1944.

40. Arnold Van Gennep, *The Rites of Passage;* London, Routledge and Kegan Paul, 1960 (first published in 1909). See also W. L. Warner, *The Living and the Dead;* New Haven, Yale Univ. Press, 1959; especially Chapter 9; and Habenstein, in footnote 22, for a discussion of funerals as "dramas of disposal."

41. See Goody, in footnote 2, for the specific material on the LoDagaa. For the general theoretical treatment, see Hertz, in footnote 13, and also Emile Durkheim, *The Elementary Forms of the Religious Life;* Glencoe, Ill., Free Press, 1947; especially p. 447.

42. Hertz (see footnote 13) took the multiple funerals of primitive societies as the strategic starting point for his analysis of mortality and social structure. See Goody (in footnote 2) for a discussion of Hertz (pp. 26-27), and the entire book for an investigation of multiple funerals among the LoDagaa.

43. I have been unable to locate precise statistics on the comparative frequency of funerals. The following data are suggestive. In a year and a half, Goody attended 30 among the LoDagaa, a people numbering some 4,000 (see footnote 2). Of the Barra people, a Roman Catholic peasant folk culture in the Scottish Outer Hebrides, it is reported that "most men and women participate in some ten to fifteen funerals in their neighborhood every year." See D. Mandelbaum, "Social Uses of Funeral Rites," in *The Meaning of Death,* in footnote 35; p. 206.

Considering the life-expectancy in our society today, it is probable that only a minority of people would attend one funeral or more per year. Probably most people during the first 40 (or even 50) years of life attend only one or two funerals a decade. In old age, the deaths of the spouse, collateral relations, and friends become more common; thus funeral attendance in modern societies tends to become more age-specific. For a discussion of the loss of intimates in later years, see J. Moreno, "The Social Atom and Death," pp. 62-66, in *The Sociometry Reader,* edited by J. Moreno; Glencoe, Ill., Free Press, 1960.

44. For a discussion of funerals among the Romans and early Christians, see Alfred C. Rush, *Death and Burial in Christian Antiquity;* Washington, D.C., Catholic Univ. of America Press, 1941; especially Part III, pp. 187-273. On funerals in the medieval and preindustrial West, see Bertram S. Puckle, *Funeral Customs;* London, T. Werner Laurie, 1926.

45. See Eissler, in footnote 17; p. 144: "The religious dogma is, with relatively rare exceptions, not an essential help to the psychiatrist since the belief in the immortality of the soul, although deeply rooted in man's unconscious, is only rarely encountered nowadays as a well-integrated idea from which the ego could draw strength." On the basis of a sociological survey, Gorer confirms the psychiatrist's judgment: ". . . how small a role dogmatic Christian beliefs play . . ." (see Gorer, in footnote 24; p. 39). Forty-nine percent of his sample affirmed a belief in an afterlife; twenty-five percent disbelieved; twenty-six percent were uncertain or would not answer (see Gorer; p. 166).

46. The problem of sacred institutions in an essentially secular society has been well analyzed by Robert Fulton. See Fulton and Gilbert Geis, "Death and Social Values," pp. 67-75, and Fulton, "The Sacred and the Secular," pp. 89-105, in *Death and Identity,* footnote 24.

47. LeRoy Bowman interprets the decline of the American funeral primarily in terms of urbanization. When communities were made up of closely knit, geographically isolated groups of families, the death of an individual was a deprivation of the customary social give and take, a distinctly felt diminution of the total community. It made sense for the community as a whole to participate in a funeral. But in cities, individual families are in a much more limited relationship to other families, and the population loses its unity of social and religious ideals. For ethical and religious reasons, Bowman is unwilling to accept "a bitter deduction from this line of thought . . . that the death of one person is not so important as once it would have been, at least to the community in which he has lived." But that is the logical implication of his perceptive sociological analysis. See Bowman, in footnote 26; pp. 9, 113-115, 126-128.

48. Edmund Volkart, "Bereavement and Mental Health," pp.

281-307, in *Explorations in Social Psychiatry,* edited by Alexander H. Leighton, John A. Clausen, and Robert N. Wilson; New York, Basic Books, 1957. Volkart suggests that bereavement is a greater crisis in modern American society than in similar cultures because our family system develops selves in which people relate to others as persons rather than in terms of roles (see pp. 293-295).

49. In a study of bereavement reactions in England, Geoffrey Gorer found that 30 of a group of 80 persons who had lost a close relative were mourning in a style he characterized as *unlimited.* He attributes the inability to get over one's grief "to the absence of any ritual, either individual or social, lay or religious, to guide them and the people they come in contact with." The study also attests to the virtual disappearance of traditional mourning conventions. See Gorer, in footnote 24; pp. 78-83.

50. See Marris, in footnote 24; pp. 39-40.

51. Irwin W. Goffman suggests that "a decline in the significance of death has occurred in our recent history." See "Suicide Motives and Categorization of the Living and the Dead in the United States"; Syracuse, N. Y., Mental Health Research Unit, Feb., 1966, unpublished manuscript; p. 140.

52. See Eissler, in footnote 17; p. 44.

53. See Goode, in footnote 16; p. 185. Perhaps the fullest treatment is by Frazer; see footnote 17, especially Vol. I.

54. See Simmons, in footnote 15; pp. 223-224. See also Effie Bendann, *Death Customs;* New York, Knopf, 1930; p. 180. However, there are primitive societies, such as the Hopi, that attribute little power and authority to dead spirits; in some cultures, the period of the dead man's influence is relatively limited; and in other cases only a minority of ghosts are reported to be the object of deference and awe. The general point holds despite these reservations.

55. See Warner, in footnote 40; pp. 4-5.

56. The novel, *Death of a Nobody* (see footnote 39) is a sensitive treatment of how its protagonist, Jacques Godard, affects people after his death; his influence is extremely short-lived, and his memory in the minds of the living vanishes after a brief period. Goffman suggests that "parents are much less likely today to tell stories of the dead, of their qualities, hardships, accomplishments, and adventures than was true a hundred years ago." See footnote 51; p. 30.

57. In an interesting treatment of the problem from a different theoretical framework, Goffman has concluded that the sense of

contrast between what is living and what is dead in modern society has become attenuated, in large part because of the decline in exposure to death. He has assembled evidence on social differences within our society: for example, women, lower-class people, and Catholics tend to have closer and more frequent contact with death or images of the dead than men, middle-class persons, and Protestants. (See footnote 51.)

The question of what is the representative American imagery of afterlife existence would be a fruitful one for research. Clear and well-developed imageries are probably typical only among Catholics, fundamentals, and certain ethnic groups. The dominant attitude (if there is one) is likely quite nebulous. For some, the dead may be remembered as an "absent presence," never to be seen again; for others as "a loved one with whom I expect (or hope) to be reunited in some form someday." Yet the background of afterlife existence is only vaguely sketched, and expectation and belief probably alternate with hope, doubt, and fear in a striking ambiguity about the prospect and context of reunion.

58. In primitive societies ghosts and spirits of the dead range over the entire social territory or occupy central areas of the group's social space. In ancestor-worship civilizations such as Rome and China, spirits dwell in shrines that are located in the homes or family burial plots. In these preindustrial societies symbolic contact with the dead may be a daily occurrence.

Likewise, in the middle ages, cemeteries were not on the periphery of the societal terrain but were central institutions in the community; regularly visited, they were even the sites for feasts and other celebrations, since it was believed that the dead were gladdened by sounds of merry-making. (See Puckle, in footnote 44; pp. 145-146.) The most trenchant analysis of the cemetery as a spatial territory marking the social boundaries between the "sacred dead and the secular world of the profane living" in a small modern community is found in Warner, in footnote 40; Chapter 9. Yet Warner also notes that people tend to disregard cemeteries as a "collective representation" in rapidly changing and growing communities, in contrast to the situation in small, stable communities. Goffman (see footnote 51; p. 29) notes that "increasingly the remains of the dead are to be found in huge distant cemeteries that are not passed or frequented as part of everyday routines . . . [or] in cities in which our very mobile population *used* to live."

59. Feifel has suggested that American society's rejection of

(and even revulsion to) the old may be because they remind us unconsciously of death. See footnote 35; pp. 122.

60. According to Kastenbaum, the tendency of psychiatrists to eschew psychotherapy with the aged and to treat them, if at all, with supportive (rather than more prestigious depth) techniques may be a reflection of our society's future orientation, which results in an implicit devaluing of old people because of their limited time prospects. See Kastenbaum "The Reluctant Therapist," pp. 139-145, in *New Thoughts on Old Age,* in footnote 20. The research of Butler, a psychiatrist who presents evidence for significant personality change in old age despite the common contrary assumption, would seem to support Kastenbaum's view. (See footnote 21.)

Sudnow contributes additional evidence of the devaluation of old people. Ambulance drivers bringing critical or "dead-on-arrival" cases to the county hospital's emergency entrance blow their horns more furiously and act more frantic when the patient is young than when he is old. A certain proportion of "dead-on-arrival" cases can be saved through mouth-to-mouth resuscitation, heart massages, or other unusual efforts. These measures were attempted with children and young people but not with the old; one intern admitted being repulsed by the idea of such close contact with them. See Sudnow, in footnote 28; pp. 160-163.

61. Frederick J. Hoffman, *The Mortal No: Death and the Modern Imagination;* Princeton, Princeton Univ. Press, 1964; see especially Part II. In a second paper on Hiroshima, Robert J. Lifton also notes the tendency for the threat of mass death to undermine the meaning systems of society, and the absence of a clear sense of appropriate death in modern cultures. See "On Death and Death Symbolism: The Hiroshima Disaster," PSYCHIATRY (1964) 27:191-120. Gorer has argued that our culture's repression of death as a natural event is the cause of the obsessive focus on fantasies of violence that are so prominent in the mass media. See Geoffrey Gorer, "The Pornography of Death," pp. 402-407, in *Identity and Anxiety,* edited by Maurice Stein and Arthur Vidich; Glencoe, Ill., Free Press, 1960; also reprinted in Gorer's *Death, Grief, and Mourning* (see footnote 24).

The inappropriateness inherent in the automobile accident, in which a man dies outside a communal and religious setting, is poignantly captured in the verse and chorus of the Country and Western song, "Wreck on the Highway," popularized by Roy Acuff:

"Who did you say it was, brother?/Who was it fell by the way?/

When whiskey and blood run together,/Did you hear anyone pray?"

Chorus: "I didn't hear nobody pray, dear brother,/I didn't hear nobody pray./I heard the crash on the highway,/But I didn't hear nobody pray."

62. The important distinction between ideal family structures and actual patterns of size of household, kinship composition, and authority relations has been stressed recently by William Goode in *World Revolution and Family Patterns;* New York, Free Press of Glencoe, 1963; and by Marion Levy, "Aspects of the Analysis of Family Structure," pp. 1-63, in A. J. Coale and Marion Levy, *Aspects of the Analysis of Family Structure;* Princeton, Princeton Univ. Press, 1965.

63.Bronislaw Malinowski, *Magic, Science and Religion;* Garden City, N. Y., Doubleday Anchor, 1955; see pp. 47-53.

64. Emile Durkheim, *Division of Labor;* Glencoe, Ill., The Free Press, 1949.

Elisabeth Kubler-Ross

ON THE FEAR OF DEATH

Epidemics have taken a great toll of lives in past generations. Death in infancy and early childhood was frequent and there were few families who didn't lose a member of the family at an early age. Medicine has changed greatly in the last decades. Widespread vaccinations have practically eradicated many illnesses, at least in western Europe and the United States. The use of chemotherapy, especially the antibiotics, has contributed to an ever decreasing number of fatalities in infectious diseases. Better child care and education has effected a low morbidity and mortality among children. The many diseases that have taken an impressive toll among the young and middle-aged have been conquered. The number of old people is on the rise, and with this fact come the number of people with malignancies and chronic diseases associated more with old age.

Pediatricians have less work with acute and life threatening situations as they have an ever increasing number of patients with psychosomatic disturbances and adjustment and behavior problems. Physicians have more people in their waiting rooms with emotional problems than they have ever had before, but they also have more elderly patients who not only try to live with their decreased physical abil-

---

ities and limitations but who also face loneliness and isolation with all its pains and anguish. The majority of these people are not seen by a psychiatrist. Their needs have to be elicited and gratified by other professional people, for instance, chaplains and social workers. It is for them that I am trying to outline the changes that have taken place in the last few decades, changes that are ultimately responsible for the increased fear of death, the rising number of emotional problems, and the greater need for understanding of and coping with the problems of death and dying.

When we look back in time and study old cultures and people, we are impressed that death has always been distasteful to man and will probably always be. From a psychiatrist's point of view this is very understandable and can perhaps best be explained by our basic knowledge that, in our unconscious, death is never possible in regard to ourselves. It is inconceivable for our unconscious to imagine an actual ending of our own life here on earth, and if this life of ours has to end, the ending is always attributed to a malicious intervention from the outside by someone else. In simple terms, in our unconscious mind we can only be killed; it is inconceivable to die of a natural cause or of old age. Therefore death itself is associated with a bad act, a frightening happening, something that in itself calls for retribution and punishment.

One is wise to remember these fundamental facts as they are essential in understanding some of the most important, otherwise unintelligible communications of our patients.

The second fact that we have to comprehend is that in our unconscious mind we cannot distinguish between a wish and a deed. We are all aware of some of our illogical dreams in which two completely opposite statements can exist side by side—very acceptable in our dreams but unthinkable and illogical in our wakening state. Just as our unconscious mind cannot differentiate between the wish to kill somebody in anger and the act of having done so, the young child is unable to make this distinction. The child who angrily wishes his mother to drop dead for not having gratified his needs will be traumatized greatly by the actual death of his mother—even if this event is not linked closely in time with his destructive wishes. He will always take part or the whole blame for the loss of his mother. He will always say to himself—rarely to others—"I did it, I am responsible, I was bad, therefore Mommy left me." It is well to remember that the child will react in the same manner if he loses a parent by divorce, separation, or desertion. Death is often seen by a child as an impermanent thing and has therefore little distinction from a divorce in which he may have an opportunity to see a parent again.

Many a parent will remember remarks of their children such as, "I will bury my doggy now and next spring when the flowers come up again, he will get up." Maybe it was the same wish that motivated the ancient Egyptians to supply their dead with food and goods to keep them happy and the old American Indians to bury their relatives with their belongings.

When we grow older and begin to realize that our omnipotence is really not so omnipotent, that our strongest wishes are not powerful enough to make the impossible possible, the fear that we have contributed to the death of a loved one diminishes—and with it the guilt. The fear remains diminished, however, only so long as it is not challenged too strongly. Its vestiges can be seen daily in hospital corridors and in people associated with the bereaved.

A husband and wife may have been fighting for years, but when the partner dies, the survivor will pull his hair, whine and cry louder and beat his chest in regret, fear and anguish, and will hence fear his own death more than before, still believing in the law of talion—an eye for an eye, a tooth for a tooth—"I am responsible for her death, I will have to die a pitiful death in retribution."

Maybe this knowledge will help us understand many of the old customs and rituals which have lasted over the centuries and whose purpose is to diminish the anger of the gods or the people as the case may be, thus decreasing the anticipated punishment. I am thinking of the ashes, the torn clothes, the veil the *Klage Weiber* of the old days—they are all means to ask you to take pity on them, the mourners, and are expressions of sorrow, grief, and shame. If someone grieves, beats his chest, tears his hair, or refuses to eat, it is an attempt at self-punishment to avoid or reduce the anticipated punishment for the blame that he takes on the death of a loved one.

This grief, shame, and guilt are not very far removed from feelings of anger and rage. The process of grief always includes some qualities of anger. Since none of us likes to admit anger at a deceased person, these emotions are often disguised or repressed and prolong the period of grief or show up in other ways. It is well to remember that it is not up to us to judge such feelings as bad or shameful but to understand their true meaning and origin as something very human. In order to illustrate this I will again use the example of the child—and the child in us. The five-year-old who loses his mother is both blaming himself for her disappearance and being angry at her for having deserted him and for no longer gratifying his needs. The dead person then turns into something the child loves and wants very much but also hates with equal intensity for this severe deprivation.

The ancient Hebrews regarded the body of a dead person as something unclean and not to be touched. The early American Indians talked about the evil spirits and shot arrows in the air to drive the spirits away. Many other cultures have rituals to take care of the "bad" dead person, and they all originate in this feeling of anger which still exists in all of us, though we dislike admitting it. The tradition of the tombstone may originate in this wish to keep the bad spirits deep down in the ground, and the pebbles that many mourners put on the grave are left-over symbols of the same wish. Though we call the firing of guns at military funerals a last salute, it is the same symbolic ritual as the Indian used when he shot his spears and arrows into the skies.

I give these examples to emphasize that man has not basically changed. Death is still a fearful, frightening happening, and the fear of death is a universal fear even if we think we have mastered it on many levels.

What has changed is our way of coping and dealing with death and dying and our dying patients.

Having been raised in a country in Europe where science is not so advanced, where modern techniques have just started to find their way into medicine, and where people still live as they did in this country half a century ago, I may have had an opportunity to study a part of the evolution of mankind in a shorter period.

I remember as a child the death of a farmer. He fell from a tree and was not expected to live. He asked simply to die at home, a wish that was granted without questioning. He called his daughters into the bedroom and spoke with each one of them alone for a few minutes. He arranged his affairs quietly, though he was in great pain, and distributed his belongings and his land, none of which was to be split until his wife should follow him in death. He also asked each of his children to share in the work, duties, and tasks that he had carried on until the time of the accident. He asked his friends to visit him once more, to bid good-bye to them. Although I was a small child at the time, he did not exclude me or my siblings. We were allowed to share in the preparations of the family just as we were permitted to grieve with them until he died. When he did die, he was left at home, in his own beloved home which he had built, and among his friends and neighbors who went to take a last look at him where he lay in the midst of flowers in the place he had lived in and loved so much. In that country today there is still no make-believe slumber room, no embalming, no false makeup to pretend sleep. Only the signs of very disfiguring illnesses are covered up with bandages and only infectious cases are removed from the home prior to the burial.

Why do I describe such "old-fashioned" customs? I think they are an indication of our acceptance of a fatal outcome, and they help the dying patient as well as his family to accept the loss of a loved one. If a patient is allowed to terminate his life in the familiar and beloved environment, it requires less adjustment for him. His own family knows him well enough to replace a sedative with a glass of his favorite wine; or the smell of a home-cooked soup may give him the appetite to sip a few spoons of fluid which, I think, is still more enjoyable than an infusion. I will not minimize the need for sedatives and infusions and realize full well from my own experience as a country doctor that they are sometimes life-saving and often unavoidable. But I also know that patience and familiar people and foods could replace many a bottle of intravenous fluids given for the simple reason that it fulfills the physiological need without involving too many people and/or individual nursing care.

The fact that children are allowed to stay at home where a fatality has stricken and are included in the talk, discussions, and fears gives them the feeling that they are not alone in the grief and gives them the comfort of shared responsibility and shared mourning. It prepares them gradually and helps them view death as part of life, an experience which may help them grow and mature.

This is in great contrast to a society in which death is viewed as taboo, discussion of it is regarded as morbid, and children are excluded with the presumption and pretext that it would be "too much" for them. They are then sent off to relatives, often accompanied with some unconvincing lies of "Mother has gone on a long trip" or other unbelievable stories. The child senses that something is wrong, and his distrust in adults will only multiply if other relatives add new variations of the story, avoid his questions or suspicions, shower him with gifts as a meager substitute for a loss he is not permitted to deal with. Sooner or later the child will become aware of the changed family situation and, depending on the age and personality of the child, will have an unresolved grief and regard this incident as a frightening, mysterious, in any case very traumatic experience with untrustworthy grownups, which he has no way to cope with.

It is equally unwise to tell a little child who lost her brother that God loved little boys so much that he took little Johnny to heaven. When this little girl grew up to be a woman she never solved her anger at God, which resulted in a psychotic depression when she lost her own little son three decades later.

We would think that our great emancipation, our knowledge of science and of man, has given us better ways and means to prepare ourselves and our families for this inevitable happening. Instead the days are gone when a man was allowed to die in peace and dignity in his own home.

The more we are making advancements in science, the more we seem to fear and deny the reality of death. How is this possible?

We use euphemisms, we make the dead look as if they were asleep, we ship children off to protect them from the anxiety and turmoil around the house if the patient is fortunate enough to die at home, we don't allow children to visit their dying parents in the hospitals, we have long and controversial discussions about whether patients should be told the truth—a question that rarely arises when the dying person is tended by the family physician who has known him from delivery to death and who knows the weaknesses and strengths of each member of the family.

I think there are many reasons for this flight away from facing death calmly. One of the most important facts is that dying nowadays is more gruesome in many ways, namely, more lonely, mechanical and dehumanized; at times it is even difficult to determine technically when the time of death has occurred.

Dying becomes lonely and impersonal because the patient is often taken out of his familiar environment and rushed to an emergency room. Whoever has been very sick and has required rest and comfort especially may recall his experience of being put on a stretcher and enduring the noise of the ambulance siren and hectic rush until the hospital gates open. Only those who have lived through this may appreciate the discomfort and cold necessity of such transportation which is only the beginning of a long ordeal—

hard to endure when you are well, difficult to express in words when noise, light, pumps, and voices are all to much to put up with. It may well be that we might consider more the patient under the sheets and blankets and perhaps stop our well-meant efficiency and rush in order to hold the patient's hand, to smile, or to listen to a question. I include the trip to the hospital as the first episode in dying, as it is for many. I am putting it exaggeratedly in contrast to the sick man who is left at home—not to say that lives should not be saved if they can be saved by a hospitalization but to keep the focus on the patient's experience, his needs and his reactions.

When a patient is severely ill, he is often treated like a person with no right to an opinion. It is often someone else who makes the decision if and when and where a patient should be hospitalized. It would take so little to remember that the sick person too has feelings, has wishes and opinions, and has—most important of all—the right to be heard.

Well, our presumed patient has now reached the emergency room. He will be surrounded by busy nurses, orderlies, interns, residents, a lab technician perhaps who will take some blood, an electrocardiogram technician who takes the cardiogram. He may be moved to X-ray and he will overhear opinions of his condition and discussions and questions to members of the family. He slowly but surely is beginning to be treated like a thing. He is no longer a person. Decisions are made often without his opinion. If he tries to rebel he will be sedated and after hours of waiting and wondering whether he has the strength, he will be wheeled into the operating room or intensive treatment unit and become an object of great concern and great financial investment.

He may cry for rest, peace, and dignity, but he will get infusions, transfusions, a heart machine, or tracheotomy if necessary. He may want one single person to stop for one single minute so that he can ask one single question—but he will get a dozen people around the clock, all busily preoccupied with his heart rate, pulse, electrocardiogram or pulmonary functions, his secretions or excretions but not with him as a human being. He may wish to fight it all but it is going to be a useless fight since all this is done in the fight for his life, and if they can save his life they can consider the person afterwards. Those who consider the person first may lose precious time to save his life! At least this seems to be the rationale or justification behind all this—or is it? Is the reason for this increasingly mechanical, depersonalized approach our own defensiveness? Is this approach our own way to cope with and repress the anxieties that a terminally or critically ill patient evokes in us? Is our concentration on equipment, on blood pressure our desperate attempt to deny the impending death which is so frightening and discomforting to us that we displace all our knowledge onto machines, since they are less close to us than the suffering face of another human being which would remind us once more of our lack of omnipotence, our own limits and failures, and last but not least perhaps our own mortality?

Herbert Blaney

THE MODERN PARK CEMETERY

In landscape architecture, as in others of the fine and structural arts, the object is to build better, more usefully and more beautifully. This is as true of cemetery building and cemetery administration as of town planning, real estate development and park building.

Those closely in touch with the construction and care of cemeteries must be keenly aware of the possibilities of making the cemetery a spot of perpetual beauty and charm. Many of the older graveyards of the country present a view of shapeless, ill-kept roads and lawns or grassless mounds, a meaningless jumble of freakish, decaying headstones and dreary, moaning cedars, pines and spruces. The modern park-like cemetery presents a very different aspect. In every phase of its development the ultimate harmonious beauty and cheerfulness of appearance are kept in mind.

Let us compare briefly some of the salient features of cemeteries that have undergone a change within comparatively recent years and that make for more naturalistic scenic beauty, restfulness and permanency of charm.

General Plan and Road System

The "road and block" plan for the modern cemetery is similar to that of a modern real estate development. The

---

"The Modern Park Cemetery" by Herbert Blaney, *The American City,* April 1917, pp. 395-400.

sections or blocks are as large as is convenient and are formed by pleasantly curved roads laid out on easy grades following the contour of the ground. In older cemeteries one frequently finds roads or wide gravel paths encircling small sections of from one to five lots, thus causing great waste in salable lot space. Curves impossible for modern automobile traffic, and a "choppy," formless landscape appearance are also thus produced. The modern cemetery drive or avenue is like a park road. It is no wider than is necessary to satisfy the demands of traffic, and winds thru attractive park scenery, always bringing one conveniently near each lot.

In many older cemeteries, particularly in the West, the stiff gridiron plan of roads and lot lines was formerly used, but this has been entirely superseded in modern design by the more pleasing curved roads and irregular-shaped sections even where the topography is flat. An excellent comparison of the two methods of drive platting is seen in the plan for enlarging a cemetery in a small Mid-Western city, where the informal arrangement has been used for the newer sections.

Although paths are provided to give access to all lots, the path can be followed only by the lot markers, for the entire section, paths included, is a smooth, gently rolling lawn, unbroken save for pleasing monuments and planting.

Monuments

There is a fortunate growing tendency away from gaudy and freakish display in all fields of applied art. This is happily noted in the use of monuments in the cemetery. The idealist would abolish all gravestones, perhaps would favor universal cremation, but since one is entitled to his individual views on these subjects, we must recognize that there is still, and always will be, a demand for lot burials and stone markers.

The modern park cemetery has fewer monuments, and in some sections none are permitted to rise above the ground, bronze and stone tablets being used. Headstones, where used to mark the individual grave, are set flush with the ground. If the records of the superintendent are carefully kept and stored in a fireproof vault, there remains scant excuse for the headstone, as each individual grave can always be accurately located.

The character and design of monuments is much improved. The early settlers used slate slabs, but these fast reach decay, most of them being illegible to-day. The mania for the "shaft" and "statuesque" monuments so rampant in the middle and last part of the last century is happily past. The modern cemetery admits only those monuments meeting the approval of the trustees.

Curbings, iron fences and seats, urns and idle figures of rococo design are also in the discard.

While we cannot dispose of existing monuments in our cemeteries—for even the most humble piece of stone represents the deep sentiment of some bereaved one—we can strive with new burying grounds and with newer sections of older cemeteries to restrict and direct the erection of stonework along saner and more esthetic lines. This can be done in the publicly owned as well as in the privately owned cemetery.

Perpetual Care and Planting

The modern cemetery is in reality a park, with its broad expanses of smooth lawn partially shaded by beautiful trees and enframed and adorned by masses of hardy flowering shrubs and vines, all forming a pleasing setting for artistically designed and well-placed monuments. This is indeed a contrast to the appearance of many older cemeteries where small "chopped-up" sections of lawn, often dishevelled and weedy, are bound in by iron fences and crumbling stone curbing and spotted over with numerous stones, few worthy the sculptor's art.

Perpetual care is the magic instrument in the organization of the modern burial ground which ensures forever the maintenance of every phase of the cemetery's physical make-up and the preservation of the landscape beauty so jealously guarded in the newer grounds. This perpetual care of the cemetery is ensured by the income from a fund created by setting aside a certain percentage of all lot sales. Such a provision is placed in the deeds for all lots so that all portions of the cemetery will always have uniform and adequate care.

The introduction of floral interest only in the form of hardy flowering shrubs and perennial-and-wild-flower garden areas, well-conceived in the cemetery's plan, places the horticultural side of the cemetery design on a par in modern thought with the engineering phases of the cemetery's construction.

An Instance of Modern Cemetery Planning

In Bloomington, Ill., a city of about 40,000 people, a group of men saw the urgent need of better and more extensive cemetery facilities. They accordingly organized as a development company and purchased a pleasantly rolling and partially wooded tract of thirty acres at the edge of the city. Their task was to suitably develop this area as a modern cemetery.

This development, embodying all of the desired characteristics mentioned above, proceeded quickly and economically along the following lines. A glance at the results thus obtained may be helpful in guiding other cities and trustees in their efforts to build cemeteries better.

1. After obtaining a deed to the land, the first step was the employment of a landscape architect to advise in and direct the development work.

2. Under the landscape architect's direction a topographical survey was made of the entire tract, showing grades and all existing trees.

3. Comprehensive plans for the future construction and landscape development of the entire thirty acres were prepared, show-

ing avenues, lots, service buildings, and all landscape features. These plans represent the ideal to which the trustees will work in years to come.

4. After determining the portion to be immediately developed, work was begun on laying drains and building the roads, and the sections were carefully graded and seeded. Lots were staked and permanently bound with concrete markers.

5. During the first planting season after the grading was completed, trees, shrubs, vines and hardy flowering plants were planted thruout the entire developed area.

6. The property was enclosed by a wire fence with heavy boundary plantings. Brick entrance gates were built, and the office, superintendent's house and stables are in process of erection. A chapel is provided for, and it is expected this will soon be erected by memorial bequest.

An ultimate development plan directs all future growth of the cemetery, both as to laying out lots and planting, so that the effect shall always be a perfectly coordinated whole.

The roads are adapted to automobile traffic, ample room being provided at drive intersections for the automobile funeral to turn. The avenues are uniformly 16 feet in width and constructed with 12 feet of well-built gravel roadway and a 2-foot concrete gutter on each side. This gutter conducts the rain water to frequent drain inlets, and serves the secondary purpose of holding the gravel in place and maintaining an even edge to the road.

The drives divide the cemetery into comparatively few sections, averaging 200 feet in width and not more than 600 feet in length. The entire section between the roads is graded as a broad, smooth expanse of lawn, no mounded graves or lots or sunken gravel paths to mar this beauty. The planting is so arranged as to divide each section into a series of bays in which a few well-placed monuments will be set off and enframed in shrubbery and trees.

There is no stiff and rigid system of lot and path lines. Along the avenues two tiers of lots extend parallel to the drive. The interior of the section is platted arbitrarily in some adapted rectangular system. Where the paths are inconspicuous and form an integral part of the broad lawn, the lot lines are indistinguishable, so the arrangement does not influence the landscape effect.

The lots are in the following uniform sizes, excepting where the avenues curve sharply or at corners:

24 x 24	feet,	admitting	of	16	graves	and	monument
20 x 20	"	"	"	12	"	"	"
12 x 18	"	"	"	6	"	"	"
12 x 12	"	"	"	4	"	"	"
9 x 12	"	"	"	4	"	with no monument	

Along the curved driveways, at drive intersections and at certain focal points, larger lots are provided for mausoleums and special monuments. These are planned to accentuate and terminate pleasing vistas along the drives and thru the plantings.

Absolutely no space is lost to use. The lots front directly upon the drives. Odd-shaped and triangular lots, necessarily having some space where no grave can be located, are still in large demand, as they usually offer exceptional opportunity for landscape treatment. Some may have the idea that shrub plantings immediately upon the lots render these lots of smaller use, but the shrubs can be planted directly upon a grave, or if a new grave must be dug, then the shrubs can be temporarily taken up and replaced after the burial.

Along the boundaries of the cemetery the irregular-shaped sections will be mainly used for single graves. No monuments will be permitted upon such graves, a careful record being kept of every burial and the exact location of the grave. In these sections, stone bounds are placed at intervals, so that the location of every grave can be definitely determined and described. Small stone or bronze slabs level with the ground will be permitted to mark the graves in this section.

Thruout the cemetery only one monument will be permitted on any one lot. The location for this is determined on the general plan, and an effort is made in planting the shrubs to give a background for each stone so that no two will appear in close proximity, marring the effectiveness of each and giving a "stone-pile" effect. The absence of headstones appearing above ground allows the single monument to appear to better advantage on the unbroken lawn.

Where it is desired to keep an open lawn vista, a restriction against all monuments above ground is made. In this case a bronze or stone slab can be placed level with the grass, as is done frequently in a Chicago cemetery. It is the author's belief that this type of flat stone can be developed as artistically as the vertical monument.

At Park Hill, receiving-vaults are located in the basement of the office building. These are of steel encased with reinforced concrete and are recessed in the foundation wall with only a small portion projecting into the vault room. An evergreen and vine-bordered walk leads one to this vault room. The service yard and superintendent's cottage are secluded in one corner of the property, hidden from view by tall plantings of trees and shrubs.

It is in the provisions for planting that Park Hill Cemetery justly ranks in the forefront as a park cemetery, for hardy permanent plants are alone permitted and the trustees have in the very beginning so completely planted trees and shrubs over the entire property that it becomes a bird haven and a spot of landscape beauty at the very outset. Grandeur and sublimity are added to the landscape effect by the ancient existing trees and will be further enhanced after a few years by the growth of the newer plantings.

Dr. Wilhelm Miller has characterized the cemetery lot bedded with geraniums and coleus as "the gateway to bad taste," but the modern cemetery, with its naturalistic shrubbery groups and open lawn vistas, and with monuments fittingly enframed with lacy green, must surely measure up to his ideal of "A Gateway to the Great Hope."

In prohibiting flower beds on the lots and graves, the builders of the modern cemetery are not excluding a flower interest. Thousands of spring bulbs, such as crocus, squills, and narcissus, can be naturalized amongst the boundary plantations and beneath the shrub groups on the lots. In

Park Hill, a naturalistic informal perennial-and-native-flower garden has been laid out to lend interest to the burial park and to serve as an example to the lot owners of the real value of native and hardy flowers.

With expert and comprehensive plans at the start, and intelligent and far-seeing administration and upkeep, the modern cemetery becomes an important link in the better park areas of the city, besides serving for all time with the highest degree of efficiency the needs of a burial ground.

PASSING:

AN EPILOGUE

Charles O. Jackson

DEATH IN AMERICAN LIFE

For Americans in the twentieth century, connection between the world of the dead and that of the living has been largely severed and the dead world is disappearing. Communion between the two realms has come to an end. It is a radical departure because for three centuries prior, life and death were not held apart. Meaning flowed freely between the two. It is radical also in that the movement toward withdrawal from the dead reversed a strong trend apparent through most of the nineteenth century in which the place and role of the dead in the world of the living was increasing significantly.

The material in Parts One and Two of this volume has sought to suggest that this trend was a corollary as well as consequence of the decline in what has been called the "pilgrim" posture toward life.[1] In this view the world was merely a wilderness to be suffered as preparation for the truly significant "eternal" home. But that posture gradually weakened. Even though the pilgrim rhetoric continued, death was increasingly perceived in the first half of the nineteenth century within a context of growing attachment to the "wilderness" as well as within some unease about the true destiny of the dead. The latter unease was encouraged all the more by the implications for the human spirit in contemporary scientific directions such as Darwin's "heartless" theory.

As the preceding selections illustrate, once death began

to become less acceptable, the living demanded that it be domesticated, its harsh reality muted and beautified. The living became more unwilling to conclude their relationship with those departed. They would also seek comfort through a substantial reduction in social distance between the dead world and the living world. Indeed, at least by the last quarter of the nineteenth century, the two realms had become highly intertwined.

One dramatic expression of this movement was to be found in the antebellum "rural cemetery movement." If initial motivation for this application of landscape gardening technique to the graveyard was consideration of public health, the cemetery came to signify much more. Amid its beautiful and rustic environment with personalized plots, there would be positive proof for both the dead and the living that the latter truly cared. Such burial grounds would also become places of leisure for the living who found in them a source of assurance, succor, and moral instruction.

Nor was the cemetery the only evidence and example of the closing between the dead and living worlds in the nineteenth century. Personal care of the body of the deceased had always been a prime responsibility of family and friends. This continued throughout the century. The home continued to be the typical location of the wake and became so for the funeral. Professional undertaking services obtained some popularity by the last years of that century, but the responsibility over the body which the family was willing to delegate to such a functionary was limited. Many clearly felt that the body deserved more respect than to be handed over to strangers for final disposition. What became substantially new in the relationship with the dead, however, was the increased attention and resources which the living world gave to preservation and aesthetic presentation of the body.

Even by the early nineteenth century there was public interest in burial receptacles which would provide greater and more durable protection for the corpse than did the then-standard wooden coffin. By the eve of the Civil War, beauty in receptacles was a growing popular concern. A logical extension of this trend was the inception of protective embalming, and later cosmetic application to the increasingly precious body. The former received initial impetus in preservative and sanitation services offered by private entrepreneurs to families of victims killed in the Civil War. Both practices were only gradually accepted, and remained limited in popularity even by the close of the century.

The pattern of increased investment of life resources and time in the dead may be further observed in the growth of elaborate funerary practice, stylized display of grief, and supporting death paraphernalia in that century. While varying in degree with geographic locale and social strata, this complex included such matters as tightly defined periods of social mourning, precise strictures on dress, and wide variety in items of death etiquette, from mourning cards to the post-death "memory" picture of the corpse. This elaboration of the ritual complex was not unique to the United States in the period, and much American practice had been imported from abroad. A distinctive trend in the latter, however, was to move away from the gloom and somberness of the imported mourning style toward the gracious and beautiful.[2]

The observation that death and the dead, considerably groomed and polished from their rough appearance of earlier years, were allowed increasingly substantial demands on the lives of the living in the nineteenth century is borne out in other ways as well. Not only did death become a major theme in the popular culture of the antebellum period, but large numbers of Americans involved themselves in movements which may be viewed clearly as efforts to draw the afterlife more closely into the living world. One was the vogue of spiritualism where actual communication occurred between the dead world and living world. This movement reached peaks in the 1850s and again in the 1870s. In the unprecedented measure of interaction between the two worlds offered by this movement, there was final proof that "passing on" was almost merely that, a matter of status change.

A second direction was the popular inclination, encouraged by many religious leaders and a significant amount of literature, to inquire into the most minute detail of heavenly existence. The general result of this scrutiny was the transformation of the once awesome spiritual world into a state much like that of life in middle-class America. Nor did these efforts escape recognition by contemporary observers. An 1884 review critical of several such "literary inquiries" described the trend as the "Annexation of Heaven" by hauling "into boundless space the baggage of this world."[3] The dead, who inhabited that realm, moreover, were increasingly perceived in the folk culture, if not theology, as never far away. They waited and watched the lives of the living with concern, both groups secure in their expectation of future reunion on life terms. As Ann Douglas has perceptively observed in her treatment of this subject, there was in all this a clear commitment to the denial of death as a separate state.[4]

Americans of the twentieth century no longer live their lives with the well-defined relationship to and interest in the dead world which came to characterize the nineteenth century. Nor is this change to be totally bemoaned. The nature of the earlier association was in many ways restrictive on the living, naive, and premised in part upon the unhappy, grim reality of a very high mortality rate. Death could hardly be denied. There was too much of it around, particularly among the young. Even at the close of the century, life expectancy at birth was only forty-seven years, and infant mortality was approximately 162.4 per 1,000 live births. Precisely when reversal of the previous life-death relationship began is difficult to establish, but it was clearly under way by the opening of the twentieth century. The subsequent dichotomizing of the living and dead worlds so apparent in contemporary society was a product of many factors. An early ingredient was the previously noted view of human life and death implied in the new science which Charles Darwin symbolized. Many Americans reacted initially to that threat by further commitment to a closer relationship with the dead in ways just described. Many also would gradually find that such accommodation was less and less meaningful as their traditional religious certitude weakened before the force of natural scientism.

More subtle than the new science in changing the relationship of the life and death worlds, though at least as drastic in consequence, were the forces of urbanization, bureaucratization, mobility, and demographic change which caused death and the dead world to fade radically from sight as well as in impact. A number of scholars have spoken to the consequence of one or more of these factors. Two very able and pertinent analyses have been provided in Part Three of the present volume. It is therefore only necessary to mention these consequences briefly and to underscore their collective effect.[5] Mobility separated and subsequently acted to diminish emotional involvement or investment among family, relatives, and friends. After a period of separation, even death meant less. The secondary and functionary personal relationships, characteristic of the urban setting, have meant that, in general, death would have much less personal impact than was the case in small close-knit communities of the past.

City life also encouraged bureaucratic solutions to the problem of the dead as well as the dying, as it encouraged similar solutions to other social problems. Death and the dead became the province of the hospital and the funeral home. Medical advance has made the former a superb instrument of health care delivery, but there is reason to question that location as a place to die. It may well be that the prospect of death in this closeted, alien setting, where individual personality tends to be subordinate to technique and medical device, has made recognition of one's mortality all the more frightening and difficult to accept. In any event, transfer of primary responsibility over the dying and the dead from the family to these two agents has reduced direct exposure to mortality for many people. Placed in the hands of institutional specialists where contact was routine and impersonal, moreover, death and the dead in the present century came to interfere much less than ever before with the main stream of life.

Death has also become less visible because increasingly it is the elderly who do the dying. This is a consequence of the drastic reduction in child and mid-life death in the decades of this century. The elderly tend to be those members of the family least important functionally to its continuation. By the time their parents die, children of the elderly normally live apart from them and have established an immediate family of their own as the center of emotional investment. The aged tend also to be, in varying degrees, already disengaged from the actual operation and ongoing life of the society. Therefore in this group, death has the least effect on survivors as well as the societal order. Social visibility of death and the dead is thus reduced.

The latter consequence has been accelerated greatly in the past twenty years as a result of the extensive age-grading and isolation of the elderly via the retirement city/home movement. Moreover, death has become less visible in this century because it is less prevalent. The mortality rate in the United States has declined from 17.2 per 1,000 population in 1900 to a current low of slightly less than nine per 1,000. As Robert Fulton has observed, increasing life expectancy and declining mortality rates have produced in America a "death-free generation." For the first time in history a family may expect statistically to live twenty years without the passing of one of its members.[6] In all such ways then has death itself faded in visibility and impact, which in turn has made the maintenance of any sense of meaningful connection with the dying or those already gone all the more difficult.

Yet the dynamics and impersonal forces described above are not the whole story. In larger perspective, the dead world has been lost because an increasingly secular-minded society has actively chosen to abandon it. While secularization is, of course, a force long evident in the history of western civilization, it can also be fruitfully understood here as a continuation of the previously discussed reaction against the pilgrim outlook. The secular trend may be related as well to the "mortality revolution" which began to occur in the period just preceding the Industrial Revolution.

Calvin Goldscheider argues that the decreasing level of death in modern society and its removal as a daily threat to the social order have brought about a weakened interest in the traditional sacred understanding of death. When life was precarious, and death was frequent as well as mysterious, social institutions were greatly needed to explain death. With the gradual decline in mortality as a pressing social concern, there was simply much less interest in it or the "sacred" context in which it was placed. Goldscheider suggests further that in order to remain vital even religious institutions have had to redefine or secularize their content. Rewards for religious adherence could no longer be located in other worlds or lives, but would be placed increasingly in quality of life in this world.[7] Perhaps the "mortality revolution" may also help to explain the loss of concern with the theme of natural death and its meaning apparent in philosophy and literature at least in this century.

In any event, a dimension of the secular vision in America and elsewhere in the West has been that death became a taboo topic. The precise cause of that taboo, as well as the general death-avoidance which characterizes American society in this century, has been a source of much recent scholarship. Fulton and Geis, as well as Geoffrey Gorer, have probably identified the most fundamental factor. In a culture which will support no longer the certainty of afterlife, natural death became too frightening to contemplate or discuss.[8] Whatever the cause, the taboo is most significant. Little relationship is possible with a realm which we are actively attempting to forget. Moreover, the gradual erosion of certainty about, or even concern with, the afterlife has made meaningful relationship all the more difficult because the living literally do not know where their dead are. Without a defined location, understandable in human terms, the deceased are truly lost.

The social withdrawal from the dead implied in the above comments is equally evident in a variety of other ways. The depersonalized nature of the modern cemetery is one case. "Perpetual care" has largely released the living from physical need to visit the gravesite. The "Memorial Park" movement underway as early as the 1920s went a step further. It substituted small ground-level bronze plaques for the ornate headstones of the nineteenth century. It eliminated epitaphs and the traditional coffin-size "mounds"—a constant reminder in earlier days of death's reality. Only the random pieces of statuary and other limited adornment in such "parks" betray the true nature of the site to passersby. The readily identifiable garden cemetery of the previous century, with its highly personalized gravesite expressive of the individual, was designed to encourage association with the dead. The Memorial Park is not.

A similar withdrawal from commitment to the dead is apparent in other forms of death response. Gone are the elaborate rules of social mourning so important in the previous century. Gone also are the formal mourning costume and supporting paraphernalia of the past. As William Kephart noted in his study of Philadelphia, only one of the once-standard mourning shops remained in that city by 1950.[9] The process of restricting the time and space given over to the dead has progressed to the point that any open expression of grief over loss has become something to be avoided. The elaborate Victorian funeral began to fade in the World War I era. While the American funeral remains by most standards a gaudy and expensive affair, it has come in for heavy criticism since the fifties. Such rites are said to be too time consuming, too disruptive of city traffic, too barbaric, and so forth.

As comments in Part One of this volume make clear, criticism of funerary activity is not new, but the volume and heat behind it in recent years are.[10] The gradual rejection of social mourning as well as the growing reaction against elaborate funeral practice may be a quite natural consequence of present death demography. Robert Fulton argues that contemporary feeling about the inappropriateness of the traditional funeral can be related to the fact that it is the elderly who largely do the dying now. For earlier noted reasons, deaths within this group tend to be "low-grief" in type for survivors, and require only minimal acknowledgment of the passing for emotional closure. Anything beyond this seems unwarranted.[11] Presumably the same case could be made on other forms of ritual display. On the matter of the loss of social-mourning custom, Sybil Wolfram concludes that the primary cause is to be found in the decline of the significance of kinship ties, a matter already apparent by the close of the nineteenth century.[12] This may also be true. Whatever the causes, however, the central point is this. In the present century, Americans have steadily moved to reduce the degree of time and resources which they must provide the dead.

So for all practical purposes, the dead world has become detached in contemporary society from the living world. Natural death, at least, has increasingly faded from view. The single, though perhaps in the long run, major challenge to these developments has been an apparent new surge of interest in the topics of death and dying which became visible in the 1960s. Why such an interest should develop in a cultural setting where death was so alienated from life remains open to speculation. Drawing an analogy with earlier sexual taboo in America, a common observation has been that the taboo in such a vital area was simply bound to collapse sooner or later. Essentially, the position taken here is that "the time" came with the 1960s, just as it did for sex in an earlier decade. Of course, this view begs the matter of cause and in many ways rings far too simplistic. More satisfying have been efforts to relate the awareness behind that literature to the force of recent medical issues, such matters as legal definition of death, and the implications of transplant surgery. It has also become common and not without logic to relate concern with death and dying to the general growth of social sensitivity toward quality of life which emerged in the 1960s.

Robert Kastenbaum and Ruth Aisenberg have discussed in some detail the matter of recent interest in death among "mental health specialists." Their conclusions are thought provoking and would appear to apply to broader groups than merely the one cited. Basically, those conclusions are five: (1) We are more threatened by the prospect of mass death than ever before. (2) Particularly as a result of developments in the mass media, we are less isolated from violent death. (3) The mental health professions have been established long enough now to have developed a large senior echelon of individuals who have experienced brutal death, the death of loved ones, and are now also confronted with interpreting their own approaching mortality. Application of this point to a larger public would be that interest among specialists, especially in published form, could generate broader interest. (4) We now recognize that our simple faith in the problem-solving ability of material progress has been unwarranted. Unacceptable human suffering and unnecessary premature death will not be vanished so easily. (5) We have begun to suspect that our very way of life may have lethal components and requires careful scrutiny.[13]

A noteworthy attempt at historical approach to the appearance of the new interest has been made by intellectual historian Philippe Ariès. Placing that phenomenon in the general context of western thought, he has concluded that the death literature is uniquely American. It has no European equivalent. Its development was possible because the modern western tendency toward interdicting, or in some way denying the presence of death in this century, was never quite completed in the United States. The American way with death has been to sublimate it, to transform it and put make-up on it, particularly through the arts of the funeral industry, but never to make it totally disappear. Because American society, unlike industrialized Europe, never completely accepted the interdict, it was the single place where the interdict could be successfully challenged.[14] This analysis may well be very perceptive and important. As earlier noted, the thrust of the American accommodation with death in the nineteenth century was always toward a setting beautiful to see and feel. A belated though logical dimension of this thrust was embalming and cosmetic concern with the body. The fact that such practices have been retained and further developed in the twentieth century, even though the mood which produced it had evaporated, does suggest that this peculiarly American aberration may be highly significant.

Whatever the full dynamics behind the new death interest, in retrospect, the prototype for the literature at least can be found in Herman Feifel's 1959 edited volume titled, *The Meaning of Death.*[15] This collection of interdisciplinary essays was not only a valuable contribution in a neglected area, but has come to stand as an historical watershed, a "grand divide" between death as a taboo topic and death as the subject of an astonishing amount of scholarship and popular interest since that event. Indeed, as one scholar has observed, more material appeared on the subject of death and bereavement in the five years following Feifel's work than had appeared in the previous one hundred years.[16]

The new interest in and literature on death has taken several major directions: concern with the conditions of death, including the related matters of euthanasia and the right to death with dignity; concern with suicide prevention; concern with the needs of the bereaved; and concern with generally decontaminating the topic of death in American culture. There is, however, a growing interest in even such unlikely areas, for a highly secular society, as the question of post-death existence.[17] Perhaps the best, and surely the most popular example of the new literature is Elisabeth Kubler-Ross' 1969 volume, *On Death and Dying.* The book is based on extensive work with terminal patients and its concern is the dynamics of the dying process. In it, the author identifies five stages through which patients may typically pass: denial, anger, bargaining, depression, and acceptance.

The concept of "stages" has not been totally accepted but this is hardly the single contribution of the volume. Even more significant is Kubler-Ross' careful delineation of the significant role that loved ones or caring professionals may play in the lives of the dying. The quality of the dying process for the terminal patient, as well as the way it is experienced by survivors, may depend greatly on the nature of the interaction between the two. If that relationship is based on an openness and honesty wherein full sharing of feelings is encouraged, a mutual acceptance of the separation can be accomplished. Indeed, such "working through" with a dying loved one may well have major and positive consequence for facing one's own death.[18] As does much of the new literature, Kubler-Ross then illustrates and stresses yet another aspect of death as social event, a concept discussed in the introduction of the present volume.

It is yet too early to make firm assessment on the permanence or significance of the new death interest. There are those who believe it marks a fundamental reversal in the national mood towards the topic of death. Perhaps this will prove the case. Perhaps we are witness to the initial stages of a third major shift in the American vision of death. Perhaps in the course of it even the dead will be reintegrated in some meaningful way into the living world. Reducing the current social distance between life and death might prove a very significant step, for there is good reason to suspect that the cost of abandoning the dead world has been great. A first comment on this subject is that we treat the dying badly. We avoid them, isolate them, and generally approach them as if their status were an embarrassment. Without attempting to establish which has been cause and which has been effect, historically it may be observed simply that such treatment is not surprising in a culture where life and death are so profoundly alienated. Second, accepting death is a difficult matter even under the best of circumstances, and the present American perspective on the dead world most probably increases that difficulty. Having made little place in life for the dead and having had little experience with even the subject of death, the individual can only perceive that event as totally alien, surely therefore all the more terrifying. Because natural death is accorded only minimal place in the culture, that culture in turn can provide essentially no resources to the individual which might assist one in meeting one's own death or that of others.

Third, much has been said in contemporary America about the need for self-identity and the difficulties of establishing it. While the matter is complex, one traditional dimension of identity has been the understanding of a clear relationship, individually and collectively, to the generational stream from past to future. The ability to do this has been significantly weakened in recent years, and that problem has surely at least been aggravated by the steady movement toward denying the dead world a role in the living world. This denial is after all a rejection of both our past and future. If the dead are simply gone and insignificant as those presently alive are soon to be, the chain of historical continuity is broken at every link. Finally, we have gone a very long way toward eliminating the presence of the dead world from life, but death does come, and in the end our vision of it is a powerful informing agent in our vision of life. Because the world of the dead is largely understood as irrelevant to our lives, death tends to become without significance and absurd. Because we have this perspective on the end of life, it becomes difficult to avoid the same view on all life because it is lived in the face of death.

Yet assuming there have been costs from the present relationship between life and death, is it truly realistic to expect that the dead can be accorded a significant place in modern society? We live after all in a very secular, temporal, youth-oriented culture, and one in which there are many impersonal forces working against closer association. Certainly a return to such an elaborate interaction between the living and dead worlds, as that which characterized the late nineteenth century, would be unlikely and indeed not desirable. This accommodation also carried serious social costs for the living. If there is reason to question the present state of things, moreover, it does not arise from need to restore any previous order, but rather because of the extreme nature of our present withdrawal from the dead. Dealing with the problem, therefore, is less a matter of developing specific claims for the dead on the life world than one of obtaining popular recognition that death and the dead should be a concern of the living. The unhappy alternative is that we continue to live as well as die in a societal setting where the tragedy of human mortality seems increasingly irrelevant, where denial has become a national art, and where dying is an alien unnatural humiliation. As previously suggested, the recent surge of interest in the topics of death and dying could mark the beginning of that necessary recognition, which in turn might reverse the twentieth-century pattern. If judgment is premature, we may at least hope.

NOTES

* Portions of this essay draw heavily on material previously published by the author in *Omega: The Journal of Death and Dying* under the title, "Death Shall Have No Dominion: The Passing of the World of the Dead in America."

1. Cyclone Covey, *The American Pilgrimage: The Roots of American Religion and Culture* (New York, 1961).

2. Robert Habenstein and William Lamers, *The History of American Funeral Directing* (Milwaukee, 1955), p. 393.

3. Anon., "The Annexation of Heaven," *Atlantic Monthly,* 53 (January 1884), pp. 135, 143.

4. Ann Douglas, "Heaven Our Home: Consolation Literature in the Northern United States, 1830-1880," *American Quarterly,* 26 (December 1974), pp. 514-515.

5. Leroy Bowman, *The American Funeral: A Study in Guilt, Extravagance, and Sublimnity* (Washington, D.C., 1959), ch. 10; Robert Blauner, "Death and Social Structure," *Psychiatry: Journal for the Study of Interpersonal Processes,* (November 1966), pp. 378-394; Robert Fulton, "Death, Grief and Social Recuperation," *Omega,* 1 (February 1970), pp. 23-28; Richard Kalish, "The Effects of Death Upon the Family," in Leonard Pearson, ed., *Death and Dying: Cur-*

rent Issues in the Treatment of the Dying Person (Cleveland, 1969), pp. 79-107.

6. Fulton, "Death, Grief and Social Recuperation," p. 25.

7. Calvin Goldscheider, *Population, Modernization, and Social Structure* (Boston, 1971), pp. 130-131.

8. Robert Fulton and Gilbert Geis, "Death and Social Values" in Robert Fulton, ed., *Death and Identity* (New York, 1965), pp. 67-68; Geoffrey Gorer, "The Pornography of Death," *Encounter,* 5 (October 1955), p. 51.

9. William Kephart, "Status After Death," *American Sociological Review,* 15 (April, 1950), p. 641.

10. See, for example, Jessica Mitford, *The American Way of Death* (New York, 1963).

11. Fulton, "Death, Grief and Social Recuperation," 23-28.

12. Sybil Wolfram, "The Decline of Mourning," *The Listener,* 75 (May 26, 1966), 763-764.

13. Robert Kastenbaum and Ruth Aisenberg, *The Psychology of Death* (New York, 1972), pp. 234-236.

14. Philippe Ariès, *Western Attitudes Toward Death from the Middle Ages to the Present* (Baltimore, 1974), pp. 94-102.

15. Herman Feifel, ed., *The Meaning of Death* (New York, 1959).

16. Fulton, "Death, Grief and Social Recuperation," 24.

17. See Charles Panati, "Is There Life After Death?" *Family Circle,* Vol. 89, No. 11, (November 1976), 78, 84, 90.

18. Elisabeth Kubler-Ross, *On Death and Dying* (New York, 1969).

A NOTE ON FURTHER SOURCES

There is as yet no historical counterpart to the recent enormous proliferation of literature on the topics of death and dying in contemporary America. Beyond a handful of pertinent books, such material which does exist is difficult to locate and miscellaneous in form. It typically appears as single chapters or a few pages of comment in large studies and as random articles in unrelated journals. An appropriate conclusion for the present volume might be, therefore, some comment on the whereabouts of additional published sources which would prove informative for further examination of response and attitudes toward death.

With regard to the overall relationship of death to life in the American past, there have been only three volumes of significance published in the past twenty years. While segments from each of these works are used in the present collection, all three are sufficiently important so as to warrant brief comment. The oldest is Robert Habenstein's and William Lamers' *The History of American Funeral Directing,* which was published in 1955. It was issued under the auspices of the National Funeral Directors Association and, while valuable, is by intent a chronicle of the funeral industry rather than cultural responses to death. The second and most important is Philippe Ariès' *Western Attitudes Toward Death: From the Middle Ages to the Present.* Highly synthetic in nature, this volume provides an excellent perspective on American death behavior within the larger context of western thought. Given this focus, however, particulars of national histories must be neglected. The most recent volume is David Stannard, ed., *Death in America,* an expanded edition of the winter 1974 issue of the *American Quarterly.* Coverage of death behavior in the United States is limited to six well-done period or thematic essays. Also useful as a general introduction to the history of death in the United States are essays by Monroe Lerner and by Calvin Goldscheider on long-term demographic trends. Both may be found conveniently in Edwin Shneidman, ed., *Death: Current Perspectives.*[1]

With regard to death-related activity in seventeenth- and eighteenth-century North America, two useful background articles are Elizabeth Thomson, "The Role of Physicians in the Human Societies of the Eighteenth Century," and Erwin Ackerknecht, "Death in the History of Medicine." Both discuss the new concern in that period over "true" versus "apparent" death. While not totally germane here, an interesting parallel to this line of thought is in the speculation among the philosophers about prolongation of life, and the relationship of that thought to the doctrine of progress. This is well developed in the pertinent parts of *The Evolution of Prolongevity Hypotheses to 1800* by Gerald Gruman.[2]

More directly pertinent to death-related behavior in the American colonial period is Margaret Coffin's *Death in Early America,* a somewhat misleading title since comment extends across the nineteenth, and at points into the twentieth centuries. The volume is written for popular consumption, is lacking in scholarly development, and is vague on chronology, but it is worth examination. Several article-length pieces also deserve mention, both because of their own value and because they point up in their focus a major problem in study of the period. The problem is that so much of the available literature is focused on the Northeast. David Stannard has provided an excellent essay on the general dynamics of death anxiety among the puritans. It should be followed by reading also his "Death and the Puritan Child." New England custom is the focus, in addition, of chapter six in John Draper's *The Funeral Elegy and the Rise of English Romanticism.* While a bit rambling, Martha Fales' essay, "The Early American Way of Death," presents some interesting data on mourning rings and their changing nature.[3]

Perhaps the most informative material on changing death perspective in the period is to be found in tombstone sculpture, an area unlike most aspects of death-related activity, where there has been historical interest for a substantial period of time. With the exception of Dickran and Ann Tashjian's *Memorials for Children of Change,* recent articles on this subject are more interpretive than the existing book-length scholarship. Among the more informative are Avon Neal and Ann Parker, "Graven Images: Sermons in Stone," published in *American Heritage,* and Edwin Dethlefsen's *American Journal of Physical Anthropology* piece, "Colonial Gravestones and Demography."[4]

The above material points up also the direction of changes in tombstone sculpture during the early nineteenth century. Full appreciation of the significance of those directions requires, however, a clear understanding of the dynamics involved in the rural cemetery movement. Two most useful sources on this subject are Stanley French, "The Cemetery as Cultural Institution: the Establishment of Mount Auburn and the 'Rural' Cemetery Movement," and Thomas Bender, "The 'Rural' Cemetery Movement, Urban Travail and the Appeal of Nature." The former takes the broader view. Noteworthy as well is Frederic Sharf's examination of the movement through artistic trends in the prototype "rural" cemetery, Mount Auburn outside Boston, in his "The Garden Cemetery and American Sculpture." The variety and, by present standards, extravagance which developed in nineteenth-century burial ground art may be examined in Edmund Gillon, Jr., *Victorian Cemetery Art.* The volume includes 260 photographs of cemetery sculpture from the New York and New England areas.[5]

Nineteenth-century spiritualism may be examined in two volumes, Geoffrey Nelson's *Spiritualism and Society* and Howard Kerr's *Mediums and Spirit-Rappers, and Roaring Radicals.* The former provides theoretical materials on origin and dynamics of the phenomenon. It also allows some comparison of spiritualsim in the United States with that in England. The latter looks at spiritualism in creative literature up to 1900. While her own thesis is more complex, the sharp reduction in social distance between the living and the dead through the "Americanization" of the afterlife is well illustrated in Ann Douglas', "Heaven Our Home: Consolation Literature in the Northern United States, 1830-80," although proper appreciation for that trend really requires at least some examination of pertinent novels by Elizabeth Stuart Phelps. Her *Gates Ajar* is now readily available, having been recently reprinted with a well done introduction by Helen Sootin Smith.[6]

Very little in the way of published material is available which might serve to sum up, or detail overall, the complex system of funerary behavior, formal display of grief, mourning practice, and supporting death paraphernalia which ultimately developed in the nineteenth century. Perhaps the most useful existing chronicle is in the pertinent chapters in the Habenstein and Lamers volume. There are several such studies of similar developments in England, however, which can be helpful in understanding the intricacies to which the growing commitment of life resources could go. One is John Morley's *Death, Heaven and the Victorians.* Another is James Curl's *The Victorian Celebration of Death,* which does include some limited comment on the United States. This volume is marred, however, by the author's peculiar commitment to the old Victorian cemetery. A useful contrast to the elaborate form suggested in these sources is the pattern among rural Americans of limited resources described in chapter fifteen of Thomas Clark's *Pill, Petticoats and Plows.*[7]

Philippe Ariès' volume previously cited, as well as his "The Reversal of Death: Changes in Attitudes Toward Death in Western Societies," provide excellent treatments of the emergence of death denial and death as taboo topic in the twentieth century. Geoffrey Gorer's classic essay, "The Pornography of Death," also examines the emergence of death as a taboo topic. The matter of denial has come in for extensive comment of recent years, with most observers asserting that a high degree exists in American culture. One examination of the denial-acceptance debate is Dumont and Foss, *The American View of Death,* in which the authors seek to find a middle ground between those two positions. Their analysis is badly weakened, however, because they begin with a distorted vision of the debate as a dichotomy of mutually exclusive alternatives. A well-developed argument for the existence of a substantial acceptance of death in contemporary life may be found in Talcott Parsons and Victor Lidz, "Death in American Society."[8]

On the consequences of such matters as bureaucratization and demographic change on dying and death impact, several sources warrant examination. One is Ariès', "A Moment That Has Lost its Meaning," a summary of major observations on the declining significance of death as event, published in the June 1975 issue of *Prism,* the whole of which is devoted to death. This article is an abridged excerpt from Ariès' book. Other rewarding scholarship is: Vanderlyn Pine, "Social Organization and Death" in *Omega,* a journal given over entirely to the topics of death and dying; Robert Fulton, "Death, Grief and Social Recuperation," also in *Omega;* Robert Fulton and Gilbert Geis, "Death and Social Values," in Fulton, ed., *Death and Identity;* Paul Reiss, "Bereavement and the American Family," in Austin Kutscher, ed., *Death and Bereavement.*[9]

A major expression of twentieth-century withdrawal from the dead has been in the trend toward deritualization of death. One dimension has been the loss of social mourning ritual and discouragement of even private show of grief, examination of which is provided in Geoffrey Gorer's *Death, Grief and Mourning.* The data for the study is British but Gorer believes quite correctly that the pattern described applies equally well to the United States. A good critical review of his thesis is available in Sybil Wolfram, "The Decline of Mourning," in *The Listener.* While criticism has not had the extreme consequences on last rites it has had in Western Europe (described by Ariès as taking the least possible notice of death), it has been a persistent note in this century. More recently it has put the funeral industry significantly on the defensive, and encouraged a minority to offer so-called cut-rate funeral/burial arrangements. It may be observed in significant amount by simple perusal of the *Readers' Guide to Periodical Literature* under the topics of death, funerals, and burial, as early as the 1890s where funeral costs become part of the argument for cremation. No better examples of the more recent increase in ferocity of that criticism is to be found than in the scathing commentaries of Jessica Mitford and of Ruth Harmer.[10]

One measure of the relationship of the living and the dead is the cemetery. W. Lloyd Warner has provided a fascinating account of the social role fulfilled by the cemetery as illustrated in one New England community. While the essay is based on twentieth-century data its value is in description largely of what such burial grounds once did, since that role has changed appreciably. Also recalling an earlier accommodation between life and death, though one which lingers in limited degree in isolated rural areas, are two recent oral history collections, *Foxfire 2* and William Montell's *Ghosts Along the Cumberland.* Both are recollections by southern mountain people largely, it appears, of the years prior to World War II. What comes through readily from these spokesmen of a bygone order is a pattern now thoroughly obsolete: death as community deprivation and obligation, home-centered funerary activity, open expression of grief, and a clear acceptance of mortality in self as well as others. An example of a contemporary area only recently fully subject to the secular/temporal trends as well as urban forces of this century, and one still in transition toward the radical life-death alienation which characterizes modern America is reported in Christopher Crocker's essay, "The Southern Way of Death."[11]

Finally, the chief problem to be faced by those seeking some understanding of the new death literature is the sheer bulk of this material. Thus, one fine example of that literature, O. A. Brim et al, *The Dying Patient,* cites over three hundred pertinent recent works. A necessary beginning point, however, would be with Herman Feifel's seminal volume, *The Meaning of Death* and Elisabeth Kubler-Ross' *On Death and Dying.* A good cross-section of the new scholarship which would be readily available is Schneidman's earlier noted edited work, *Death: Current Perspectives.* A well developed statement on the need for death education is Daniel Leviton, "The Role of the Schools in Providing Death Education." Several significant questions about the directions of the new literature are raised in Gwynn Nettler's provocative, if somewhat labored review essay in *Social Problems.*[12]

NOTES

1. Habenstein and Lamers, *The History of American Funeral Directing* (Milwaukee, 1955); Ariès, *Western Attitudes Toward Death* (Baltimore, 1974); Stannard ed., *Death in America* (Philadelphia, 1975). There are two additional volumes which are aimed directly at death-related behavior and thought in the United States. Both include useful historical observation but neither has history as a primary concern. They are Richard Dumont and Dennis Foss, *The American View of Death* (Cambridge, 1972) and Arien Mack, ed., *Death in American Experience* (New York, 1973). Quality among essays in the latter varies considerably; Lerner, "When, Why, and Where People Die," pp. 138-162 and Goldscheider "The Mortality Revolution" (an abridgement), pp. 163-189, both in Schneidman, ed., *Death: Current Perspectives* (Palo Alto, Calif., 1976).

2. Thomson, "The Role of Physicians in the Humane Societies," *Bulletin of the History of Medicine,* 37 (January 1963), pp. 43-51; Ackerknecht, "Death in the History of Medicine," *Bulletin of the History of Medicine,* 42 (January 1968), pp. 19-23; Gruman, *The Evolution of Prolongevity Hypotheses to 1800: Trans. Amer. Phil. Soc.,* 56, Pt. 9 (Philadelphia, 1966), pp. 74-91. Also of possible interest is Gerald Gruman, "The Rise and Fall of Prolongevity Hygiene," *Bulletin of the History of Medicine,* 35 (May-June 1961), pp. 221-229.

3. Coffin, *Death in Early America: History and Folklore of Customs and Superstitions of Early Medicine, Funerals, Burial and Mourning* (Nashville, Tenn., 1976); *Historical Review,* 78 (December

1973), pp. 1305-1330; Stannard, "Death and the Puritan Child," *American Quarterly,* 26 (December 1974), pp. 456-476; Draper, *The Funeral Elegy* (New York, 1929, 1967), ch. 6; Earle, *Colonial Days* (New York, 1899), ch. 14; Fales, "The Early American Way of Death," *Essex Institute Historical Collection,* 100 (April 1964), pp. 75-84.

4. Tashjian, *Memorials for Children of Change: The Art of Early New England Stonecarving* (Middletown, Conn., 1974); Dethlefsen, "Colonial Gravestones," *A.J.P.A.,* 31 (Winter 1969), pp. 321-334. Other less valuable sources are: Harriette Forbes, *Gravestones of Early New England and The Men Who Made Them, 1653-1800* (Princeton, N.J., 1973); Allan Ludwig, *Graven Images: New England Stonecarving and Its Symbols, 1650-1815* (Middletown, Conn., 1966); Ivan Sandrof, "As I Am Now So You Must Be," *American Heritage* 11 (February 1960), pp. 38-43; Sonia Marsal, "Mortality Writ in Stone: Early New England Gravestones," *Americas,* 16 (August 1964), pp. 22-30; Avon Neal and Ann Parker, "Graven Images: Sermons in Stones," *American Heritage,* 21 (December 1969), pp. 18-29.

5. French, "The Cemetery as Cultural Institution," *American Quarterly,* 26 (March 1974), pp. 37-59; Bender, "The 'Rural' Cemetery," *New England Quarterly,* 47 (June 1974), pp. 196-211; Sharf, "The Garden Cemetery," *Art Quarterly,* 24 (Spring 1961), pp. 80-88; Gillon, *Victorian Cemetery Art* (New York, 1972).

6. Nelson, *Spiritualism and Society* (New York, 1969); Kerr, *Mediums and Spirit-Rappers* (Urbana, Ill., 1972); Douglas, "Heaven Our Home," *American Quarterly,* 26 (December 1974), pp. 496-515. Pertinent works by Phelps are *Beyond the Gates, The Gates Between,* and *Within the Gates.* See Phelps, *The Gates Ajar,* ed. Helen Sootin Smith (Cambridge, Mass., 1964). Noteworthy also is Mark Twain's lampoon on the Phelps'-type vision of the afterlife, "Extract from Captain Stormfield's Visit to Heaven," in Charles Neider, ed., *The Complete Short Stories of Mark Twain* (Garden City, N.Y., 1957), pp. 564-597.

7. Morley, *Death, Heaven and the Victorians* (Pittsburgh, 1971); Curl, *Victorian Celebration of Death* (Detroit, 1972); Clark, *Pills, Petticoats and Plows* (New York, 1944), pp. 260-274.

8. Ariès, *Western Attitudes Toward Death;* Ariès, "The Reversal of Death," *American Quarterly,* 26 (December 1974), pp. 536-560; Dumont and Foss, *American View of Death;* Gorer, "The Pornography of Death," *Encounter* (October 1955), pp. 49-52. It is also included in Gorer's *Death, Grief and Mourning* (New York, 1965), pp. 192-199. Parsons and Lidz, "Death in American Society," in Edwin

Schneidman, ed., *Essays in Self-Destruction* (New York, 1967), pp. 133-171.

9. Ariès, "A Moment That Has Lost Its Meaning," *Prism, 3 (June* 1975), 27 ff; Pine, "Social Organization and Death," *Omega,* 3 (Winter 1972), pp. 149-153; Robert Fulton, "Death, Grief and Social Recuperation," *Omega,* 1 (February 1970), pp. 23-28; Fulton and Geis in Fulton, ed., *Death and Identity* (New York, 1965), pp. 67-75. Also see Fulton's introduction to Part IV, "Ceremony, the Self, and Society," pp. 333-338; Reiss in Kutscher, ed., *Death and Bereavement* (Springfield, Ill., 1969), pp. 219-221. It is interesting to contemplate the current closeted nature of death in the health-care setting within the context of a larger phenomenon which John Lofland labels the "dramaturgic revolution." In this revolution of "styles of doing things," all primal scenes, fornication to dying and death have shifted from "relatively commonplace openness to delicate concealment." Lofland uses as a case study state executions in England and the United States circa 1700 to circa 1950. See "Open and Concealed Dramaturgic Strategies: The Case of the State Execution," *Urban Life: A Journal of Ethnographic Research,* 4 (October 1974) pp. 272-295.

10. Gorer, *Death, Grief and Mourning;* Wolfram, "The Decline of Mourning," *The Listener,* 75 (May 26, 1966), pp. 763-764; Mitford, *The American Way of Death* (Greenwich, Conn., 1963); Harmer, *The High Cost of Dying* (New York, 1963). While criticism of the funeral, particularly with regard to cost, has grown steadily, it is still the case that the higher a person's status in his group or community the more his funeral ritual is likely to proliferate and expand. See Jack Bynum, "Social Status and Rites of Passage: The Social Context of Death," *Omega,* 4 (Winter 1973), pp. 323-332. The epitome of extravagant expression in the American death industry is California's Forest Lawn Cemetery, the story of which is reported in Paul Jacobs' "The Most Cheerful Graveyard in the World," *The Reporter,* 19 (September 18, 1958), pp. 26-30. A biting satirical treatment of that industry in general, and Forest Lawn in particular, is Evelyn Waugh's *The Loved One* (New York, 1948).

11. Warner,*The Family of God: A Symbolic Study of Christian Life* (New Haven, 1961), ch. 5; Eliot Wigginton, ed., *Foxfire 2* (New York, 1973), chs. 14-15; Montell, *Ghosts Along the Cumberland* (Knoxville, Tenn., 1975). Unfortunately neither Wigginton nor Montell attempts significant interpretation of the data he represents. See Crocker in Kenneth Moreland, ed., *The Not So Solid South*

(Athens, Ga., 1971), pp. 114-129. Note, for example, Crocker's observation that in his research locale, unlike patterns in large urban hospitals, visiting does not taper off once the "dying" category is applied. Rather, the reverse is true.

12. Howard Freeman, Orville Brim, and Greer Williams, eds., *The Dying Patient* (New York, 1970); Feifel, ed., *The Meaning of Death* (New York, 1959); Kubler-Ross, *On Death and Dying* (New York, 1969); Schneidman, *Death: Current Perspectives;* Leviton in Betty Green and Donald Irish, eds., *Death Education: Preparation for Living* (Cambridge, Mass., 1971); Nettler, "On Death and Dying," *Social Forces,* 14 (Winter, 1967), pp. 335-344.

INDEX

ABOUT THE EDITOR

Charles O. Jackson, professor of history at the University of Tennessee, Knoxville, specializes in American social and cultural history. He has written articles for such journals as *Military Affairs,* the *South Atlantic Quarterly,* the *Journal of the History of Medicine,* and *Voices: Journal of the American Academy of Psychotherapists.* His previous book-length works include *Food and Drug Legislation in the New Deal.*